Blacks and the
Populist Revolt

Blacks and the Populist Revolt

Ballots and Bigotry in the "New South"

●

Gerald H. Gaither

●

THE UNIVERSITY OF ALABAMA PRESS
University, Alabama

ACKNOWLEDGMENT

This book would not have been possible without the cooperation and assistance of many people. The initial stimulus came from Dr. Ralph Haskins, The University of Tennessee, Knoxville. Sincere thanks are due also to the librarians of various institutions for their assistance in the face of ever increasing demands upon their patience and stamina. The conscientious and dedicated services of these individuals has reinforced my belief in the existence of "southern hospitality."

I owe particular appreciation to Dr. Sheldon Hackney, who shared unselfishly his statistical data, for the development of the enclosed election analyses and for the preparation of the Introduction, which synthesizes the major ideas and trends of modern populism.

Looming over the enterprise has been the unseen presence of the godfather of Southern History, Professor C. Vann Woodward, whose works originally inspired this study and assisted me greatly in arriving at my understanding of Populism. While I have largely disagreed with many of his conclusions, this in no way lessens my sense of indebtedness.

Library of Congress Cataloging in Publication Data
Gaither, Gerald H.
  Blacks and the Populist Revolt.
  Bibliography: p.
  1. Populism—Southern States. 2. Negroes—
Southern States. 3. Southern States—Politics and
Government—1865–1950.   I. Title.
F215.GTA   320.9'75'04   75–6904
ISNB 0–8173–4726–7

CONTENTS

TABLES AND FIGURES

PREFACE

My initial interest in the racial complexion of Southern Populism was developed from a M. A. thesis ("The Negro in the Ideology of Southern Populism, 1889–1896," The University of Tennessee, 1967). Viewing the problem in historical perspective, that study suggested the necessity for a deeper and broader view of the movement. Fragmentary findings on Populist action and *prima facie* racial creed in a regional setting suggested a complexity far beyond the depth of previous historiography. Therefore, this book is an attempt to further fill the gap in political history during the period of the Southern Populist revolt from 1889–1896 in the eleven states of the old Confederacy. Several monographs and biographical accounts adequately cover the state level for the period under consideration, but no full scale account encompassing the entire region is available. There remains also a hiatus in Southern historiography concerning the blacks' role in the Populist movement. It is hoped that this study will partially fill these gaps and supply a regional portrait of Populism's biracial experiment.

In evaluating the attitudes of the Southern Populist movement toward the Negro, twentieth century historians have expressed three divergent viewpoints. The progressive historians of the 1920s and 1930s regarded the black man as a puppet, a willing tool with which the opposition emasculated the agrarian movement. The black man, according to this school, was a docile drone who sold his vote for whiskey or a few dollars.

By the 1950s, however, members of the new consensus school of historiography tended to view the black as an important class ally in the overall agrarian movement. To such interpreters of the Southern scene, the Negro's role within the Populist movement was more important than earlier assumed, and the relationship thus developed between the two races was seen as a viable alternative to the demagogic racism of the twentieth century. The Black Revolution, it seemed, had challenged historians to detect a continuous thread of interracial harmony in the American past, particularly in the South where oppression and exploitation of the black man had shaped so much of our history.

This interpretation has been challenged in more recent years by other voices who question the "myth" that a viable interracial coalition could ever have existed between the politically and economically insecure blacks and a more secure white agrarian class. More recently, the existence of any fruitful communication between the races is being challenged, specifically as a result of "institutional racism" in American society. Placing their emphasis on race rather than class, such voices as Charles Crowe, Lawrence Friedman, and Robert Saunders have set out to dispel the "myth" of racial harmony woven about the early Populist character.

Yet, Southern Populism would seem to be a many faceted crystal which does not fit easily into any set historiographical formula. In technique as well as in approach, this book has sought a renewed emphasis upon complexity, to examine

what the sociologist Pierre L. van den Berghe called "*Herrenvolk* democracy"—
the vast gap between egalitarian rhetoric and the crude contrasts in black-white
relations.[1] This volume tests these twin themes and attempts to sort out the myths
surrounding Populism and the Negro.

Populism is remembered rather romantically these days as a noble rising of "the
people" and this "New Populism" has resulted in a renewed verbal attack on the
conflict of interests at the bottom of the American pyramid. Amidst the rhetoric of
the day a New Jersey advertising man named Daniel Gaby has declared himself
"the Populist" senatorial candidate, explaining at impressive length that he wants
to resolve this age-old conflict between "poor blacks and working whites." Like
the old Populism, this new movement spiels the same attractive rhetoric to exploit
frustrations and build a base of working class support. Based on such a foundation
of "natural interest" it is difficult to visualize the new Populism lasting any longer
than the old—and for pretty much the same reasons. Because of these events, new
works on Populist racial attitudes take on a renewed importance.[2] In its coarser
illiberal form, the new Populism, like the old, could turn out to be the same old
backlash in disguise, for visceral prejudice all too often overpowers economic
interests in America. "Race in the South, as in the nation," Carl Degler has
observed, "has always overwhelmed class."[3]

Degler is right in stressing the continuing power of racist ideas in America—for
racism effectively precluded the old Populism from uniting groups of deprived
people who had only recently been at each other's throats. But for all its ambivalence, its rhetoric confusion, and social reaction, Populism strongly suggested an
abuse of economic power and an overpowering mania for money as the central
theme of Southern history; and its legacy survives in a certain facile school of
historians of the South. "The mania for making a fast buck, or even a slow buck, is
so widespread in the Deep South today," according to a modern analyst, "that it
remains in fact more troublesome than racism; the mind of the South is much more
preoccupied with it."[4] In the same view, another observer has concluded that
"money rather than ideology had been [the Southerner's] main motivation since
slavery."[5] Thus, Populism is an "ism" which has currently resurfaced in many
different forms but in a decidedly more respectable position. Its proponents'
repeated insistence on judging the movement on the basis of popular images and
stereotypes rather than its historical record makes this current vogue all the more
unfortunate. Perhaps in a small way this book may serve as a corrective.

INTRODUCTION

Populism has become such a protean term in American political life that one might infer that Populism was a central and victorious tradition rather than a brief episode of agrarian protest in the 1890s that failed to bring either power or economic relief to the small farmers of the South and the prairie states. Publicists of the left and of the right compete for the use of the term to describe their particular version of the common man's deepest desires and discontents, and politicians ranging from George Wallace to Fred Harris and Ronald Reagan to Ramsey Clark campaign with varying degrees of justification under the Populist banner. It is one of history's wonderful tricks.

The new Populism comes in many surprising shades, but antielitism is its common color. From the right, for instance, Kevin Phillips in *Mediacracy: American Parties and Politics in the Communications Age* argues that the old American commercial and industrial elites have been surpassed in power by an emerging new elite whose members dominate the "knowledge sector," those institutions having to do with the creation, manipulation, and dissemination of knowledge. In contrast to the old economic elite, the new elite is overwhelmingly liberal, though its center of strength is still in the Northeast. The new Populist majority (which is arising in opposition to the new elite, according to Phillips) will derive largely from the old Populist areas in the West and the South but it will be located in suburbia and among urban ethnic communities rather than on isolated farms. William A. Rusher, publisher of the *National Review,* calls for a similar Populism of the right in his book, *The Making of the New Majority.* Rusher's "Great Coalition" will be formed of the "economic conservatives" of the Republican Party and the "social conservatives" (Southerners, blue collar workers, ethnics). In addition, Rusher's rhetoric is redolent of the old Populist dichotomy between "producers" and "nonproducers," though the new nonproducers are not the bankers and Robber Barons but the intellectuals, bureaucrats, and welfare parasites.

At the other end of the political spectrum, the locale of protest has also changed, as one can see from the fact that Jack Newfield and Jeff Greenfield issued their new "Populist Manifesto" in 1971, not from Kansas or Georgia but in *New York Magazine* and in an Op Ed piece in the *New York Times,* as well as in a book published by the eastern communications establishment. As sophisticated alumni of the New Left, critically sympathetic to the humanizing and democratizing goals of the movement in the 1960s, Newfield and Greenfield called for a biracial movement of lower-income people in the United States to redistribute wealth and power in a more equalitarian way. "Unlike the New Left or the proponents of Consciousness III, populism recognizes that concentrated power will not be defeated by blowing up a few men's rooms or by wearing bell bottoms to a Grateful Dead concert. It will be effectively challenged when enough of us realize that corporate power, just like excessive government power, is a threat to democratic society. And the tactic for this challenge is a political coalition of economic self-interest among black and brown Americans, working-class whites, and the best reformers.''

Though they originate from fundamentally different urges, these competing forms of the new populism share a clear antielitist thrust. In this, they are historically faithful. At its core, populism is antielitist. It is the old American belief in the ability of the common man to govern himself, coupled with the belief that those currently in positions of power are serving special interests rather than the common interest. The Populist answer is usually to replace the elitists with authentic members of the folk and to redistribute wealth and power changes in the political system. Such Populist motivations have played a part in the growth in the government's role as a regulator of economic activity and in the agitation for various techniques of direct democracy to make the political system more responsive to the popular will. In these ways, Populists have argued, corporate power and corporate subversion of government power could be checked.

In addition to the antielitism which is common to all forms of populism, a central concern with biracial politics links the old Populists and the new, the Populists of the Left and of the Right. Newfield and Greenfield unambiguously place their hopes for success on the ability of the new populism of the Left to create a successful biracial political coalition, but they charged the original Populists with racism, xenophobia, and paranoia in an unqualified way that cannot be supported by the historical record which is given its most comprehensive treatment by Gerald H. Gaither in this book, *Blacks and the Populist Revolt*. From Gaither's careful attempt to portray the full range of Populists' reality in the 1890s with regard to race, one gets a much more complicated picture which is difficult to summarize in a neat generalization. Racism was a pathology that abounded in America in the late nineteenth century, but Gaither's narrative shows more completely than any previous history that Populists were afflicted in no greater degree than the population at large. On the contrary, the burden of the evidence and testimony runs in the other direction.

Between the end of Reconstruction in the 1870s and the creation around the turn of the century of the one party system based on legal disfranchisement in the white primary, a period of a continuously deepening depression in staple crop agriculture, the South was the scene of intense political conflict between the Democratic and Republican parties, a conflict modulated by a third party movement. Blacks continued to vote in large enough numbers to make the Republican party a continuing threat and to hold out the promise of victory to any independent movement which could put together in a single coalition discontented black and white farmers. Such movements, of which the People's Party in the 1890s was the foremost example, actually won one statewide election in Virginia in the 1880s and in North Carolina in the 1890s and came very close in such states as Georgia and Alabama.

Politics in nineteenth century America was more an ethnic than a class phenomenon. An emerging generation of quantitative historians over the last decade has been documenting the extent to which cohesive cultural traditions have been the most significant determinate of lasting political identity in America. The racial factor in southern politics was an especially extreme form of this "cross of culture," one that was disregarded by the independent movements and populism, and one on which the modern Right Wing Populists are depending.

Although the evidence is sketchy and inconsistent, there is probably enough in Gerald Gaither's treatment to substantiate the claim that Populists sincerely tried to construct a biracial, class-oriented political party. Blacks served in the party's hierarchy at every level, albeit in limited numbers, and white Populist candidates made rational appeals for black votes. Gaither's portrait is consistent with that of C. Vann Woodward in *The Strange Career of Jim Crow*. Writing in 1955, Woodward asserted that, "it is altogether probable that during the brief Populist upheaval of the nineties Negroes and native whites achieved a greater comity of mind and harmony of political purpose than ever before or since in the South."

No scholar has claimed that the Populists were advocates of social equality between the races. Theirs was a very pragmatic, or perhaps purely expedient, appeal for political cooperation based on the idea that poor whites and poor blacks had the same economic problems. "This was an equalitarianism of want and poverty," Woodward writes, "the kinship of a common grievance and a common oppressor. As a Texas Populist expressed the new equalitarianism, 'they are in the ditch just like we are.' " Gerald Gaither is careful to point out that one of the major stumbling blocks to racial cooperation in the Populist movement was the difference in class interests between landless blacks and small land-holding whites.

Nevertheless, some real biracialism existed within Populism. The most striking example of biracial political cooperation at the local level has been produced by Lawrence C. Goodwin of Duke University using oral history sources to reconstruct the story of Populism in Grimes County, Texas, which was the culmination of a black-white coalition, based on intricate family alliances dating back to Reconstruction. The relationship between whites and blacks within Populism is symbolized by the fact that in Grimes County the Populist sheriff was white and one of his deputies was black, rather than vice versa. Successful in the county elections of 1896 and 1898, the biracial Populist coalition was brutally repressed by the White Man's Union using physical intimidation, terrorism, and murder to gain a landslide victory for white supremacy in 1900.

White Democrats interpreted Populism as a threat to white rule and more importantly, in this writer's opinion, as a threat to the rule of a particular group of whites. As soon as politically possible, therefore, steps were taken to remove the threat by removing the black voter. Between 1889, when Florida enacted a poll tax and 1908 when Georgia adopted a disfranchising constitutional amendment, every Southern state took steps to restrict the electorate. This was also a period of tense racial conflict; lynching reached its tortuous peak in 1893 and 1894, and blacks were being proscribed from area after area of life. About 1910, the informal and fluctuating patterns of race relations of the 1880s was replaced by rigid, uniform, and statutory segregation. Though historians have argued over which class of whites was most responsible for the disfranchisement of black voters, the evidence is clear that in every state the most effective opposition to disfranchisement came from Populists. This was probably not racial altruism, but it does indicate that lower economic groups are not always so blinded by racial prejudice that they cannot see their own self-interest.

As subsequent history demonstrated, it was not in the economic interests of lower income whites to have blacks proscribed from politics, especially inasmuch as the same legal and structural barriers lowered the level of white participation as well. V. O. Key, Jr., in his classic study, *Southern Politics in State and Nation,* argued convincingly that the southern delegation to Congress, and presumably other successful southern politicians as well, were more conservative than the general southern public because lower income groups were relatively inactive in politics. The one party system, and the personal factionalism it bred, contributed to the lack of responsiveness of elected officials to the needs of their poorer constituents. This accounts for the lower "social pay-out" of the political system. The lack of structure and organization also created an atmosphere in which demagoguery was necessary in order for a maverick or a politician in a hurry to get the attention of the voters and lure them to the polls.

Key's major theme with regard to southern politics was that race, even after disfranchisement, was the strongest factor affecting political behavior and, more significantly, that racial issues were raised and manipulated in order to mute class antagonisms that lay smoldering beneath the surface. Such diverse commentators as Robert Sherrill and Kevin Phillips agree with Key, though they follow the implications in different directions. Phillips, in *The Emerging Republican Majority,* argues that the correct Republican Party strategy is to appeal to the South and its solid block of presidential electoral votes by emphasizing social issues (e.g., race) and not economic issues. Sherrill's muck-raking essays in *Gothic Politics in the Deep South* reek of the dualistic Populist critique in which the oppressed masses are exhorted to overthrow the privileged classes who are using racial phobias to keep the masses down. Race is the smokescreen which hides the economic self-interest of the masses from themselves.

The old Populist dream of a class-oriented, biracial alliance is one that has long been shared by other American radicals and was particularly popular during one phase of the Civil Rights movement. The solidarity of the oppressed was an attractive sentiment among middle class, white, New Left students who were constructing a myth of themselves as members of the proletariat. In the summer of 1963, when the Student Nonviolent Coordinating Committee was still an interracial and integrationist movement trying to organize black communities in the South, Students for a Democratic Society launched the Economic Research and Action Project which sent teams of young people to organize northern white working-class neighborhoods. ERAP loosely coordinated its activities with SNCC in an attempt to be an interracial movement of the poor.

This and other alliances between black and white radicals during the 1960s was an uneasy relationship at best, for reasons too complex to pursue here. Suffice it to say that the persistent arguments between black and white radicals was over the question of whether America's pathological condition was the result of race or class oppression. White radicals argued that class was the major issue and that the ruling class in America had always used ethnic diversity to prevent the working class from organizing. Black radicals would reply that whites had the luxury of believing in the fundamental nature of class because they were not black. This is the oversimplified gist of Harold Cruse's insistence in all of his works on the needs for a black cultural revolution. In any case, the emergence of black power after 1966 separated the black and white movements and each subsequently splintered into violent ineffectiveness.

A left cataclysmic view of the grass roots history of the movement since 1966 might find the trend in Lowndes County to be typical. Lowndes County, in Alabama's black belt, was the scene of two infamous Civil Rights murders. It was also the county selected for the target of a new political organization effort by Stokeley Carmichael in 1966 after the passage of the Voting Rights Act the previous year provided some hope that black voters could be registered. The Lowndes County Freedom Organization, whose symbol was the black panther before the group in Oakland had discovered the symbolic importance of that animal, was thus the first political experiment in black power. Soon, however, Stokeley Carmichael left Lowndes for more global roles and the LCFO was merged into the National Democratic Party of Alabama, an anti-Wallace and mostly black statewide group. Soon, with the addition of black voters to the roles, politics were biracial and taking place within the regular Democratic party. John Hulett, the black sheriff, tentatively supports George Wallace for the obvious reasons, as did Mayor Johnny Ford in nearby Tuskegee. The separate black organization no longer exists in Lowndes.

On a larger scale as well, the Civil Rights Movement, the one man one vote decision of the Supreme Court, and the Voting Rights Act of 1965 have worked their wonders. In 1960, there were only 1.4 million black voters in the 11 southern states, primarily in the Rim South, comprising 28% of the black voting age population. By 1974, there were 3.7 million black voters in those states, almost 70% of those eligible. About 2% of the 79 thousand public officials in the South are now black. This is a low figure when compared to the 20% of the population that is black but it is significant in view of the lily white nature of public offices in 1960. Half of the black office holders in the nation are in the South and the South now boasts 3 black members of the House of Representatives: Barbara Jordan of Houston, Harold Ford of Memphis, and Andy Young of Atlanta. Perhaps a more graphic representation of the change is the picture of George Wallace crowning a black homecoming queen or Strom Thurmond introducing his new black legislative aide.

Do such advances indicate that a new day dawned, and, if so, is future progress for blacks to be gained through racially homogeneous and third party movement or does the future lie in the direction of biracial alliances as in the radical myth or biacial alliances dominated by middle-class leadership and interests?

Only 102 of the more than 1,000 counties in the 11 southern states, and only one of the cities of the region, have black majorities. No one seriously argues that separatist politics is the long-term answer for southern blacks. The question is whether or not coalition politics will work for blacks, in the sense of producing social and economic benefits for the masses, unless the black part of the coalition is as highly organized, as aware of its own self-interests, and as disciplined as the white part of the coalition. Stokeley Carmichael and Charles Hamilton in their book, *Black Power,* argued that blacks needed to create an independent base of power before entering into alliances with other groups to obtain specific goals of mutual interest. Left unanswered was the question of what happens in the meantime.

In the meantime, however, we do have some interesting examples of biracial coalitions that are successful. In Atlanta, Maynard Jackson was elected with white support though the coalition is hardly of the Populist variety. It depends instead on the well worked middle class power networks that have extended across the racial lines in Atlanta for some time. Barbara Jordan is supported in her Houston constituency by a significant segment of whites as well as by blacks and Chicanos. More importantly, Chandler Davidson's analyses of nonpartisan elections over the last decade show that working-class whites do not automatically vote against black candidates and will join black voters to support liberal candidates of both races if important bread and butter issues are at stake. In New Orleans, Mayor Moon Landrieu maintains power through the skillful use of very traditional political techniques in favor of the white and black political organizations, which joined to put him in office. Over the past decade in New Orleans, though the picture is somewhat mixed, when racial and economic liberalism were combined in a single candidate, biracial labor coalitions appeared. In a more militant vein, there was the famous Charleston hospital strike, fought and won by an integrated union.

One must either dismiss all the biracial success stories as meaningless to the lives of the common black man or entertain the notion, contra Carmichael and Hamilton, and contra Rusher and Phillips, that under certain conditions coalition politics will work without a prolonged period of separatism and consciousness raising.

What one thinks those conditions for success are depends in part upon what one thinks of the attitudes of working-class whites on race. Most historians maintain, and Gerald Gaither agrees, that the original Populism failed in the 1890s because the conservative whites were successful in convincing poor whites that a vote for Populism was racial treason and that the fate of all Anglo-Saxons depended upon white solidarity within the Democratic Party. Some whites, significantly those under the greatest economic pressure, and furthest removed from racial pressure (i.e., poor whites in white counties), were able to violate the taboo and plunge into the politics of economic self-interest. Others clung to the Proto-Dorian bond and followed their traditional leaders from the elite orders of society. Clearly then, working-class whites are more amenable to supporting a biracial coalition when the salience of racial issues is low and that of economic issues is high.

The attitude of blacks is obviously also important. Will they suspend their distrust of whites long enough to vote for a common candidate? Even white radicals are suspect to blacks. Just as there was some racial scapegoating on the part of bitterly frustrated white Populists in the 1890s after being defeated by fraud, violence, and conservative white manipulation of the black vote, there was an increase in the cynicism of blacks about the intentions of white reformers. For instance, Lynchburg, Virginia, sported a highly participatory political arena in the 1880s. Toward the end of that decade, the Knights of Labor even briefly gained control of that small city by running a biracial, working class ticket and appealing to the working man of both races. Later, after a flurry of Populism in the state, a working man's party was formed in Lynchburg for the municipal elections of 1897. The ticket (consisting of two professional men, two grocers, two shopkeepers, an old reformer who was an insurance agent, and four artisans), which had direct links with the old Knights of Labor party, made a strong and direct appeal in a series of mass meetings for black votes. Soon, however, a prominent black began endorsing the Democratic ticket and holding rallies for its conservative white candidates. As one of the black leaders told a black mass meeting, every time a group of whites get disgruntled, they rebel against the Democrats and "calling themselves 'working men' or 'Populists' endeavor to secure the support of the colored men in their effort to get office." The Working Man's Party lost the election and did not do especially well in the black ward. This is an example of the alliance between blacks and Bourbons against the rednecks, to put it in inelegant terms. White Democrats worked very hard throughout the South in the 1890s convincing blacks, especially blacks in influential and vulnerable positions, that they had more to gain from upper-class white people than from rednecks. James Q. Wilson and Edward Banfield, among contemporary political scientists, argue that this Bourbon-black combination represents the best tactic for blacks, and their argument fits the frequent findings of social scientists that racial tolerance among whites increases with income and education. Atlanta is an example of a city in which this pattern exists, but it may depend for success on the existence of a large, old well-established and well-organized black bourgeoisie which is not available to the same degree in other cities. It also may be true that biracial coalitions do not depend on tolerance but on perceived self-interest.

Despite the many hazards in the limited payoff thus far, it is clear the biracial coalitions of various kinds are working in different parts of the South under an assortment of conditions. The millennium certainly has not arrived and no true radical would claim any of the existing examples as a sort of populistic working-class movement that will eventually lead to liberation.

The original Populism was a response to inadequate economic growth, a condition which leads the poor to complain about the division of wealth and power. For all their turbulence, the 1960s and early 1970s were not primarily a period of class-oriented movement. They were, for the most part, an economic boom time and they spawned various movements against cultural repression: of blacks, students, women, Indians, homosexuals. It may well be that a period of slower economic growth into which we are now entering will stimulate class antagonisms to the extent necessary to foster neopopulistic reform movements.

On the other hand, if the ecologists, the consumer advocates, public interest lawyers, and the Club of Rome report are right, we are in for a new era of declining average levels of consumption in which the most important issues may be those having to do with such things as water quality, air quality, and a vast array of public services. If we do reach an era of economic stasis, the strains within our political system will be severe. Because people with lower incomes are likely to have different priorities from people with higher incomes, there is bound to be a period of turbulence and some conflict between groups interested in economic justice and those interested in the new environmental issues. This will accentuate the verging class interests and may well lead to a leveling trend in income distribution.

Even if one thinks that we have not reached the realistic limits of democratic governance in this country, it is not at all clear that the future of Populism is very bright. In the first place, society has changed shape now so that a large portion of it thinks of itself as middle class, with all of the complacency and inhibitions against organization which that term implies. Moreover, to the extent that the new environmental issues capture the attention of the public, the possibility of an old style, populistic, mass movement declines.

Mass movements depend on a bit of pageantry in order to mobilize people; that is why they sometimes degenerate into pure expressive politics and fake reform. The new issues do not lend themselves too well to mass appeals. This is not so much because they cannot be dramatized, for they can be dramatized to some degree, but because they are usually very technical and complex and solutions are not at all clear. In these areas, knowledge is power, and we may have to depend on the "Genteel Populist" like Ralph Nader and John Gardner's "Common Cause" to defend the public interest.

Ralph Nader is not a mass movement and to an old Populist would appear to be as elite as any Robber Baron. It may be, however, that the new issues demand so much sophistication and such continuous monitoring and tinkering that volatile mass movements do not provide an effective approach to them. This points to the need for a solution to one of the most troublesome dilemmas of a free society, which is that the most privileged groups have the most influence. That is the issue Populists have always identified as the crucial one for a democracy, and it is still there. Gerald Gaither's book helps us understand better its racial dimensions.

SHELDON HACKNEY

Blacks and the
Populist Revolt

I

THE BLACK AND THE

FARMERS' ALLIANCE MOVEMENT:

A PARADIGM FOR POPULISM

The last quarter of the nineteenth century was a period of intense agrarian ferment in the South. As prices declined, a number of organizations were created to express the discontent and aspirations of the Southern farmer. Among these organizations the Farmers' Alliance was the most important of the lot, at least by the late 1880s. It was the Alliance which ultimately served as the forerunner of the Populist Party, a political vehicle of agrarian protest.

While the *modus operandi* of the Alliance and the Populist movements exhibited different approaches, the former preferring to work within the Democratic Party and the latter creating its own independent political activity, both, nevertheless, did have something of the same purpose and membership. With the failure of one movement to achieve its purpose, the creation of the other began. "Populism in the South," according to Tom Watson, "was the legitimate offspring of the Farmers' Alliance. . . ."[1] Furthermore, because of the extensive carry-over of membership from one movement to the other, the Populist racial ideology was, to a large extent, a transference of attitudes into a similar movement, utilizing different means toward accomplishing the same goal: alleviation of agrarian grievances.[2] Because of such an inextricable relationship, the racial ideology of one movement is, indeed, inseparable from a study of the collective whole.

The white Alliance originated in Lampasas County, Texas, as early as 1874 or 1875 as a cooperative effort in purchasing supplies, furnishing effective opposition to land sharks and cattle barons, and preventing cattle rustling.[3] There soon appeared on the scene C. W. Macune, a man with extensive plans and ambitions for the Alliance.[4] Under his charismatic leadership, the organization spread rapidly across the South, introducing itself in Macune's words, as "a strictly white man's nonpolitical secret business organization."[5]

As the order spread eastward, it encountered other organizations of similar aims and nature. Obviously the most expedient process of expansion was a union of forces with these organizations. Perhaps the most important of these mergers was made with the Louisiana Farmers' Union in 1887. With this union the National Farmers' Alliance and Co-operative Union of America, commonly referred to as the Southern Alliance, came into official being. In 1888, a similar merger with the Agricultural Wheel was proposed. After considerable debate, consolidation was finally agreed upon in December, at a gathering of delegates in Meridian, Mississippi.[6]

In the early days of the Alliance movement, the black, as a potential recruit, received only minor consideration. With Reconstruction and the hardening of racial attitudes, the prerogative of the group or individual to express discontent was largely governed by the common denominators of racial solidarity and the Democratic party in the South. In the mind of the white South, any aberrant action in white ranks was viewed suspiciously as an attempt to revive the "horrors" of Black Reconstruction.[7] It was not only expedient but necessary for the Alliance to early disregard the Negro.

In 1882, the prevailing spirit of racial distrust, along with a hostile barrage of propaganda, were probably the motivating factors that caused the Alliance to restrict officially its membership to whites and to discourage strongly its membership from becoming involved in or endorsing any "distinct party."[8] While the Alliance chose not to admit blacks into its ranks, with three-fourths of the Negro population engaged in agrarian pursuits it was imperative to create a parallel black organization, if for no other motivation than self-interest.[9] It was impossible to establish a profitable agricultural system in the South while the Negro acted as a potential competitor and a cheap source of exploitable labor. The small white farmer soon realized that he could rise no higher on the ladder of prosperity than his black counterpart. As the *National Economist,* the official organ of the Southern Alliance, observed in 1891,

> No one realizes better than [the Southern white farmer], if he allows sharpers to swindle the colored man by paying him excessively low prices for his cotton, by taking advantage of his necessity for money, . . . such low prices will tend to keep prices low until [the white farmers] . . . are compelled to sell . . . and . . . perpetuate the low prices. The fact is that the law of self preservation compels the Southern white farmer to . . . hold [the Negro] out of the clutches of the exploiter. . . .[10]

Thus while expediency necessitated the black's early exclusion from the order, it also required that he later be included in the grandiose agrarian design.

The Northern Alliance was also instrumental in promoting the idea of a Negro order in the South. Unlike its Southern counterpart, the Northern Alliance accepted the philosophy that anyone, regardless of color, should be included in the movement if born on the farm or involved in an occupation that related to agrarian pursuits.[11] Because of economic and geographical considerations, as well as the concentration of Negro population in the South, a Northern-based Colored Alliance would have been of little value from an organizational standpoint.

Milton George, editor of the *Western Rural* of Chicago, promoted the delicate task of organizing a Negro order in the South. He reasoned that the farmer class should organize to protect its interest and that a working coalition with the Negro agricultural class could only serve to further this goal. Thus, a combination of self-interest and self-consciousness were the chief progenitors of white interest in the Colored Alliance. Its creation cannot be said to have been inspired by any one single motivation, unless it was the elevation of the farmers' declining status.[12]

The Colored Alliance was founded December 11, 1886, in Houston County, Texas.[13] Attracted by ritual, secrecy, and the possible economic benefits of the order, the membership of the organization at the local level rose substantially. Within a few days it had spread to such an extent throughout Houston and neighboring counties that it was deemed necessary to call a convention at Good Hope Baptist Church in Weldon to discuss the possibility of a sub-Alliance merger. All of this took place within a mere eighteen days after the founding of the first local, indicating its magnetic quality to the black masses. The delegates "unanimously agreed" that "union and organization" were absolute necessities to the "earthly salvation of the Negro farmer".[14] The convention also set forth a "declaration of purposes," stating its reasons why a separate Colored Alliance was necessary, and outlining goals the organization hoped to achieve. With the adoption of this declaration, the entire convention of "sixteen colored men and citizens of Texas," signed the document and adjourned.[15]

The Colored Alliance was well aware of the difficulty involved, and the lack of desire by many blacks of integrating with the white Alliance. They recognized the necessity of loyalty to the Southern racial norm, be it black separatism or white supremacy; and as such, any organizational integration was highly undesirable to both organizations. The principal if not the entire impetus for this Colored Alliance separatism was the increasing emphasis blacks in the 1880s were putting upon self-help, economic development, and racial organization as a temporary tactic to attain wealth and power, which would in turn, it was believed, result in the subsequent granting of equal rights by the whites out of respect. At bottom, it was the black separatist counterpart to the "gospel of wealth" philosophy which permeated most white attitudes of the period.[16] The economic self-help drive was paramount in the Colored Alliance, and its concerted emphasis was particularly fitted to give the organization an even more conservative cast toward integration than it otherwise would have had at this time. The blacks did, however, make it clear from the very beginning that they desired ideological integration and unity of broad purpose with the white Alliance, through any means that would be mutually beneficial to both races. One resolution stated rather succinctly:

> That though we are organizing separate and apart from the Farmers' Alliance now existing in Texas, composed of white members, we believe it will be to our interest to work in harmony with that organization. That we ask the members of the white Alliance throughout the United States to aid us in perfecting our organization.[17]

R. M. Humphrey of Lovelady, Texas, "a white man, a Texas Baptist preacher who spent some years in missionary work among the Negroes," was elected

General Superintendent and presented with the awesome responsibility of organizing and spreading the Colored Alliance gospel throughout the South. An obscure itinerant preacher, Humphrey was virtually unknown up to this point and with the later decline of the Colored Alliance he faded back into obscurity. Described as "an elderly man of large frame and portly person, with plain speech and a free blunt manner," he was reportedly wanted by the blacks because "of his ability and because of their confidence in him as a friend of the race." Privately, however, his position was probably more as an alternate white spokesman who could openly express a militance that would be denied to blacks. In addition to his missionary work, Humphrey brought with him about "twenty-five years" experience in agriculture during which time he had employed "a lot of Negroes, good colored people." It was said that he "used" to be a Democrat although he had voted "a few republican tickets, but mighty few."[18] Undoubtedly Humphrey was aware of the magnitude of his task as well as the meager chances of making a success of the order. This was, he wrote later, an organization that "had no money, no credit, few friends, and was expected to reform and regenerate a race which, from long endurance and oppression and chattel slavery, had become extremely besotted and ignorant."[19]

Despite such seemingly insurmountable obstacles, Humphrey apparently possessed the necessary missionary zeal and initiative required of his office. The order presently began to spread to other states with newly organized branches adopting the Texas pattern and purpose, adding some slight modifications to fit local problems. One can only surmise whether this early success was due mainly to the magnetism of the black self-help philosophy, the organizational talents of Humphrey, the destitute condition of the black farmer, or a combination of the three.

Once the Colored Alliance achieved interstate proportions, it became legally necessary to obtain a federal charter. A convention of the various state Colored Alliances was assembled in Lovelady on March 14, 1888, to discuss the procurement of this charter. After some debate, it was decided to regard the Colored Alliance as a trade union for legal purposes. A charter application was then forwarded to the necessary authorities, using this classification. The federal government apparently concurred with the definition of the order since a charter was granted and duly filed with the Recorder of Deeds in Washington.[20] Thus, the Colored Farmers' National Alliance and Cooperative Union was born.

As the Colored Alliance moved toward the possibility of becoming in fact as well as in name a nationwide organization, it encountered a variety of forces and attitudes. A brief examination of selected Southern state orders will reveal a number of important points about the movement, not the least being the diverse Southern white attitudes toward the different orders. While little is known about the Alliances' organizational methods, it seems probable that it imitated the white Southern Alliance, sending forth organizers in teams, probably recruited on the state level. According to Leonidas L. Polk, president of the Southern Alliance, "most of its organizers [were] white."[21] However, this statement was not true in all states. In Tennessee, for example, whites were barred from any official

1870: Bale of Cotton brought $120

1880: Two Bales of Cotton brought $120

1890: 2 and 2/3 Bales of Cotton brought $120

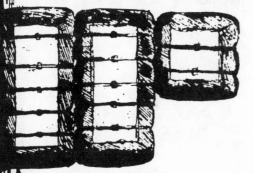

1894: 4 and 4/5 Bales of Cotton brought $120

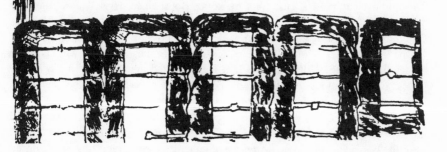

FIGURE 1. POST-CIVIL WAR DEFLATION
(From *People's Party Paper,* October 5, 1894.)

organizing of Colored Alliance lodges unless commissioned specifically by the state's General Superintendent.[22] Conversely, the opposite situation ostensibly occurred in Alabama. A white Texas organizer who came to the state in 1889 expressed his hope "that the Farmers' Alliance men everywhere will take hold and organize or aid in organizing the colored farmer, and placing him in an attitude to co-operate intelligently and systematically."[23] This indicates, at least in Alabama, that a certain unity of endeavor existed from the start between the orders of both races, with regard to recruiting and organizing the Negro farmer.

The Alabama blacks had expressed little more than quizzical interest in the Alliance movement until the consolidation of the Wheel and Alliance in Meridian, Mississippi, in December, 1888. At the Meridian meeting the white Alliance stated its desire for the creation of a separate Colored Alliance. Considering the poverty of the region, the concentration of black population, and this gesture of approval by the whites, it would indeed have been surprising if an organization had not resulted. Thus, with white aid and sympathy, the Alabama Negro took immediate advantage of this opportunity.[24]

It appears that black orders came into existence in Alabama as early as January, 1889, only a month after the white Alliance expressed the need for such orders. Moreover, by the summer of the same year the membership had reportedly reached 50,000. In the formative years of the Colored Alliance, the Alabama whites gave their hearty approval of the order.[25] If the hapless black farmer could improve his lot, it would doubtless yield a rich harvest in white ranks as well! As one newspaper expressed it: "The white and colored Alliance are united in their war against trusts, and in promotion of the doctrine that farmers should establish cooperative stores, and manufactures, and publish their own newspapers, conduct their own schools. . . ."[26] However, this early rationale of the movement dissolved when the Alliances became associated in the public mind with political developments.

The eventual downfall of the order was brought about by the political complexities of the state movement. The state, especially the Black Belt, reacted violently against any attempt on the part of the blacks to enter politics. Because of the "almost paranoid accusations by some Bourbons" as well as a show of disapproval from the conservative faction of the white Alliance, the Alabama Colored Alliance movement began to decline by 1892.[27]

One of the outstanding characteristics of the Tennessee order was its close association with the Colored Wheel. It was reported that "a great many of our [black] brothers belong to both orders."[28] Early efforts to bring Tennessee blacks into the Alliance fold were conducted during the summer of 1888 by C. A. Vaughn of Detroit (Tipton County).[29] While the presence of the Colored Wheel prevented the expected membership response, the combined movement of the two orders, nevertheless, achieved a notable degree of general success, reporting 387 Colored Wheels and Alliances by October, 1888.[30]

The willingness of the Tennessee Negro farmer to participate in the Alliance and

Wheel is attested to many times in the official state organ, the *Weekly Toiler*. As one state lecturer remarked:

> The colored people show an eagerness for information and enthusiasm for our cause and principles, which is unsurpassed by any audience I have ever addressed. I am convinced that the colored farmers of Tennessee, if properly educated will make active working members of the order. The prejudices growing out of their former condition of slavery are gradually disappearing. . . .

He went on to express his hope that "the white brethren will . . . treat them kindly" and show them "that our fight is a common fight for their interest. . . ."[31]

Yet, the Tennessee Colored Alliance suffered a chronic failing, common to many state Alliances—a shortage of funds. While the white Alliance permitted the black members to trade through the Memphis and Nashville Exchange, it was hoped that the Colored Alliance would establish its own business concerns. The *Weekly Toiler* exclaimed that the black order of the state should "blush with shame" at its failure to raise funds to establish its own Exchange. While the Colored Texas Alliance was reportedly worth $135,000 "above all liabilities," the Tennessee order had not managed to raise a "mere" $10,000.[32] In the light of the order's noted enthusiasm for the agrarian doctrines, it seems likely that their failure to establish a separate exchange was due to financial inability rather than any laxity of support.[33]

Despite this strong dependence on the white Alliance for moral and financial assistance, no major rift in policy or purpose initially occurred between the two orders. At their August, 1890, state convention in Pulaski, the Colored Alliance made clear its plan to "cooperate with the white people of the state. . . ." The *National Economist* expressed its belief that the Negro farmers of Tennessee, "under the wise counsels of their grand old leader" Humphrey were "laying a basis for the final adjustment of the race question. . . ."[34] Like the Colored Alliance, the white Alliance put great stress on economic activity in solving the race question. Underlying all this was the assumption that wealth and morality would negate racial prejudice.

The success of the Colored Alliance, and of the Tennessee Alliance movement in general, was constricted by the role the Negro order purportedly played in the state's politics. Though the Negro was never the nemesis in Tennessee politics that he was in other Southern states, the Democrats, nonetheless, managed to conjure up visions of "Black Republicanism" in the collective mind of the state's white electorate. Charges were made that the Tennessee Alliance was organizing the Negro to create a Republican ascendancy; but in light of the fact that most of the white Alliance members in the state were Democrats, this allegation seems unfounded. As in Alabama, the supposed interrelationship of the Negro, the Alliance, and the Republican Party presented the Tennessee Democrats with a potent weapon which proved to be the nemesis of the Tennessee Colored Alliance. During the 1890 election campaign especially, there was "a bitter and mendacious war" waged against the Alliance, because of its "aggressiveness" for "Alliance principles." Particularly vitrolic against the Alliance was Josiah Patterson, the "big brained old champion of Bourbon Democracy," who was a chief contender for the Democratic gubernatorial nomination. Making no appeal to the "ideal one gallus, copperas breeches man with the hoe," Patterson dwelled on the twin issues of the agricultural depression, attributing it to the farmers, and the demagogic rhetoric of a "white man's government."[35] Charges were made that the Alliance was organizing the Negro to create a Republican "ascendancy," but since most of the white Alliance members in the state were Democrats, this allegation seems unfounded. Furthermore, Tennessee Alliance men supported the state laws of 1889 to disfranchise black voters. The assertions of the opposition do not logically follow. The Colored Alliance leadership, in turn, had declared that "we are not for politics [party], we are for the man," preferring to measure candidates by the Alliance yardstick of performance rather than any party label. How much the blacks had turned away from the party of their fathers is largely a matter of conjecture. Nevertheless, such volatile charges presented the Democratic opposition with a formidable propaganda coup against the Colored Alliance. The enervating effects of this political campaign took its toll on the Tennessee Colored Alliance membership, which by its own admission had dropped from a July peak of 100,000 to 60,000 members in December, 1890, near the end of the campaign.[36]

In South Carolina, the Colored Alliance movement was inspired by a forerunner, the Cooperative Workers of America, a subsidiary of the Knights of Labor. Black locals were organized in 1886–1887, with the intended goal of raising the state's black agricultural force to a higher minimum wage, reportedly fifty cents per hundred pounds of cotton picked. Since any effort to organize the Negro was viewed with a jaundiced eye, the meetings of the order were clandestine and nocturnal, usually in Negro churches, with sentries posted to warn the members of any approaching intruder.[37] Despite these clandestine efforts, the movement soon aroused the suspicions of the whites, if for no other reason than the unusual manner in which the meetings were held. Was this the root of a black conspiracy? Were there plans to overthrow the state government in one swift move? Curious fear enveloped the white community—a state of mind which was reflected in an attack on all forms of racial organization.

During May, 1887, in Greenville County, an armed "posse" of white men took it upon themselves to investigate forcibly the activities of a local black order that had been secretive in its actions. The secretary was forced to surrender his membership list, consisting of only seventeen names. When each member was interrogated separately, it was discovered that the Negroes had joined the movement in anticipation of getting their rations at half price and with the possible idea of striking for a wage of a dollar a day. The community heaved a sigh of relief, but this was presently replaced with white indignation at such proposals. The threat of lynching was imminent; such black "insolence" could not be tolerated. White wrath soon rendered the state organization completely ineffective.[38]

With this organizational vacuum and the existence of the same grievances, the Colored Alliance found fertile ground for its beginnings in South Carolina. As early as September, 1888, in the immediate wake of the Cooperative failure, the Colored Alliance made its timely invasion of the state. Under the direction of T. E. Pratt of Cheraw, the order spread throughout the state, and by February, 1890, reportedly had 237 organized clubs and 30,000 members statewide.[39] While the white population of the state initially displayed neither enthusiasm for nor fear of the black order, the Colored Alliance did, however, on occasion receive sympathetic reactions from the white Alliance movement.[40]

Even though the Alliance experienced rapid growth up to 1890, the order began to flounder seriously by the fall of 1891, the immediate reasons being involvement in political and economic affairs. During the 1890 election with the rise of the Tillman machine, the Republicans, as well as a faction of the anti-Tillmanite Democrats, in their desperation turned to the Negro and the Colored Alliance for political support, but with little apparent success.[41]

Despite the Colored Alliance's nonpartisan nature in this effort, the existence of a Negro order in such numbers aroused the political fears of all factions. An abortive attempt in the fall of 1891 to create a general strike among the Negro cotton pickers resulted in a failure for the Colored Alliance. As we shall see later on this strike, not only from whites in the South Carolina Alliance, but in the rest of the South, resulted in intense hostility. After these two ventures, the animosity of the white community destined the order to oblivion; and after 1892, all mention of the organization disappears.[42]

While these three sketches of various state Colored Alliances are hardly definitive, they do, nonetheless, provide us with the opportunity to take note of certain general characteristics at the grassroots level. As is now clear, the Colored Alliance attracted support quickly from a broad area in the South. Within months after the first Texas sub-Alliance was founded, locals were to be found in nearby Arkansas; and within months after the founding of the national chapter, state organizations were to be found in widespread areas of the South.

The rapid manner in which these orders came into being was probably due more to the inordinately hard times experienced by the blacks rather than to any public relations effort of the central office in Houston. Aided by this unfortunate situation, the order symbolized "the substance of things hoped for, the evidence of things not seen" to the oppressed white, as well as to the black farmer.[43]

An economic motif, then, threaded through the Negro's attraction to the Alliance. During these years the Negro began to play a more responsible role in his immediate orbit. By the fall of 1891, it was reported "throughout the South [that] the colored man has been able to get more money for his cotton and pay less for his bacon."[44] It is difficult to measure the full extent of black economic development from the scanty literature, but it appears that the Negro's control over the economic essentials necessary for self-help and economic development were increasing.

While his progress was slow, very slow, there was a degree of tangible proof that the agrarian black masses, through self-help, might rise out of their oppressed economic state. For a brief time the vitality of the black farmer's emphasis on economic self-help and group success did appear to be a viable way to eliminate prejudice. If the white agrarian refused to grant the black this privilege, he would ostensibly be forced to pay an increasingly high price in terms of economic disorders which would disrupt the entire price and labor index of the South. Always in the background, the threat of self-interest loomed as an ever present reminder to the white Alliance that it could not fight the battle alone. In order to prosper, the white farmer reluctantly realized that he "must take with him all engaged in that occupation."[45]

The Colored Alliance, as has been noted, depended to a great extent upon the good will of the white South at large. Unfortunately, when black Alliance initiative conflicted with what the white community viewed as being in its best interest, as in South Carolina, the dispute was more often than not resolved to the disadvantage of the Negro.

Though in theory the Colored Alliances were of a nonpolitical and nonpartisan nature, the presence of such a large organized body of black voters conjured up the specter of Black Republicanism and the lingering fear of a political coup. By 1890–91, when many orders had participated in politics, the Bourbons began to subject the Alliance to an intense "ghost dance . . . of 'Negro supremacy.'"[46] By the fall of 1890, an election year in many states, a Virginian Allianceman remarked that "the great gun of white supremacy has been loaded and primed and trained upon our ranks. . . ."[47]

The Bourbons hoped—futilely, as it later developed—that this appeal to poor white agrarian prejudice, always just under the surface, would stem the mounting tide of political rebellion in the Alliance ranks. If, as a result of these tirades, the Conservatives could heal the split in white ranks and isolate the blacks, a class combination of considerable weight could be removed from the political landscape. The racial prejudices of the poor whites were being courted vigorously in an effort to divest them of any thought of organizing around any ideology except white supremacy.

Whether the Alliance movement concurred with the political philosophy of the Bourbons was of lesser importance than the fact that the proposals the Bourbons espoused had not come to be an accepted norm of regional conformity. When any constructive agitation emanated from the Alliance, especially the Negro order, these reforms were often regarded as a political tactic to revive Black Republicanism. For the Negro to become involved in or even merely accused of using political means to achieve his goals usually resulted in internecine strife—at the expense of the Colored Alliance in this case.

Financial dependence was also a determining factor which militated against the possibility of the Colored Alliance's establishing a firm independent policy of self-help. While some state exchanges, notably Texas, did achieve a marked degree of financial stability, most, as in Tennessee, found themselves dependent upon the financial good will of the white Alliance. If the white orders failed to take an active interest in their black brethren, the Negro orders were apt to founder. It should be noted here, however, that the white Alliance leadership, regarding the blacks as "an infant race just growing into manhood," expressed a marked degree of paternalism for the Colored Alliances.[48] Class or self-interest, as we have seen, forced the white rank-and-file to render aid to the black orders. All elements, despite the diversity of their racial philosophy, had the same end in mind: the uplifting of the farmer class through self-help, economic development, and racial organization.

Since Negroes as a group were financially destitute and unable to support large co-ops or exchanges—a condition exacerbated by poverty—it appears that many members of local orders rendered only token financial assistance to their clubs. The *National Alliance,* under Humphrey's editorship, counseled the order to stop "buying [Alliance] badges and regalia and all that kind of thing" and pay up their dues and subscribe to the paper to keep themselves better informed. While emphasizing the fact that "the [Colored] Alliance was organized to do you good," it was rather sharply pointed out that this had to be a reciprocal process.[49] While the extent of the practice is not known, the financial straits of the order were such that the neglect of only a small parcel of the membership would create financial havoc in any local chapter.

When viewed with an objective eye, the purported strength of the Colored Alliance appears to have been exaggerated. While faulty membership tabulations on the local level and misquoted press releases could have been added to the advertised total, the Colored Alliance administration must take the blame as the chief perpetrator of these claims.

In August, 1891, it was reported that "over 2,000 sub-Alliance charters have been issued for Colored Alliances since the Ocala convention [of December, 1890]."[50] In June of the same year (1891), the National Alliance reported that "more than 1,600 voters join the Colored Alliance every day that the sun rises."[51] If this astonishing rate of growth had continued for as long as a year, it would have produced approximately 595,000 new "voters"—a sign of potent growth, indeed, if true! If Humphrey authorized these figures—and we must assume he did as a result of his position—he probably made no personal gain as a result. While such prevarications are "unusual," to say the least, for a Baptist missionary, his only intentions were probably to gain influence and attract prospective members, all in hopes of furthering the order.

Equally as perplexing a problem is the difficulty of ascertaining the aggregate strength and geographic distribution of the Colored Alliance. An 1891 membership analysis by the General Superintendent revealed the following breakdown: 300,000 females, 150,000 males under twenty-one years of age, and 750,000 adult males, out of a total membership of nearly 1,200,000 "in more than twenty states."[52] As of December, 1890, however, the Colored Alliance president, J. S. Jackson, a black man, reported that the order represented only twelve states but had a membership of two million black farmers[53]—800,000 more than Humphrey would report nearly a year later (see Table I). The picture is further confused when the *Progressive Farmer,* quoting Humphrey from an interview, credited the organization with a membership of 1,200,000, and representing thirty states rather than twenty as reported by Jackson.[54] Ironically, these last two statements were made within two weeks of each other!

The diversity of these statements points out rather clearly that the extent of the order was probably unknown, even among its own officers. Moreover, in their eagerness to display an impressive total, the officers probably exaggerated their membership claims with the intent of currying political favor. It is highly doubtful that a member, once accepted by the order, was ever dropped from the roll whether his membership was in good standing or not. As previously noted, the dereliction of some members in paying their dues probably detracted from the whole but with no obvious difference being indicated by the officials.[55]

Near the end of 1891, rapid deterioration was evident in the order's size and effectiveness. One student has indicated that the order "collapsed about the end of 1891."[56] This viewpoint is further substantiated by a black paper, *The Republican,* which made the comment in January of 1892 that the Colored Alliance went "up like a rocket and down like a stick, a mere pull, a fizzle and she is gone."[57] While the order lingered through 1892, it never again possessed its former degree of importance. After 1892, the Colored Alliance was but a shadow of its former self in both strength and importance.

TABLE I

Colored Alliance Membership, 1890

	Membership		Discrepancy
State	July, 1890	December, 1890	Score
Alabama	75,000	100,000	+25,000
Arkansas	100,000	20,000	−80,000
Florida	20,000	*	*
Georgia	100,000	84,000	−16,000
Louisiana	20,000	50,000	+30,000
Mississippi	60,000	90,000	+30,000
North Carolina	100,000	55,000	−45,000
South Carolina	50,000	90,000	+40,000
Tennessee	100,000	60,000	−40,000
Texas	150,000	90,000	−60,000
Virginia	50,000	50,000	0
Totals	825,000[a]	689,000[b]	−116,000

*Figure not available.

[a]*Appleton's Annual Cyclopedia, 1890,* 301.

[b]*Progressive Farmer,* December 23, 1890; *Western Rural,* December 13, 1890, in Saloutos, *Farmer Movements,* 81; *Atlanta Constitution,* December 4, 1890, in Jack Abramowitz, "Accommodation and Militancy in Negro Life, 1876–1916" (Unpublished Doctoral dissertation, Columbia University, 1950), 30.

The diversity of opinion about the extent and strength of the Colored Alliance exemplifies the difficulty of reaching a conclusion. Historians have assessed the membership of the order from 800,000 to 1,300,000, depending on the individual and the period of interpretation.[58] The figure of 1,000,000, however, in all probability represented the peak strength of the National Colored Alliance. Evidence from both primary and secondary sources points to the fact that this peak was reached during the early months of 1890. (See Table I.)

The bulk of the order was concentrated in the South Atlantic and Gulf states, with the remainder scattered in Delaware, Ohio, Illinois, Indiana, Missouri, and some few clubs in Nebraska.[59] All states of the South eventually possessed orders but in varying degrees of strength.

A combination of factors brought about the downfall of the Colored Alliance. Internal dissension created a certain amount of disunity. As of late 1889, two Colored Alliances were in existence, both competing for the support of the Negro farmer. Minor differences existed in the orders, not only in their rituals but in their methods as well. Antagonism between the two groups became so pronounced that it was reported to have "divided our churches, broken up our schools, embittered our communities and created discord in our families. . . ."[60]

In early 1890, the two orders decided to compromise their differences. In the discussions that followed, R. M. Humphrey represented one group and Andrew J. Carothers the rebel group. Out of this conference the proclamation of a merger between the two orders was announced. It was also decided that the national headquarters would remain at Houston and the official name of the order would be retained as the Colored Farmers National Alliance and Cooperative Union. February 22, 1890, was set aside as "a day of thanks and prayer," for the merger to be cemented in friendship. Alliance stores and exchanges were also urged to enter into the festivities on this special day of reconciliation.[61]

No sooner had this dispute been settled than another schism occurred in the South Carolina Colored Alliance in 1890. Under the leadership of W. J. Grant of Charleston, an independent state group was organized.[62] While little is known about the results of this schism, it appears that it proved to be an abortive effort with few practical accomplishments. It is probable that the South Carolina order, as with Texas, nursed its wounds and returned to the fold.

At a time when black solidarity was called for in the agrarian campaign, it is painfully evident that personal grievances and psychological disunity created a degree of estrangement within the order. Such a division of loyalty further served to change the complexion of strained Alliance finances. These small divisions of loyalty were important, for they included enterprising leaders and members who were not afraid to take the initiative. Such a dissident group comprised a significant minority in this as well as any other movement.

In addition to the problem of divided loyalties, the Colored Alliance, due to economic circumstances and membership pressure, was forced into taking a rather unpopular stand in behalf of its members. As previously noted, the economic potential of the order attracted a large segment of the early membership. In accordance with this fact, the order was forced to dedicate itself to a great extent to a philosophy of uplifting the Negro farmer. Back of such a commitment lay a heritage of nearly three centuries of prejudice and poverty which worked against the achievement of such a program. Once the organization dedicated itself to such a goal, however, it was forced to produce some tangible results—or, obviously, it could not long exist. When any institution fails to respond to an expressed mandate, it tends to lose viability. The Colored Alliance officials recognized this fact and their efforts during these years were directed toward achieving some tangible part of this philosophy.[63]

If the white farmer felt the pinch of declining prices, the Negro experienced it even more. A slow process of economic erosion had mitigated the possibility of the Negro's developing an adequate financial margin by the 1890s. The presence of the few black farmers who did command a comparative degree of prosperity only served to distress the average Negro tenant farmer. In the spring of 1890 the *National Alliance* noted that many of ''our wives are barefoot, our children naked and our home[s] mere hovel[s].''[64] In South Carolina, a hostile critic of the blacks sympathetically reported that ''I have not seen an all wool blanket among them in years. Their clothing is mostly of thin cheap material, especially the women, and children.''[65] Testifying before the Senate Committee on Agriculture and Forestry, Humphrey, who had traveled widely among the black communities of the South-
. . . noted that ''the great majority of the colored farmers of the South . . . and their women spend the season in cotton fields, with a single thin garment, without shoes, and they live upon the coarsest, commonest food. . . .''[66] In essence, the Negro farmer had his financial back to the wall and under such arduous circumstances the Colored Alliance membership understandably looked to the organization to provide them with some immediate measure of relief. It had nourished an agrarian philosophy of black self-help and racial self-reliance through economics but the translation of the rhetoric into reality would require a stronger, more united protest effort than had previously occurred.

There soon occurred an event of such crucial importance that the Colored Alliance could ill afford not to become involved. In the fall of 1891, a number of merchants and planters, notably in the Memphis and Charleston area, agreed to combine themselves into a series of organizations for the purpose of wage and price control. The ulterior motive behind the formation of these organizations, however, was the reduction of the wages paid to the cotton pickers of the South.[67] Such a measure would increase their profits at the expense of the lower paid agricultural workers. Since the blacks were predominantly engaged in agrarian pursuits as ''hired hands,'' they would be among those hardest hit by the scheme.[68]

Coming at a time when many black farmers were living at a subsistence level, any reductions of the prevailing wage scale, however diminutive, would push the Negro agrarian farther down the economic scale of first-class citizenship.[69] As members doubtless expressed their vehement antagonisms to the state and national chapters, the Colored Alliance was faced with the realization that it must decide on a course of action. If the order failed to aid the cotton pickers, many of whom were probably members, there could be little doubt about waning interest and membership. Furthermore, if it became involved in a dispute with the economically powerful merchant-planter class, it also stood to lose.

There were several precedents of black agrarian protest in the 1880s. Significantly, their espousal also had almost always been associated with a program demanding higher wages and better working conditions, deriving their inspiration from self-help, racial solidarity, and the sympathetic assistance of the Knights of Labor. After 1886, the Knights, admittedly in eclipse, made a major effort toward forging a working alliance with the agrarians. Thus, the black agrarian tendency toward complaint and protest had been exacerbated by contact with the Knights.[70]

A local Colored Alliance effort to redress grievances through self-help and racial solidarity had occurred in Leflore County, Mississippi, during the fall of 1889. The attempt by a black to organize a Colored Farmers' Alliance store and boycott local white merchants aroused considerable ire from whites who threatened retaliation. As a result of the Negro's efforts, approximately four hundred Colored Alliance members armed themselves in defense, but the arrival of national guardsmen reinforced by a local posse overwhelmed the blacks.[71]

The vitality of the black agrarian protest was clearly demonstrated by these efforts. But it is significant that these efforts were almost always violent, unsuccessful, and never widespread features which were probably not lost on the Colored Alliance leadership in seeking a solution to their problem.

After some slight hesitation, the Colored Alliance decided to support the cotton pickers and proceeded with plans to organize a general southwide strike on a scale unprecedented in the annals of black history. The chances of success for such a strike were not as remote as they first appeared. Even at this late stage of its development the order still had approximately 1,000,000 members; in addition, the crop involved was to some extent a perishable commodity that had to be harvested within a reasonable time. The basic problem, therefore, appeared to be one of successfully holding out until negotiations were made.

The plans of the order were clandestine; not even the white Alliance was taken into confidence. The Texas order first formulated its plan of attack. With September 20, 1891, set as its target date, the Texas order agreed not to pick cotton for less than $1 per hundred pounds plus board. Circulars were then mailed out from the National Headquarters at Houston to every sub-alliance in the South informing them of the proposed strike, what methods were to be employed, and the target date.[72]

The plan, however, appears to have suffered a setback for two major reasons: the blacks failed to strike in sufficient numbers and the target date was not properly synchronized. A minor strike was reported in the area of Florence and Orangeburg, South Carolina, for example, as early as September 10—ten days before the Texas strike date.[73] The maturity date of cotton varying throughout the critical area probably explains in great part why the overall strike date was not more closely coordinated.

While minor strikes occurred in areas of Arkansas and South Carolina, a general southwide strike never occurred.[74] By September 26, 1891, The *National Economist* noted that "one thing seems certain, *if a* [general] *strike was ordered,* it has proven a failure as it certainly deserved to be."[75] Limited funds on the part of the black community and imminent economic coercion on the part of the powerful merchant-planter class probably contributed to a last minute withdrawal of the proposed strike.

An independent daily, the New York *Herald,* viewing the whole situation somewhat humorously, remarked,

> This is not what the [white] Alliance expected when it kindly consented to receive colored men as members. A black man's vote being as good as another, when it is counted, it was thought well to secure as many colored votes as possible to take part in the grand strike against capital. But the colored man struck for himself. Who says he never learns anything?[76]

The strike, however, was no laughing matter to Leonidas L. Polk, president of the Southern Alliance. He soundly condemned the plan as an attempt by one group to advance itself at the expense of the whole farmer movement.[77] Coming under attack by the press as favoring the strike in his actions and speeches, Polk very acidly replied in the negative, stating that he knew nothing about the matter except what he read in the newspapers. Furthermore, he advised the white farmers to let their crops stand in the field "rather than pay over fifty cents per hundred pounds to have it picked."[78]

When all is said and done, the Colored Alliance experienced only failure and public disfavor out of this venture. When these are added to internal dissension, growing political distrust on the part of the Bourbons, and growing disappointment on the part of the black community toward its program, survival of the order was hardly expected. It seems probable that the last vestiges of the black order were ultimately absorbed into the Populist movement. The black, like his white counterpart, was coming to realize that independent political action was a necessity to achieve his ends. As the blacks were becoming disillusioned with the Colored Alliance program of self-help, the consideration of politics as a more viable alternate solution developed within the inner councils of the Alliance conventions. Central to understanding this shift is an examination of the search for policy.

II

THE SEARCH FOR POLICY:

THE ROOTS OF RACIAL CONFLICT

The Alliance as well as the subsequent Populist movement sought to realize its goals through a series of combinations—the agrarian West, South, and the blacks—and such diverse elements would naturally harbor proclivities toward internal dissension, both sectional and racial. Thus, interracial comity and formal structure ostensibly underwent excess tension during the convention phase of the Alliance movement as a result of greater racial contact and official policy formulation by the Alliance leadership. In this facet of its development, the Alliance was particularly vulnerable to disaffection, not only by proselytized blacks potentially subject to greater prejudice, but by whites as well. Such potential circumstances of discontent could have rendered the broad movement especially receptive to debilitation or, conversely, could provide fertile soil for the germination and growth of the movement. Any analysis of the Alliance movement, therefore, must of necessity be accompanied by some discussion of the inner conflicts, exemplified by individuals and groups, of the order's conventions. The blacks' shift toward the Populist movement was nurtured during this experience, despite a tendency toward group separatism. The burden of this chapter, therefore, is to note the role of the blacks in these events, however circumscribed, as they foreshadowed the Populist revolt.

As the Alliance diffused throughout the country, North and South, the mood kept reasserting itself for a centralized effort to wage battle against the more formidable centralization of the opposition. As of December, 1889, a joint meeting of the two regional orders had been called at St. Louis to discuss the possibility of consolidating the Northern and Southern Alliance movement. At this meeting, according to one observer, there were delegates from twenty-eight states representing over two million "white and colored" constituents, "all acknowledging the same evils to exist and seeing the necessity for the same remedy." With "shoulder touching shoulder as brothers," they proceeded to discuss the knotty problems of unification.[1]

Although the agrarians of both regions openly called for planting "the white rose of peace on the grave of sectionalism," the translation of the rhetoric into mutually agreed upon policy proved no mean task.[2] Three major sectional enigmas surrounded the question of consolidation: the name of the proposed order, the exclusion of blacks as members by the Southern Alliance, and the Southern policy of maintaining strict secrecy. Previous to the St. Louis meeting, the Southern Alliance (so called) had changed its name to the Farmers' and Laborers' Union and subsequently elected new officers and drew up a new constitution. The Northern Alliance objected to the new name and suggested instead the National Farmers' Alliance and Industrial Union, "possibly to satisfy the Wheel or to offer a bait to the forces of labor. . . ."[3] The problem of nomenclature was readily solved and the Southern Alliance proceeded to incorporate it into the constitution. Since it "was a condition thought necessary by the brethren from the Northwest," the Southern Alliance was also willing, under duress, to remove the word "white" as a membership qualification, leaving to each state any decision about the eligibility of blacks as members. However, only whites would be allowed to serve on the Supreme Council, the national legislative body of the Alliance. As a final concession, however, the Southern Alliance insinuated that blacks would be allowed even into the sacred Supreme Council if it would help facilitate consolidation.[4] Clearly, a much more formidable obstacle than race was the problem of secrecy. On this point the South remained adamant. Experience had indicated that the tendency for unfriendly elements to infiltrate the Alliance had been prevented through secrecy. By monitoring the membership and carefully limiting the applicants to the farmers' "natural allies," the Southern Alliance had a hold on its membership that the Northern Alliance was never able to achieve. All further attempts at concession ended in stalemate, the question of secrecy being "the sole cause."[5]

The old shibboleths of race, party loyalty, and sectionalism, as well as the southern disposition for secrecy of operation precluded the possibility of consolidation at this time. Of all these reasons, it seems rather paradoxical that sectionalism rather than racism proved perhaps the most significant. According to Professor Woodward, "the old bloody-shirt feeling was more prevalent among the Northern delegates than among the Southern."[6] If sectionalism was prominent in the North, certain observers believed they saw its decline in the South. "Hostility to the Northern people has almost disappeared," Lord Bryce commented of the Southern climate.[7] Less optimistic but still hopeful, President Macune correctly prophesied that "Sectionalism in this country will continue," but he predicted that it would "assume a different form from that which has so long afflicted the [Southern] people, and have another purpose."[8] In varying degrees, these predictions were both true, but the agrarian agitation, as Macune foresaw, would cause the region's agrarians to adopt a more conciliatory tone in the immediate future. The immediate failure of the white orders to combine had negated the first steps toward organizational integration of the two regions in their fight for common ends.

Representatives of the Colored Alliance from several states (Tennessee, Florida, Texas, Alabama, Mississippi, North and South Carolina, Kentucky, and

Indian Territory) were in session at St. Louis at the same time as the two white Alliances. Committees were exchanged with various white organizations as a gesture of friendship. The black Alliance was extremely delighted with its white visitors, regarding them in Humphrey's words as "ministers of light and salvation" to the black race.[9]

In the main, there was a studied effort at St. Louis to point out the possible contributions of both races cooperating, despite the continued emphasis on separatism as a solution to the race problem. Humphrey, the General Superintendent, espoused such a program of cooperation as he spoke before the white bodies. The blacks, he added, did not deny that "a large percent" of the goods bought and raised by the two races were in common and, as stated at the Meridian meeting in 1888, there should be "race co-operation" as "mutual interests may demand."[10] The threat of self-interest always loomed as an ever present reminder to both races that they could not achieve a program of agrarian reform alone. However, it should not be forgotten that this marked tendency toward reform was not held to the exclusion of racial separatism.

As an example of racial self-help, the Georgia Colored Alliance took advantage of this meeting to implement a plan to establish a black land investment company. This plan was put into action on their return from the convention, and by May, 1890, it was reported that "quite a number" were in operation in the state.[11] In their constant emphasis on the acquisition of property, such efforts were particularly significant as practical applications of the black self-help philosophy.

Despite the propensity of the white Southern Alliance to compromise their previous policy of segregation, the Colored Alliance, nonetheless, still did not wish to consolidate with its white counterpart. In its 1888 convention, the order had adopted a resolution "that white organizations shall positively prohibit the administration of colored men to membership, and colored organizations shall prohibit the admission of white men to membership."[12] While reasserting this philosophy of black separatism at St. Louis, the black Alliance did reaffirm its wish to establish "the most intimidate confederation with the white Alliance."[13] And, quite aside from the policy of economic cooperation, it is significant that the black Alliance continued its early policy of separatism despite the whites' stated readjustment of membership qualifications. On the surface, this may seem to indicate a turning away from the agrarian goal of class progress, but it actually represented a strong grasp of reality, for it embodied a distinction between economic self-interest and the sensitive race question. The process represented a practical code of anticipated reality also, for no Southern state apparently voted later to include blacks as members.[14]

The whites at St. Louis were farsighted enough not to open themselves to the volatile charge of "social equality" by their Bourbon critics. Furthermore, the white agrarians' own regional and lower class dispositions to prejudice made it exceedingly difficult for them to translate their stated membership principles into practice; for, like all normal human beings, they too had a natural craving for social acceptance—a state of mind which would have precluded their new policy of interracial cooperation. "The color line cannot be rubbed out," Terence Powderly exclaimed of the South. Speaking before the St. Louis convention, he added that "the Southern people are capable of managing the negro question for themselves." Repudiating social equality, he suggested to the Alliance only that blacks "be protected" when they become "a lever with which to oppress the white man. . . ."[15] Clearly, like the blacks, the whites were expressing racial interests first and group interests second.

If nothing else, the St. Louis meeting of 1889 had demonstrated to what lengths the Southern Alliance delegates were willing to compromise in order to implement economic reform. These men were practical farmers who wanted to revamp their class and personal interests; passion and prejudice could yield few financial returns to the man with an empty pocket. Regional racial values were played down— subordinated to the more impervious reality of economic self-interest. Here was an expedient strategy of economic realism upon which the future structure of political salvation might be built.

It is significant, then, that the shadowy racial and sectional unity in the three Alliances was not totally abandoned at St. Louis but was to be subordinate to a more practical contemplation and have a second airing at Ocala, Florida, on December 2, 1890. Although all three groups had debated in open forum their desire for reform, the Colored and Northern Alliance were generally too skeptical of Southern domination to welcome unification unreservedly, and their skepticism was manifested in the halting manner in which unity was pursued at St. Louis. In a movement so fluid much could be gained, albeit in a crude way, through longer exposure to the sobering everyday economic circumstances experienced by the agrarians.

Delegations from all the Southern states were present at Ocala on December 2 with expectations of later arrivals from as far away as California. The Colored Alliance also had decided to hold its annual meeting at Ocala with the white Alliance. Manifesting the dominant pattern of separatist thought, the blacks assembled in a separate body.[16]

On their arrival the blacks were met with the usual committee visitations from the white organizations, bidding them welcome. In return, the black Alliance appointed committees to each of these bodies to express its "good will and fraternal regard" for these orders. Brought face to face with further unwelcome economic hardships since St. Louis, the blacks seemed far more concerned at Ocala with a type of unity somewhat akin to a confederation rather than an integrated union of forces. A proposal was made by the Colored Alliance to these various white committees, suggesting that they meet and form a confederation "for purposes of mutual protection, co-operation, and assistance." This was readily agreed to by the white orders—a conspicuous example of sharpened class consciousness and self-interest which derived its inspiration from economic influence—and a joint session met to discuss the proposal. An agreement was presently reached and "heartily endorsed" by all.[17] Each organization pledged itself to the need for "common citizenship . . . commercial equality and legal justice" toward all men black or white. In a burst of conciliatory optimism, Humphrey announced that "this agreement will be known in future ages as the burial of racial conflict, and finally of race prejudice."[18]

Keeping in step with the expressed atmosphere of racial conciliation, the Supreme Council of the Southern Alliance voted unanimously to adopt the following resolution toward blacks:

> We recommend and urge that equal facilities, educational, commercial, and political, be demanded for colored and white Alliance men alike, competency considered, and that a free ballot and a fair count be insisted upon and had for colored and white alike. . . .[19]

Yet, upon inspection this statement still emphasizes moral character ("competency considered") as a prime necessity of political ability. Furthermore, such abstractions were easily stated but there is little to suggest, including the black Alliance's separate assemblage, that this was little more than a recrudescence of the old separate-but-equal doctrine, despite the black's tendency toward more open recognition of interracial cooperation.

However, not all such stated abstractions were so harmonious between the two orders. As peculiar racial interest began to put increasing stress on economic cooperation, the contradictions inherent in this shaky alliance soon surfaced. Despite its earlier abstract emphasis on "a free ballot and a fair count" for black and white, the white Southern Alliance adopted a resolution on the second day (December 3, 1890) which "most soundly condemned" the Lodge Federal election or "Force Bill" as being "partisan in spirit . . . and . . . partisan in application."[20]

> Resolved . . . That we do most solemnly protest against the passage of the Lodge election bill, and we most earnestly petition our Senators to employ all fair and legal means to defeat this unpatriotic measure. . . .[21]

The Colored Alliance, while tending to stress the economic approach to the exclusion of political interests, nevertheless did inculcate political protest and agitation as a part of their philosophy of self-help and racial solidarity. Thus, seeking to work out their own salvation in a hostile environment, they took as their political keynote a "free ballot and a fair count" which could be realized through the Lodge Bill. It was not surprising, therefore, that on December 5, 1890, the black order, by a unanimous vote, adopted the following resolution: "That we, the delegates of the National Colored Farmers' Alliance do hereby . . . urge upon Congress to pass the Lodge election bill, and let it apply to all sections. . . ."[22] Clearly, the Colored Alliance's "object" in favoring the bill "was to have protection of the ballot boxes. . . ." The blacks, while not entirely satisfied with the Force Bill, "wanted something guaranteeing every man a free vote and an honest count."[23]

The Force Bill aroused considerable ire in the white Southern press but the stated positions of the two Alliances were a striking symbol of the political redemption of two races who ostensibly shared a special class-interest. In the first place, the whites put greater emphasis on accommodation with the region's political norms, while the blacks stressed civil rights, political agitation, and economic radicalism. The attempt to hold to the ideology of agrarian class interest thus separated along racial interests.

The Colored Alliance also entered a strong protest to Congress concerning the passage of the Conger Lard Bill, designed to check the adulteration of lard. Cotton seed, "the colored man's crop," used as an admixture to pure lard, had reportedly dropped from twelve to fourteen dollars a ton the previous year to six to nine dollars in late 1890 at the time of the Ocala meeting. "No legislation ever introduced into Congress, with the exception of the laws fastening slavery upon us," according to the black Alliance president J. J. Jackson, "has been so injurious to the colored race as the so-called Conger Bill."[24]

A conflict of interests existed between the two orders concerning a number of other issues. The subtreasury plan was generally approved by both organizations, but the blacks adopted a more radical position on the single tax issue. The single-tax concept was explicitly advocated by the Knights of Labor at Ocala, represented by Terence Powderly and A. W. Wright of Toronto. More specifically, it was Wright who promoted the single-tax philosophy to the blacks and "they swallowed whole" the idea.[25] As an adjunct, the landless blacks expressed the viewpoint that "land is not property; can never be made property . . . the land belongs to the sovereign people."[26] Conversely, the white farmers as early as 1889 were "chary" of the "single tax tendencies" of the Knights, which inhibited "any closer union" between the two orders. As a corollary, the Alliance proposition to lend money on lands received only minor support from the blacks because they viewed themselves as a landless group whose major desire was for the government to "take care of the product[s] of our labor. . . ."[28] These issues are particularly significant, because it was this gap between small land-owning whites and landless blacks that made it impossible for the doctrine of class development to be acceptable to both groups.

The threat of independent political action, latent since the St. Louis convention, became a crucial issue at Ocala as had been predicted. The white Alliance in general, unlike the mid-Western and black delegates present, voiced strong objections to such a course of action. They still preferred to bore from within through the Democratic party—the party of "white supremacy."

The Colored Alliance, however, under the urgings of Humphrey, took an unequivocal stand in favor of a third party. "From the very first," Humphrey optimistically announced, "the Colored Alliance has been strongly in favor of the third party movement."[29] Here again, he overstated the blacks' earlier emphasis on the third party approach, but criticism of the Republican party was becoming significant by the 1890s. Blacks, according to Humphrey, were willing to withdraw from the Republican party because of a "lack of justice" resulting from the inequities of political patronage and a pro-business Congress which was opposed to the black farmers' interest.[30] Thus, by 1890 the black Alliance, discouraged by the trend of political events, was more receptive to political insurgency than the white Southern Alliance. Perhaps an even more fundamental dichotomy was the fact that the blacks were more inclined to look to the federal government for protection of person and patronage than were the whites who looked for protection of property and higher prices for their products. The frustration of black political ambitions through the Republican party caused a rechanneling of their initiative toward a party which, ostensibly, would espouse the Negro's cause.

The question of forming a third party had resulted in a compromise at Ocala. Despite the urging of the blacks and the white Kansas delegation, most of the white delegates seemed to agree with Leonidas L. Polk, who urged caution on the third party question, suggesting that "the greatest and most essential need of our order" at this point was "education"—by which he probably meant creating awareness "among the masses upon those questions which mostly relate to their interests."[31] It was officially decided to postpone a final decision until February, 1891. While independent political action was not totally agreeable to all factions, black or white, at this time, political thinking had certainly taken on a new warmth by the beginning of 1891.

The most conservative elements, such as the Mississippi Colored Alliance, were yet "not in favor of a third party." Although they wanted "the common good . . . benefit of the farmer and national reform," they believed that this could best "be brought about by our own choice of candidates."[32] In substance, it was a question of the right men with reform ideas working through the establishment. Race also played a prominent part in preventing greater expression of the third party policy. "In the South," a Georgia paper explained, "whatever may be the condition of affairs the farmers and the Alliance men are compelled by circumstances to carry out their views and reforms through the Democratic party. There are some things more important than reforms that merely affect the pocket."[33] These and similar warnings filled the columns of Southern papers, testing the sincerity of the white farmers' belief in white supremacy. Also, the recent 1890 election had initially reinforced the view that reform could be accomplished within the Democratic party. Controlling "no less than eight" legislatures, four governorships and "numerous" minor offices throughout the South, the white Alliancemen understandably endorsed the existing system during the months immediately following the election.[34]

On the whole, the accommodators dominated at the Ocala meeting but the process of working within the two major parties was proving a failure in the long run. Once elections were over, the Alliance membership had little control over its legislators. According to the Reverend J. L. Moore of Crescent City, Florida, Superintendent of the Putnam County Colored Farmers' Alliance, "The wily politicians see and know that they have to do something, therefore they are slipping into the Alliance, and the farmers, in many instances, are accepting them as leaders; and if we are to have the same leaders, we need not expect anything but the same results."[35] It was becoming obvious to the agrarians of all leanings that they must move toward a new horizon and create their own party machinery. These were the conditions that helped ignite the Populist movement.

A recapitulation of the salient facts surrounding the Alliance movement reveals several defects that would make interracial cooperation difficult, if not impossible, in the emerging Populist movement. First, the Alliance failure reveals the traditional paucity of interracial class consciousness among the poor and disadvantaged of the South, one of the very un-Marxian burdens of Southern history. True, for a time it did seem that the agrarian movement might succeed in creating a genuine class feeling, a coalition among blacks and whites, but in the end this was eroded by racism, antithetical interests, and economic expediency. Ultimately, this proposed coalition of blacks and whites was quite patently the product of a Machiavellian motivation of racial self-interest which in the final analysis dictated the direction that would be taken. Both the Alliance and Populist membership, according to C. Vann Woodward, were "always more interest-conscious than class-conscious" but in the case of black and white, as we have seen, the interests were contradictory.[36] The agrarian rhetoric, for all its focus on the farmers' problems, assumed the same position on the part of both races at the bottom of the economic structure. From the outset the white agrarian movement, which has been called "the South's third estate," was basically "composed of employing farmers" whose main endeavor was to abate the steady deterioration of their "middle class" economic position as producers; and, conversely, the blacks as employed toilers were understandably less concerned with pursuing policies that were contrary to their group interests.[37] A coalition basically composed of blacks who sought more compensation for their labor and whites who conversely sought more for their products seemed destined to fail because of antithetical ends. The volatile actions of the white Alliance toward the black cotton pickers' strike indicate that black laborers were welcome as long as they promoted or enhanced the interests of their white mentors and made no effort to better themselves outside the white Alliance paradigm.

Secondly, the Alliance experience graphically reveals how broadly stated principles are subject to economic tergiversation under the tension of practical application. Although both black and white agrarians were avowed inflationists, at bottom their positions were at odds: the blacks were seeking to reduce their accumulated debts while the whites were seeking higher prices for the products of their labor. In 1889, a North Carolina black emigration convention captured in proper perspective these differing interests when it attacked the white Farmers' Alliance for keeping wages low and inhibiting black political rights.[38]

Thirdly, the Alliance interracial experience illustrates in a painfully dramatic way the fragility of racial liberalism which is often fused with both liberal and illiberal tendencies at the same time. Thus, while the agrarians readily perceived the evils inherent in such materialistic groups as large planters, bankers, and industrialists, they apparently saw nothing morally wrong with promoting a narrow self-interest over their rhetorical commitment to a broader secular humanism. Espousing a motto of "Equal Rights to All and Special Privileges to None," the Alliance's sentimental rhetorical appeals to conscience were not characterized by a sustained revamping of actions. When self-interest vulgarizes philosophical underpinnings, it tends to become the handmaiden of caprice, the purveyor of the crassest sort of opportunism and racism. Such was the case with the agrarian coalition when volatile episodes dramatized the tensions and con-tradictions that lurked just beneath the surface.

Lastly, and perhaps most important for the emerging Populist movement, the two Alliances disagreed on the two major political issues of the latter nineteenth century which offered substantial aid and comfort to downtrodden blacks: the Blair Education Bill and the Lodge Federal Force Bill.[39] Indeed, given the political structure and the nature of Southern race relations at the time, it was exceedingly unlikely that the racial differences on these two important issues were isolated incidents. At bottom, the sycophantic public utterances of the Alliance did not reflect the varied economic interests and shifting political emphases of blacks and whites. Time would reveal that the emerging Populist movement was faced also with these same obstacles in its effort to form a political coalition with the blacks.

III

TIME OF TRIAL, TIME OF HOPE:

THE BIRTH OF SOUTHERN POPULISM

The steady drift toward political autonomy was not a new issue in the Alliance movement of the 1890s. From its very inception and throughout its earlier existence, it had contained elements, both black and white, which believed that their salvation could best be found through independent political activity. The experience of the Colored Farmers' Alliance in Alabama stands as a case in point: entering the state in July 1889, a segment of the organization under "Frank Davis, a solvent and successful negro farmer," sought to confine the Alliance to "business" and to eschew politics. Conversely, a more radical group sought to resort immediately to politics, but were "dispersed" by the more conservative element.[1] In some ways the most important part of the Alliance movement was the gradual change in its political philosophy toward a third party. Prior to the Alliance experience, there were other precedents that helped create a heightened awareness of politics as a potent reform force for the farmers—notably the Agricultural Wheel, the Louisiana Farmers' Union, and the Greenback-Labor campaigns of the 1870s and 1880s. These movements served as an important corrosive in undermining the restrictive effects of the Democratic party on the Southern agrarian mind. In short, Populism was not a sudden political aberration but the culmination of a pattern of agrarian protest which had existed since Reconstruction.[2]

It was the Democratic party, however, that represented the dominant political ideology of the white South throughout the final quarter of the nineteenth century, and as such, in whatever direction it moved, the majority of the South's inhabitants was sure to follow. By the same reasoning, in whatever direction it refused to follow, the South would not long continue. "To be anything but a Democrat," Tom Watson later lamented, "was in public opinion to be a traitor to the section and the white race."[3] You "may strike the wife of your bosom while her arms are locked in love's embrace about your neck, or your little child as it lisps its evening prayer at its mother's knee," one former governor of Georgia declared, "but for God's sake, don't strike the dear old Democratic party."[4] The explanation for this absolutist quality on the mind of the white South is understandable when it is examined as something other than a uniquely political mechanism. As one Democratic North Carolina editor explained:

> The Democratic party at the South is something more than a mere political organization striving to enforce an administrative policy. It is a white man's party, organized to maintain white supremacy and prevent a repetition of the destructive rule of ignorant negroes and unscrupulous whites. . . . The safety of the South . . . as well as the conservation of free institutions on these shores, depend upon the strength, unity and perpetuity of the Democratic party.[5]

Because of their fascination with this logic, most whites seem to have taken for granted the bland assumption that the continued maintenance of the Democratic party was a racial necessity. "In the South," a Georgia paper pointed out, "whatever may be the condition of affairs, the farmers and the Alliance men are compelled by circumstances to carry out their views and reforms through the Democratic party. There are some things more important than reforms that merely affect the pocket."[6] These and similar public warnings filled the columns of Southern newspapers testing the white farmer's belief in white supremacy. In substance, allegiance to party was regarded as more important than allegiance to principle in the South of the 1890s.

Even stronger perhaps than the need to conform to the Southern political norm was the need to meet the approval of Southern society at large. The rigid value structure offered few opportunities for the individual to buck the tide of political solidarity and racial pride. Furthermore, the white farmer of the South was subject to the same prejudices and complexities as those around him in his own cultural realm. A set of rigid racial priorities had long served as the rationale for political inaction in the South. The solidarity of one's race, it was assumed, was more important than political reason. Finally, one must note the psychological and compensatory role conformity played in the farmers' more immediate orbit. In the face of insult, it provided dignity; in place of accusations of "Negro supremacy," it provided acceptable arguments. Discussing the Southern white farmers' dilemma of "revolt or conformity," Professor Woodward has stated:

> Changing one's party in the South of the nineties involved more than changing one's mind. It might involve a falling off of clients, the loss of a job, of credit at the store, or of one's welcome at the church. It could split families, and it might even call into question one's loyalty to his race and his people.[7]

Faced with such adamant opposition from significant authority figures, it would indeed not be surprising if the Populist movement had never taken hold at all in the South. Equally as difficult were the individual experiences of insurgents and the psychic strains they encountered in their daily lives. Perhaps some insight into the anxiety suffered by the Populist leadership can be gained from the melancholy recollections of Milford Howard, a Populist senator from Alabama:

> It will give you some idea of this bitterness when I state that my own father would
> not hear me speak and said he would rather make my coffin with his own hands than
> have me desert the Democratic party. This has been more than thirty years ago but
> some of the old feeling still slumbers and I have never been and never will be forgiven
> for my fall from grace.[8]

Describing the tone of his third party experience, Howard "doubt[ed] if in all the
political campaigns of this country there was ever as much vituperation, filth and
vindictiveness unbottled as was ever turned loose upon [my] head" as during this
era.[9] Similarly, in Georgia, Tom Watson's brother was secretary of a meeting that
publicly denounced Watson as a traitor.[10] In his private journal, Watson describes
the constant threat of injury he faced as a Georgia Populist:

> It was almost a miracle I was not killed in the campaign of 1892. Threats against my
> life were frequent and there were scores of men who would have done the deed and
> thousands who would have sanctioned it. Fear of the retaliation which my friends
> would inflict prevented my assassination—nothing else.[11]

Such actions also constituted an integral part of the less significant personalities
involved in the movement. In Guntersville, Alabama, for example, a group of
Alliancemen who had brought their produce to market were derisively greeted by
local housewives as a group of "nigger lovers and nigger huggers." In disgust the
farmers gathered up their produce and "reported to their families and neighbors
the estimation placed upon them by much of the populace."[12]

The sacred, like the secular, was considered also a part of Southern institutions.
Southern white Protestantism had long adhered to a narrowly conceived
evangelism which eschewed the social criticism as espoused by the Populists. To
the church Populism represented a challenge to the hegemony of traditional
religion in Southern life and, as such, orthodox religion heaped bitter condemnation on the reform element.[13] In Nolenville, Tennessee, for example, the Reverend Douglas Anderson preached a sermon to the church's third party brethren,
urging them to "abandon their evil ways and return to the fold of the Democratic
party before it was too late."[14] A Raleigh religious publication despaired of the
"suffering in the land" but did not think Populist interference could provide a
solution. "The poor ye have with you always," it insisted.[15] The Populists were
well aware of the intimate connection between the pulpit and the politician, and of
the reasons for it. "Too often," one Populist declared, "the modern money
changer and usurer pay the bulk of the preacher's salary."[16] Another third partyite
had a more cogent explanation: "Most preachers," he bluntly asserted, "are
Democratic."[17] Sacred critics found Populism wanting and gave little comfort to
the individual parishioner who deviated from traditional relationships.

Even the institution of marriage was not safe from the increasing militancy of
Southern opinion as the agrarian protest gained momentum. At the marriage of
"Mary-Ann" (Marion) Butler to Fannie Faison in Raleigh, North Carolina, in the
fall of 1893, the newly married couple was escorted from the church to the local

depot by a "large" jeering and howling mob of Democrats who beat tin pans and uttered cat calls. Throughout the whole affair, the Democratic hecklers expressed their "wonder" as to how any "decent woman" could go so far as to marry a Populist![18] Further instances of such actions are frequent in the annals of Populist literature but these obtuse examples should suffice to point out the social ostracisms and mental anguish of being connected with the Populist movement. There was in the experience of these individuals a revealing prophecy of things to come—successive waves of ostracism, which later fed the farmer's pessimism and finally led him down the gloomy road of bitterness, anxiety, and race hatred. Operating within such a preemptive climate, these widespread hostile behavior patterns must have caused even the most devoted of Populists to consider accommodation to the South's racial and political norms.

In addition to the collective emphasis placed upon regional solidarity through the South's own institutions, external events also provided an additional rationale for closing political ranks. The Democratic propaganda machine received an unintentional, but much needed, invigoration through the well-meaning efforts of Henry Cabot Lodge, a young Republican representative from Massachusetts. At the request of President Harrison, Lodge introduced on June 26, 1890, a bill designed to supervise federal elections.[19] While the bill's passage would have insured increased federal activity in Southern politics, the concomitant influence on state elections, held at the same time and place as federal elections, was implicit in its purpose. It was obvious that the measure was aimed at the South where the Negro vote kept the Southern branch of the Republican Party in power.[20] Such actions had long been contemplated by the Republicans; and after a slight victory in the congressional election of 1888, it was believed that such a proposition could now be passed.[21] In brief, the Lodge Bill stated that when fifty persons in a county of five hundred persons in a district signed a petition that unfair election methods were prevalent in their area, federal authorities could intercede and supervise the federal elections.[22] The Lodge "Force Bill," as it was quickly tagged by the opposition,[23] passed the House on July 2, 1890, but failed to reach the Senate until the 51st Congress where it was defeated by a coalition of Western "free silver" Republicans and Democrats. The price the Democrats paid for this, it was alleged, was their vote for the "Free Silver Bill" in Congress.[24]

Despite the vehement denials of Lodge, the bill quickly developed an image as a "Force Bill" and a "Bayonet Bill," intended to place "a bullet behind every ballot" cast in the South. In the public discourse of the times, any federal involvement figured as a preemptive blessing at best. Jarring notes of reconstruction nostalgia punctuated the banner of reform, and jeremiads of doom exhorted the region to turn inward to its own political defense. "The only argument on which the Democrats depended for results in '92," according to one Populist, "was the Force Bill."[25] The result was a forced reassessment of the region's mores—an accelerated quest for self-definition through a reaction to what was regarded as external partisan politics. In the Southern mind, this bill came to personify all the old injustices related to the dark days of Reconstruction. Old memories were revived and retold to the younger generation. Since memories of the Civil War and Reconstruction, even at this late stage, still darkened the horizon, the Democratic leaders saw before them a chance to regain their slipping foothold among the dissatisfied agrarian elements.

The South's sense of time and history is subtle and elusive wherein the values of the past are emphasized in a way seemingly compatible with the values of the present. The result is a timeless order of the right and true which threatens to become an end in itself. Using this as a part of their defense, the Bourbons sought throughout the Populist revolt to create and articulate a necessary sense of unity in the South—a state of mind which demanded political conformity as a fulfillment of this ideal. The investing of sanctity in regionalism and the past by the Bourbons decidedly helped rob the Populist movement—which sought to change past political policies—of its greatest efficacy. The uncomfortable vagueness created with such issues as the Force Bill resulted in a sense of discomfort in many Populists. Consider the harsh admonitions of W. J. Cash:

> The eyes of his old captains were ominous and accusing upon him. From hustings and from pulpits thousands of voices proclaimed him traitor and nigger-loving scoundrel; renegade to Southern Womanhood, the Confederate dead, and the God of his fathers; champion of the transformation of the white race into a mongrel breed. And in his own heart, as he gazed upon the evidence, it was, in ninety-nine cases out of the hundred at least, echoed and confirmed—fearfully adjudged true.[26]

If Southern Populism spread its wings and soared mightily in the frenzied years after 1891, it was certainly not with quiet confidence but with fear and trembling and even a touch of pathos. In summary, the two important early links in what was destined to be a strong chain of protest were the Force Bill and race, both integral ingredients that traditionally involved federal participation. "The one [lasting] fear of the people," said Tom Watson, evaluating the failure of the movement, "was federal interference with our local concerns [the threat of a "Force Bill"], and the consequent uplifting of the Negro [the threat of "Negro supremacy"] into a position of political influence."[27] It was upon these two basic issues that the Democrats built their plan of attack against the third party movement.[28]

In the eyes of the political insurgents, the issue of the "Force Bill" was viewed as "positive proof" that "New England" planned to revive the old issues of the "bloody shirt" and racial hatred in the South.[29] "The cry of Negro domination in Mississippi and a demand for a force bill in Massachusetts," one constituent angrily reported, "are activated by similar desires and continued for similar ends."[30] If the sections and the races would "pull together," the "nefarious schemes" of the politicians to revive "the gory ghost of sectional estrangement" would be to no avail.[31]

In January, 1891, the *National Economist,* in an effort to answer the Negro Alliance's demands for an election bill, promised the black voter "something better than the Lodge Bill." Reaffirming the promise to stand by the Ocala pledges of equal educational, commercial, and political facilities for both races, it further pledged to "guarantee the colored voter more [political] justice than has ever been shown him by any association or party"—all without the need of a federal election bill. "During the past few years," the *Economist* continued, "a silent but potent force has been at work . . . trying to bring about a [better] condition of affairs between the races."[32] The motivation behind such a statement was probably related to the Alliance's political aspirations and the continued development of a collective feeling of unity within the farmer class, both black and white.

Although the Colored Alliance strongly supported the passage of the Lodge Bill, there was room for much backing and filling, for sharp contrasts in values and norms among black as well as white Southerners as a result of circumstances and variegated philosophy. This very heterogeneity of the black population made for disagreement over what changes were needed or needed most. Rarely will those who subscribe to reform be unanimous on how it may best be brought about. In this connection, the Force Bill did not simultaneously win approval from all quarters of the black community. Some Negroes believed that if blacks desired to abolish discrimination they would have to improve their economic condition through an assertion of a segregated black self-help philosophy. This placed minimum value on political activity and insisted on patience, industry and moral elevation.[33] A Louisiana black opposed the Lodge Bill "because it is fraught with danger to the Negro; because it will be the means of rupturing those good feelings which are at present existing between the two races; because, in fact, it is but an incentive to bring about a war of races in the South." If it was passed, he predicted, the result would be a "massacre" once the federal government tried to enforce the measure in the South.[34] Also, Senator John Morgan of Alabama presented a petition from a group of blacks who denounced the Lodge Bill. Booker T. Washington was one such black leader who took a public stand against the bill.[35] A number of prosperous blacks in Atlanta, including well-to-do merchants, were reportedly indifferent or opposed to the Bill.[36] In substance, a segment of blacks who believed that wealth and morality, to the denigration of political activity, would be the "salvation of the race" opposed the Lodge Bill. In a classical vein of Social Darwinism some articulate blacks, such as W. E. B. Dubois, asserted that the bill was based on the erroneous assumption that

> law can accomplish anything. . . . We must ever keep before us the fact that the South has some excuse for its present attitude. We must remember that a good many of our people . . . are not fit for the responsibility of republican government. When you have the right sort of black voters you will need no election laws. The battle of my people must be a moral one, not a legal or physical one.[37]

No less a prominent black personality than the North Carolinian J. C. Price, president of the Afro-American League, the National Equal Rights Convention, and Livingstone College opposed the Force Bill. But Price, the man Dubois classified as the "new leader" of blacks, "passed away in his prime" in 1894 and was replaced by Booker T. Washington after his famous Atlanta speech.[38]

According to Professor Meier, "articulate black opinion was all but unanimous in support of the Lodge Federal Elections Bill of 1890."[39] However, this does not appear to be true in the South. In brief, most wealthy articulate blacks "simply thought and acted like most Americans—particularly Southern Americans—of the age."[40] Such a multiplicity of Negro classes meant that there were many subgroups—a situation which resulted in many special interests and values around which reform would attract blacks must include. To infer that all blacks were receptive to such reforms as offered by the Populists is to say, in a sense, that race crystallizes politics into simple propositions, tidy arguments and equally attractive platforms. The emerging Populist movement, as we shall see, dismissed far too easily these vital elements of intraracial dissimilarity that had a profound impact on black receptivity to reform, particularly among the leaders who could evoke needed political responses from the masses.

By the 1890s a certain element of the white farmer class no longer believed whole-heartedly in the effectiveness of the Democratic Party as the party of reform for the agrarian movement. The improvident actions of the Democrats soon led the farmers to question whether or not they should formulate a new set of realistic values and political ideals of their own. This slight shift in attitude and the impending alignments which would appear during the Populist revolt were deeply rooted in the slow re-orientation of the farmer's attitude since the 1880s. By the early months of 1891 it was, to some degree, a psychological if not a physical fact that a new party was being considered in the South.

The dialogue carried on in the literature of the Farmers' Alliance of this period reveals a mood of criticism and political introspection as well as discussion of a potential third party. "Through sheer blind adherence," one North Carolina farmer sadly commented, "we hate to go back on it [the Democratic Party], no matter what an extent it has gone back on us."[41] Without quite acknowledging it, many farmers were waging a kind of war within themselves over the question of threatened "Negro supremacy," federal election interference, and the effects of a third party on these issues. In essence, their problem was one of dualism brought on by conflicting loyalties—they had to choose between their own ideals or those of the South and the Democratic Party as a whole. Belief in one, however, seemed to conflict with belief in the other; the inevitable result was a period of confusion, indecision, and a kind of gnawing unsureness.

If a new party was to be a fact, however, and the present political order overturned, it was necessary to know the prevailing climate in the larger arena of events. The Northern Alliance was simultaneously engaged in a similar kind of introspection and they, too, were taking stock of the political weaknesses and economic deficiencies of their region. Furthermore, the Northern Alliance, unlike most of the Southern order, contained an element of energetic men who, far from suffering any conscious ideological fetters, worked effectively and consistently for a third party.

The question of a third party had been raised at Ocala among the diverse groups, but no formal agreement had been reached, primarily because of the heterogeneity of opinion on the subject. In an effort to stay a hasty decision, a decision was made at Ocala to assemble in Cincinnati on February 23, 1891, for the express purpose of discussing the third party issue. The date was later changed to May 19 when it was discovered that it conflicted with the meeting of the Kansas legislature.[42]

With the arrival of the fateful day, "all of the political odds and ends of the country," as one reporter expressed it, were assembled in Cincinnati. Of the estimated 1,400 delegates, the Southern delegation numbered a mere thirty-six. Of this number, twenty-one were from Texas, while Alabama, South Carolina, Virginia, and North Carolina had no representatives.[43]

The extremely small number of Southerners was probably due to two factors. First of all, the agrarian South was not psychologically ready to divorce itself completely from the Democratic party, especially in the face of the recent outburst against such a policy. Secondly, and more related to the numerical attendance of the Southern delegation, was the lack of finances to embark on such a long venture. The stringent attempt at economy by those few attending was evidenced. "All the second and third class hotels," one newspaper correspondent reported, "are filled to overflowing."[44] A Georgia politician later estimated that "There are not one-half of the farmers of this country who can save enough money to make a trip to a convention once a year."[45] Populists continued to confront this problem of finances in one or more exasperating forms throughout their existence; and they found it quite acute when they competed with the more affluent Bourbon class in later political campaigns.

It also seemed that the few Southern delegates who attended the convention, much to the dismay of the Northern Alliance, were the most conservative element in the convention. The combined anti-third party element of the convention, through a bit of oratorical chicanery, attempted—unsuccessfully as it soon proved—to divert the impending political question by organizing a filibuster around those issues that did not involve the third party question. Ironically, one of the major leaders of this effort was James B. Weaver, later unsuccessful Populist presidential candidate of 1892.[46]

Unlike the Ocala convention, which had been held in a Southern cultural climate, there had been no planned segregation of the Colored Alliance delegates who attended the Cincinnati meeting. Such "liberal" actions, however, immediately aroused the resentment of the white Southerners. Long exposure to the harping threats of "social equality," coupled with a heritage of segregation, prompted them to work for aa segregated seating plan. To achieve this purpose despite their small representation, the Southerners proposed that a unit rule be adopted for the gatherings. Under this plan the various organizations would meet separately, discuss the issues, and cast a single vote for the measure before them. The vote for this proposition served in large part to confirm the worst fears of the white South. As the measure was "overwhelmingly defeated," the Southerners must have realized that the question of a third party coalition with the North would involve more than just politics in the final analysis. These suspicions must have been even more pronounced when Terence V. Powderly, well known Northern labor leader, spoke out for equality of opportunity and justice for both the black and white laborers of both sections. The precise racial creed of the South, as the Southerners viewed matters, would receive little consideration if a North-South coalition materialized.[47]

Symbolic efforts were made, nonetheless, by both sections to reduce the sectional and racial hatreds caused by "the late war." One of the most touching of these acts was the clasping of hands by a Union and Confederate veteran on the center stage, while a Negro delegate stood in the background between these two former enemies.[48]

It seems that this Negro was Savage, "a smart Negro politician," who had come "all the way from North Carolina" to be with "the people." He had been noticed by a Saginaw, Michigan, Allianceman who had been greatly impressed by his political astuteness. The white Allianceman managed to secure a place on the rostrum for the black delegate, and he made a "slick" speech to the audience.[49]

Despite the Negro's other various talents, he soon found himself financially destitute and unable to pay his railroad fare back to Carolina. Again employing his oratorical ability, Savage, expressing great loneliness for his home, made an impassioned plea to the convention to help him out of his financial predicament. A hat was passed for this express purpose and several small coins were collected. Savage then commented that if it had not been for the problem of finances, many more of his race would have attended the meeting. After his short speech, "much cheering" for the Colored Alliance and the work it was trying to accomplish in the South followed. Savage, after a final expression of his gratitude to the delegates, took his leave.[50]

The purpose of the Cincinnati convention, according to Ignatius Donnelly of the North Alliance, was "not . . . so much to proclaim a [political] creed as to erect a banner around which the swarming host of reform could rally."[51] A sharp division of opinion, however quickly developed among the "swarming host" over the sensitive question of a third party. Despite the vigorous urgings of the third partyites, even the most aggressive of the Southern delegates stopped short of final commitment, believing that "the people" needed more education on the subject of politics before they could be induced to leave the Democratic Party.

Since the Southern Alliance, due to its numerical preponderance, would constitute the balance of power in any farmer coalition, the radicals at Cincinnati courted the favor of the Southern delegates. The hopes of the third partyites, however, were soon dimmed when a letter from Leonidas L. Polk, president of the Southern Alliance (conspicuously absent from the Cincinnati meeting) urged the convention to give the people more time to decide on the political question. The reading of this letter, one paper reported "was received with painful silence" by the delegates.[52]

With this discouraging state of affairs, the Northern delegates quickly realized that the political question was settled, at least for now. Reaffirming the date of February 22, 1892, at St. Louis as the next meeting place, the convention adjourned, with few tangible results to its credit.[53]

Judgment of the future is always difficult at best, but if the Southerners based their measurements on those aspects of the Cincinnati meeting which seemed best to reveal future racial politics, they saw that they would have to reorient personal racial philosophies to accommodate blacks within the movement—if they combined with the Northern Alliance. The necessity of regional accommodation as a political device for personal gain had not yet manifested itself acutely in the black-white relationship. The Southerners approached the problem of racial accommodation warily, suggesting only that, at best, blacks be permitted segregated roles. An obvious illustration is the attempt to confine the political conduct to whites. A system such as proposed by the Southerners would scarcely have instilled in the blacks a sense of belonging. Therefore, one must measure how preemptive the black's presence actually was in the face of powerful regional prejudices which generated feelings of incongruence between self and regional accommodation.

It is largely against the background of increasing political ambitions and hostility that the South's third party ideology at Cincinnati must be viewed. As Democratic propaganda was increasingly calling for political and racial solidarity within the region, the frustration of political disappointment with the Democratic Party as a party of reform was causing a redirection of thought toward political insurgency. Despite acute agrarian sensitivity to the race question, the prospect of achieving long needed reform strengthened the ideology of a separate political party that would be championed by the farmer. Discouraged as the farmers were by the trend of political events, the acceptance of such a philosophy would still depend to a great extent upon its regional approval.[54] While the Southern insurgent was a growing element, it only made good sense to nourish further the burgeoning protest philosophy of the farmer to a point where he would finally strike out in his anger. This, the Alliance felt, was where the emphasis should be placed at this time—not on the racial philosophy of the Democrats.

The attitude of the movement toward the race question at this point lacked broad public philosophizing since it was in a period of formative growth; yet we can glean from the literature a few illuminating comments. "A third party will accomplish what millions of money and tons of blood have failed to do," reported one South Carolina optimist. "It will solve the race question."[55] Expressing distaste for the political "tricks of the past," one North Carolinian believed that:

> we have a prospect of being permitted to vote truly for equal rights. The giant born a few days ago in Cincinnati will sweep the fields and the hollows. Empty names of past political parties, along with their "bloody shirts" and "niggers in the wood-pile" are no more to be adored; measures, not men, are to be advocated. . . .[56]

The *Alliance Vindicator* of Sulphur Springs, Texas, in the same vein, believed that the campaign to "suppress personal, local, sectional and national prejudice" had been so successful that "only a few" people still clung to the old ideologies. "These will in time," it was predicted, "become educated up to the point where they can comprehend the situation" and the "cloak" of color "a man wears" will no longer be an "index to his character."[57] The expression of ideas on the eradication of racism, class solidarity over political solidarity, and independence of thought would continue to grow as the tension increased. The problem of conscious accommodation, along with all its psychic strains caused by regional pressures, subtle and crude, was one of the burdens that Populists carried with them as they presented their unconventional formula for interracial cooperation. Being obliged to court the black out of self-interest, doubtless they were troubled by the problem of incompatibility between self and society. Racial accommodation, in the incipient stage at this point, was to be a part of life for the movement during the next decade.

The St. Louis conference of February 22, 1892, was described by one unfriendly reporter as "an assembly of cranks composed of long haired men and short haired women" where "all sorts of ism's struggled for recognition."[58] Since the third party question had been officially prolonged until the St. Louis meeting, it was only natural that agitation on the issue was soon resumed. The division that occurred between the Southern white and Negro delegates over the third party issue at St. Louis is worthy of special recognition. R. M. Humphrey, the General Superintendent of the Colored Alliance, was now regarded as a somewhat unsavory character by the white delegates since he had authorized the Negro cotton pickers' strike the previous fall. Aware that the question of a third party would be a major issue at St. Louis, Humphrey, perhaps in an effort to boost his declining popularity in the white community, had engaged in a bit of political skulduggery to insure that the Colored Alliance vote was cast according to the dictates of white Alliance opinion.

At the Indianapolis meeting of November, 1891, Humphrey had inquired of J. L. Gilmore, a white man from Georgia, if he would "look after the colored work" in that state for him. Gilmore readily agreed to this request and further added that he would also lecture to the Colored Alliancemen whenever it was agreeable to his white constituents. Following the meeting, Gilmore was commissioned as a state lecturer for the Georgia Colored Alliance.[59]

A certain group in the state's white order, led by Gilmore's Tattnall County Alliance, feared that the Georgia white delegation to the St. Louis convention was going to be packed against favoring a third party. By manipulating the Colored Alliance vote, this faction saw a chance for the opinion of the state's whites to be represented, at the expense of the Negro order. Preparations were made for Gilmore to represent the third party element at St. Louis. As soon as the prevailing white opinion was made known to Superintendent Humphrey, he immediately forwarded Gilmore a letter, instructing him to cast the state's eleven Colored Alliance votes for a third party.[60]

At the St. Louis conference, Humphrey took further steps to insure that the entire votes of the National Colored Alliance would be cast for a third party. To guarantee this, he proceeded to pack the Negro delegation with white men, an action which was contrary to the organization's charter. A further indication of

Humphrey's character was his commercializing of the individual delegate's credentials, selling them to the whites for fifty cents each.[61] If the ninety-seven votes of the Colored Alliance were cast in favor of a third party, which Humphrey favored, the chances for its enactment would be greatly enhanced.[62]

The Georgia Colored Alliance appears to have been the most provoked of all the state orders as a result of its delegation's being packed with white men and their votes being forcibly cast, regardless of its members' wishes. In protest of such actions, the Colored Alliance refused to participate further in the convention's proceedings. Immediately thereupon Gilmore seized this opportune moment to cast the state's eleven votes for a third party. At this point, there were only five other members of the National Colored Alliance present—a situation which allowed Gilmore to assume control of the remaining eighty-six votes for the third party. In a display of protest, the entire Negro delegation then walked out of the convention, warning the white delegates that even if a new party was formed, it would receive no black votes.[63]

The Georgia Colored Alliance further protested that they had not only been treated in a demeaning manner, but that Gilmore had also persuaded them to pay his way to the convention. Gilmore promptly retorted that "not a Negro paid a cent of my expenses" to St. Louis and "if they said so, they lied."[64]

The actions of Humphrey, Gilmore, and the rest of the white Alliance members who allowed such illegal acts to be perpetrated against the Colored Alliance visiting delegation aptly testify that the Negro was welcome to participate in the farmer movement as long as he complied with the "advice" of his white mentors. Since these illegal acts were both largely covert and forced, this would seem to indicate that the Colored Alliance, or at least a sizeable segment of it, opposed the formation of a third party at this time. While it is possible that the whites thought they were "doing what's best" for their "ignorant" Negro brethren, it would seem, nevertheless, that stripping the Colored Alliance of its vote for a third party would offer few inducements for the black voter to bolt from the party of Lincoln. Finally, there was a valuable lesson for the blacks in these forced actions. Humphrey, as an employed spokesman for the black agrarians, could not in the final analysis forget that race was a great leveler in the South. In the first place he was a white man, and under tension of white ostracism, his siding with white interests demonstrated the fallacious assumption that coalitions between black people and other groups could be sustained on the basis of sentiment, morality and appeals to conscience. In short, he simply lacked the psychic strength to withstand the emasculating pressure of race. Secondly, the implicit white agrarian assumption that what was good for whites was good for blacks indicated that black voices would be expendable the moment they conflicted with their white "allies."

Not all topics involved racial and political hostility at St. Louis. Another symbolic ceremony, similar to the previous one in Cincinnati, of burying the sectional hatred of the "blue and gray" was performed for the benefit of the delegates. "If the common people could win victories on the battlefield," predicted the *National Economist* in describing the ceremony, "they can win greater ones at the ballot box.''[65] This touching scene was followed by the "weak voice" of one T. A. Powell, singing "United We Stand, Divided We Fall" to the accompaniment of a guitar. At his finish, shouts of "let's shake hands" ensued from various members of the audience, but few delegates actually participated. However, E. C. Cabel, a Negro delegate from "Kansas City and Virginia," was brought forward on the rostrum and asked to shake hands with some of the white delegates. Due to the crowd, he was able to shake hands with only those persons at the front of the platform, but he performed this service with joviality, laughing throughout the whole process.[66]

The Southerners, evaluating the political temperament of the St. Louis Convention, viewed with a jaundiced eye some of the statements and proposals of the more radical elements. The suffragist groups, demanding the vote for Negro women as well as white women, aroused the ire of all sections.[67] On the second day of the convention, Mrs. Mary Lease rather idealistically proposed, to no apparent avail, that the delegates abolish the sex line "as has been done to the color line."[68] Furthermore, the added pledge of Ignatius Donnelly, "to wipe the color line out of politics" also held overtones of something beyond political sentiment for the Negro.[69] Economic and political reform the Southerners obviously desired, but such proposals as these not only sounded like a program of advancement for whites but a long-range plan to assimilate the Negro and give him social advantages beyond the immediate and necessary goal of political expediency.

While wholesale participation was looked at somewhat askance by even the most reform-minded Southerner, the necessity for individual blacks to engage in the political aspects of the movement was being recognized. If one could be a reformer of racial etiquette in the South of the 1890s and still avoid the stigma of renegade and "nigger-lover," the achievement would be a pleasant one. But the resourceful reformer who astutely buttressed future needs with an appropriate moral coloration of tokenism and in hardheaded fashion held to what was the overall tried and true had the best of two worlds. He had the added satisfaction of knowing the concomitant blessings racial tokenism could potentially confer on his movement through black support and the satisfaction of being acclaimed by the white *status quo*. Thus, the necessary fusion of reform and classical self-interest was an accomplishment eagerly sought by the Southern agrarians. Such Alliance slogans as "equal rights to all and special privileges to none" were part of the shopworn folklore of reform that went back at least to the age of Andrew Jackson. But even if a charitable view is taken of the gap between such egalitarian pronouncements and the actual participation by blacks at St. Louis, the picture in reality was hardly a paragon of an uncompromising racial alliance by the white South.

Difficulties soon arose from the improvident actions of the white agrarians in limiting too strictly the participation of the blacks. For example, on the second day of the St. Louis convention, one black, W. H. Warwick of Virginia, rose "in a dignified but extremely earnest manner" and pointed out that the Colored Alliance was receiving little attention. Subsequently, he "firmly demanded" that such

The Colored man in the picture is not Dead, but Asleep, and he has a Ballot for "Harrison and the Force Bill" in his hand.   He pretends to be Dead, but he will be Awake in time to cast that Ballot in November.

Figure 2.   The Democrats Campaign with the Cry of "Negro Domination." (From Marmaduke J. Hawkins Collection, State Archives and Library, Raleigh, North Carolina.)

policies of exclusion be halted. A white delegate at the rear of the convention "flippantly" suggested that Warwick be made assistant secretary—a position of little power but possessing enough prestige to blot out the implicit moral stigma of racism leveled at the convention by Warwick. Seeing the necessity to give tangible witness to the tenor of its tenets, "the convention took the suggestion seriously. . . ." It was, surprisingly enough, a white delegate from Georgia who moved that the "colored gentleman's" nomination be made unanimous. Immediately, however, an Alabama delegate rose in protest, not because a Negro was nominated, but merely that the election should be made unanimous. The motion of the Georgian was then put before the floor, and a great "aye" resounded from "several hundred" voices, the objector from Alabama signifying the only "no" in the whole house.[70] J. Brad Beverly, a prominent white delegate from Virginia, later denied reports by the Associated Press that the election of Warwick was a joke.[71] Wrenched out of context, such acts would appear on the surface to give witness to the fact that blacks were to be among the anointed. However, the contrast between this seemingly egalitarian act and the shoddy treatment of the Colored Alliance delegates received at the hands of some of these same men when they disagreed with them is immediately obvious.

This public pronouncement for the public election of a single Negro official is not as blatantly obvious, however, as the more selfish reasons for the capture of the Colored Alliance vote. In fact, one must wonder if the members of the convention were in earnest in electing a Negro or whether this was silently viewed as a necessary concession to obtain the cooperation of the Negro. Perhaps, the South reasoned, political tokenism was a necessary evil, no matter how distasteful it might be, to protect the white farmers' interest.

By the time of the St. Louis meeting, many Southerners were coming to realize that the long awaited program of agrarian reform would not be forthcoming through the Democratic party. In addition, the stimulus of heightened financial difficulties served to push many disgruntled farmers into the third party movement. In Georgia, Texas, and Tennessee, for example, the tide of debt had been on the rise since 1889.[72] By the fall of 1891, the Tennessee Alliance movement was near collapse because of debt. Admittedly, one-fourth of the membership had dropped out of the movement, probably because of inability to pay their dues.[73] Just as the National Alliance was forced into exerting financial pressure against the Tennessee order, so it was that the general scheme of agrarian life became entangled in a web of waning finances, both personal and organizational, by 1892.

Since the Populist Party had been a political fact on the local level in many states, both North and South, as early as 1891, the prospect of achieving a program of national reform through a political revolution was beginning to receive more favorable comment in the South. By the time of the St. Louis conference (February 22, 1892), it was evident that a sizable segment of the white South viewed a third party presidential nomination as something of a necessity. The economic pinch, despite sensitivity to the race question, seems to have been the chief motivating factor, although disillusionment with the promises of the Democratic Party was also associated with the development of a collective feeling—an ideological rationalization—that economics must take precedence over political conformity.

The step preceding political reform was a nominating convention. The responsibility of selecting the place and date for the momentous occasion was delegated to a five-man subcommittee at St. Louis. Omaha, Nebraska, centrally located in the heart of the depressed midwestern farm belt, was selected as the site of the convention and the symbolic date of July 4, 1892, was set as an apt time to convene. As an obvious symbol of the new party's patriotic fervor and crusading spirit, the membership eagerly seized upon this date to declare their political independence of the two old parties to the country.[74]

Further evidence of the new order's espoused intention of sacrificing party allegiance to principle was expressed through the numerical selection of delegates to attend the Omaha conference. Each state, it was finally decided, would select eight representatives at large, and four from each congressional district. The number of delegates to be present at Omaha, it was eagerly noted, was 1,776—a most appropriate figure to be included with the date and purpose of the meeting.[75]

Whether the selection of this number was by design or accident is unknown; however, the chances against such a random total leads one to suspect that it was incorporated to add symbolic succor to the occasion. Furthermore, since the Populist Party constantly spoke of itself as a reform movement seeking to return to the principles of Jefferson and the Declaration of Independence, the promise held in such a gesture could hardly fail to be noticed by the news media, or associated in the mind of prospective recruits.[76]

When the Omaha convention convened in the summer of 1892, approximately 1,400 delegates were present, some 300 short of the magic number of 1,776.[77] Indicative of the South's changing political sentiment was the presence of "large delegations" from all the states but South Carolina—[78] an exception probably due to the charismatic influence of Ben Tillman, who had failed to bolt the Democratic Party in South Carolina.[79] Since Tillman was the undisputed leader of the state's agrarian movement, and was generally supported by the Alliance of that state, there was very little to attract South Carolinians to the Omaha convention.

Even though there was "no musty prejudice or caste system" at Omaha, the Negro had small representation at this official launching of the Populist party. It appears that there were only four black delegates, one each from Kansas and Virginia, and two members with the Texas Committee.[80] Undoubtedly, travel cost and distance were factors in keeping many black delegates away. It is also questionable whether the Negro delegates were not still discouraged over the trend of events at St. Louis earlier that year. Since it appeared that the Negro representatives at St. Louis had not supported the movement for a third party, it is possible they were still unwilling to listen to any proposition in favor of political insurgency.

A great stumbling block in the official formation of the Populist party had been the conformist psychology of the white South toward the political cry of "nigger domination." While the white Southern Populist did intend to keep the Negro socially and, to a great extent, economically subordinate, the political value of utilizing the black vote did not escape the white farmers at Omaha. According to the Columbus *Advocate,* a Negro paper, the insurgent South had decided that

> . . . The Negro will vote. That was the edict issued by the Southern delegates at the Omaha convention. One of the national committee men said, we shall vote the negroes and their votes will be counted. We know how to control and handle the negro. Already 400,000 blackmen have been enlisted in this organization.[81]

The President of the National Farmers' Alliance, Leonidas L. Polk, a North Carolinian, had pledged that the white Alliance would protect the blacks and "see that they are allowed to vote. . . . They are largely in this movement, and will be an important factor in the campaign next year."[82] The Omaha *Daily Bee* further confirmed this report when it commented that "these former Democratic leaders now say that the votes of these people shall be cast and counted. . . . The old democratic managers . . . have completely changed their attitude toward the colored voter."[83] Such was the necessity of the new political process that the struggle for the means of white reform produced attitudes more favorable than previously to the survival and development of the black vote. But the basic oulook remained unchanged: the black man was free to vote, and would receive white agrarian protection, provided the effects of his vote aided his white mentors. Consequently, Populist reform for blacks was motivated by pragmatic principles and was at bottom largely conservatism in the most reprehensible sense of the term. The thing which attracted the white Populists to the blacks was clearly the alteration of their own *status quo*. Put in a less pleasant way, the necessities of the age demanded that former racial etiquette, in relation to economics, yield to political expediency.

The Populists in their pragmatic way pointed out to the Negro that he was already in economic slavery (tenant system, lien laws, etc.) but that the Republicans and Bourbons were trying also to keep him in political slavery. "Sockless" Jerry Simpson had earlier predicted that "they [the Negroes] will vote for us" and that such a combination of the "farmer class" would constitute a potent voting force in the South.[84] Omaha would serve as the nucleus around which the overall Populist movement would soon crystalize, and such, the espoused philosophy of political self-interest advocated here would help form the basis for an attempted class combination.

The Populist and Farmers' Alliance men gathered at Omaha viewed themselves as a class apart from the "capitalists" and the "goldbugs" of the country. "From the same prolific womb of governmental injustice," they declared in their platform, "we breed the two great classes—tramps and millionaires."[85] Ideologically, perhaps even more of a fundamental dichotomy existed between the old line politicians and the Omaha agitators than the ethnic dualism between black and white in the South. The farmers, as they viewed themselves, constituted a class of underlings, and in this class was the despised Negro—an obsequious element perhaps, but nonetheless still a political factor of some weight in Southern politics.[86]

The untimely demise of Leonidas L. Polk just prior to the Omaha convention was a serious blow to the Populist cause, especially in the South. If the dictates of public opinion were honored, his future nomination at Omaha seemed assured,[87] a situation which would have placed the South in a position of party leadership in the movement. As early as the St. Louis meeting of 1892, "even the Colored Alliance" was reportedly "wheeling into line mostly for him," for which they received "hearty" cheering from the whites.[88] Whether Polk's nomination would have created a more favorable climate for the Negro in the Populist movement is largely conjecture; but judging from his past philosophy, he had little sympathy for the Negro race. While Polk had, in his own words, spent some of the "sweetest" hours of his early life with his "old black Mammy" and "little colored play-mates," he nonetheless regarded the black race as "an incubus—a solid barrier" against the forces of progress in the South. Although he had "naught but feelings of kindness" for the Negro, he would gladly "hail with delight and rejoicing his peaceful departure" from the region.[89]

Toward further accomplishing his racial philosophy, Polk formulated a plan to rid the South of the Negro's presence. First mentioned in Mississippi in 1891, the plan outlined the creation of a separate state in the West, Texas preferably, where a large uninhabited parcel of land would be cut up into forty-acre plots for Negro homesteads. To prevent unscrupulous whites from taking political advantage of the Negro, any white man who ventured into this "reserve" would be disfran-chised and disqualified from holding office.[90] While Polk expressed his intention to present his plan before the Supreme Court in hopes of having it legally implemented, it appears that he made no further efforts toward this end.[91]

These elements of Polk's thinking were not unique to him or his age but, rather, were ideals long discussed as part of the "solution" to the "Negro problem" in America.[92] Furthermore, it is all too easy to overlook the degree to which many disgruntled blacks embraced such doctrines historically in the United States. At times the search for another land seemed to be a futile, unceasing quest. Every black leader of consequence had flirted with or was receptive to the idea of colonization by the time of the Civil War.[93] Although the Civil War blunted the migratory urge, it flared back up again within the decade. By 1882, it was reported that blacks by the hundreds were "turning their faces to Arkansas and Texas. . . ."[94] In Georgia, "certain colored agents," notably the black Bishop, Henry M. Turner, were urging flight to Liberia or the west.[95] Though a product of several elements, notably persecution and increased violence, the rising philoso-phy of black solidarity and self-help in the 1880s produced several advocates, black and white, of migration and colonization. Such precarious circumstances and the approval of departure by leading blacks produced an increasingly restless migratory urge among lower-class blacks, particularly during the Populist era. According to the Reverend H. N. Payne:

Much as the colored people are attached to the places where they grew up, thousands
of them would gladly go to Arkansas, to Texas, or to any other place where they
could better their condition; but they cannot raise the money to emigrate and must
stay and suffer where they are.[96]

Such pecuniary problems necessarily produced a series of internal migrations,
notably to Kansas in the early 1880s, and several initially successful attempts to
create all-Negro "states" or towns. An example of such efforts was

the town of Judson, on Johnson's Island on the Mississippi River a little north of
Memphis, in which there is not a single white man, the owner ruling out the inferior
race. There are in the town six stores, a few shops, two churches and a school. The
island, the soil of which is quite rich, is eight miles long.

Judson, the owner of Johnson's Island, thus had "his own country," composed
solely of blacks.[97]

Many nineteenth century Americans, such as Polk, therefore embraced migration as a solution to the race problem. The increased migratory activity in the last
two decades of the century was peculiarly "correlated with the agricultural unrest
associated with the rise of the Farmers' Alliance."[98] As an agrarian creature of his
age, Polk was not victim of the folly and cupidity of a particular unique course of
action, but, rather, tried to interpret a highly volatile social problem in terms of a
traditional solution.

The death of Leonidas L. Polk had opened the door for other men of ambition
and initiative in both sections to vie for the coveted Omaha nomination; however,
his death left the South with a noticeable lack of suitable candidates, thereby
providing the opportunity for the North's influence to drive even deeper into the
political leadership of the movement. With the removal of Judge Walter Gresham,
who was supported by the South, "there was none so eligible as General James B.
Weaver of Iowa" to head up the third party.[99] The selection of Weaver, combined
with the unexpected death of Polk, undoubtedly encouraged ideological expression of a more liberal nature than would have otherwise been the case if Polk had
lived.[100]

The psychology of Omaha revealed a rationalization for political separation,
accompanied by a conflict between regional pride and overall solidarity. The
South, frustrated by its failure to lead the party's crusade, had to be courted in
order to offset any regional charges of domination. In order to counterbalance the
nomination of General Weaver, "General" James Field, representing "the best
and ruling element of Virginia Populism," was accorded second place on the
ticket.[101] While Field's selection was certainly related to the convention's aim of
developing overall political unity, much of it was probably a sort of political
opportunism, an expeditious attempt to halt any deterioration of section unity and
resentment over the selection of Weaver.

In the post-Reconstruction period, agrarian belief persisted in that concept of the
American system which rests upon the idea that reform could be realized through

the established political order; but such a view slowly dissolved, tending to become an implicit belief, an unvoiced axiom on which later Populist appeals to the third party heresy rested: reform could not be achieved through the existing system by men who viewed change as a threat to their own peculiar interests and security. In short, reform would emerge only through the efforts of a group of people, deprived both politically and economically, who became politically conscious of changes which had long been incubating and forced these changes to eventually grow into a full-blown movement. "This reform commenced where all great reforms commence," General Weaver observed, "among the poor. Necessity is not only the mother of invention but reform also."[102] Such occurrences, however, were less a stage in the career of Populism than an essential background condition for its inception. "No reform ever occurs in old organizations," asserted a Populist organ.[103]

In the initial undertaking such movements indicate their least likelihood of sustaining a genuine program of reform because of a lack of dedicated grassroots membership. To evolve into potent movements, such organizations must have wide appeal to a particular interest before they develop fertile soil for the germination and growth of reform. Relations of such incipient movements with surrounding society, if ineffective, may result in abortive actions because a more effective organization, such as the established Bourbons, creates determinants which generate dogmatic attitudes unreceptive to reform. In short, the state of ignored minorities such as the blacks who desperately needed reform can be advanced if they can project into the future and anticipate the needs and help direct such reform-minded movements.[104]

One correspondent with an eye to the Populist party proclaimed that "all political progress is made through new parties. All new parties in America," he further commented, "have believed in the equality of man before the law, and while new, they have made such progress as has dimmed in some small degree the separating lines of nationality, race and color."[105] The potential for political deprivation, however, probably provoked such actions rather than the more humanitarian determinant of idealism.[106] To a considerable extent the Southern Populist attitude toward the Negro can be viewed as a contrast between short-range emphasis on self-interest and political expedience on one hand, and long-range identification with the goals of American society on the other. In ideological aspirations, if not so much in actual motivation, the equalitarian Populist creed must have created ambivalent feelings toward the Negro in the mind of the agrarian reformer from its very outset.

In spite of increasing emphasis on political conformity, racial solidarity, and social ostracism, the robust vitality of the protest movement continued to grow after the Omaha convention. Ironically, the very pressures designed to break up the movement instead created a certain feeling of class unity in the agrarians. The cry against social injustice, human indignity, fraud at the ballot box, and the chance for an economically frustrated class to enjoy the fruits of their labor, became the motivation of Southern Populism. "Social justice, emotionally approached," according to one historian, "became the religion of the move-ment."[107]

It was understandable that the order's more articulate leadership would include equalitarian ideals in the formative Populist ideology. In actuality, however, there were two types of ideological dichotomies concerning the Negro—between the sections and within individuals themselves. In the first, the conservative Souther-ners put great stress on white economic and financial development, believing that what benefited the white man must of necessity benefit the Negro. The North, on the other hand, stressed agitation and political rights, as well as civil rights for the Negro. In the second there were distinctions within the South between those who placed reliance upon the economic self-interest approach and those, such as Tom Watson, who championed Negro protest and political action toward a land of economic and political, although not social, brotherhood.

In the attempt to hold to both of these ideologies, the lines of distinction created a dual cleavage within the Populist movement. These lines of cleavage roughly correlated with each other so that racial solidarity and self-interest tended to cluster together to form a "conservative" philosophy, while agitation for political and economic—although not social—rights tended to cluster to form a "radical" philosophy toward the race issue. In the following pages, we will survey the thoughts of the minorities during the period of Populism's ascendancy.

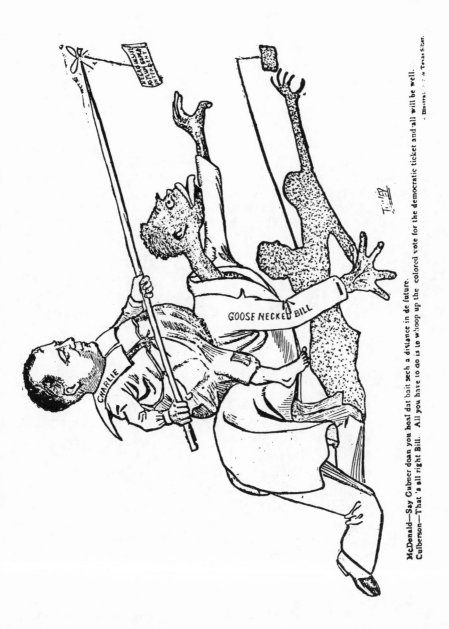

Figure 3. Democratic Solicitation of Votes Through the Negro Leadership. (From *Southern Mercury,* October 22, 1896.)

WHAT THE FORCE BILL MEANS.

Figure 4.   The Force Bill Revives Reconstruction Fears of Negro Domination at the Polls.
(From Marmaduke J. Hawkins Collection, State Archives and Library, Raleigh, North Carolina.)

Figure 5. A Vote for Cleveland Would Bring Financial and Racial Domination Upon the South.
(From *Weekly Toiler*, November 2, 1892.)

Figure 6.   The Democratic Attitude Toward the Negro Before an Election.
(From *People's Party Paper*, September 21, 1894.)

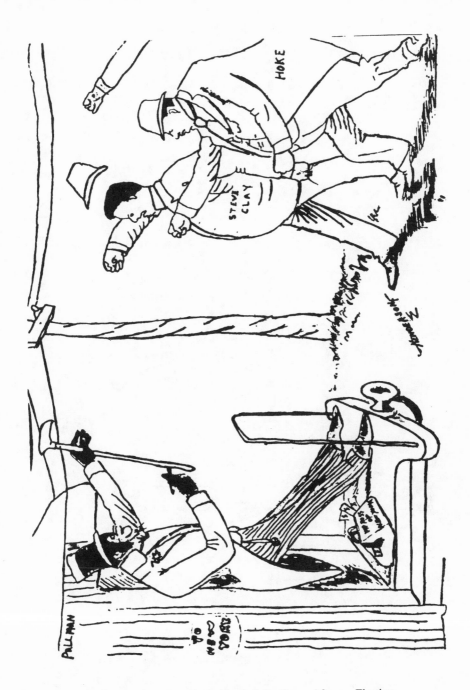

Figure 7.   The Democratic Attitude Toward the Negro After an Election.
(From *People's Party Paper*, October 5, 1894.)

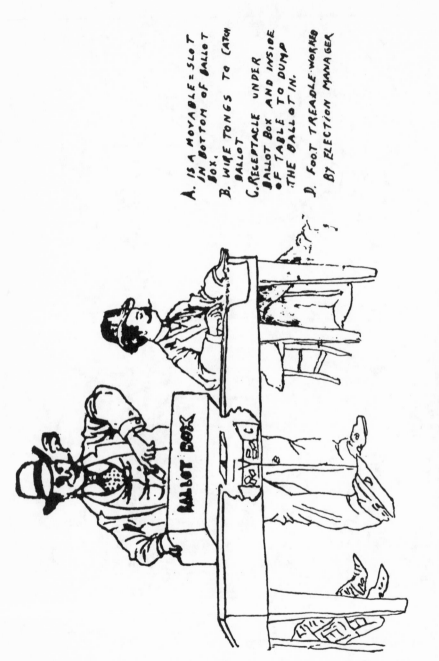

Figure 8.   Populists' Conception of Fraud at the Ballot Box.
(From *People's Party Paper*, September 28, 1894.)

Figure 9. Democratic Control of the Negro Voter.
(From *People's Party Paper,* April 24, 1894.)

Figure 10.   Populism is Absorbed by the Democratic Party after 1896.
(From *Southern Mercury,* October 29, 1896.)

IV

THE MINORITY TEMPER:

REFORM SPIRIT DURING

THE POPULIST REVOLT

If research into Southern Populism has revealed anything, it is that the racial philosophy of the movement cannot be considered independently of its framework of overt ideological expression. In order to understand more fully the workings of the Populist mind toward the blacks, it is necessary to examine its concept of agrarianism, the social ethic, and the application of power in politics.

An examination of Populist rhetoric reveals an agrarian translation of the traditional Protestant conception of wealth through work and virtue. With fervor they constantly referred back to the days of Jefferson and Jackson as their ideal paradigm of economic organization. The Texas Populist, James H. "Cyclone" Davis, often brought Jefferson's works to the political platform to serve as the final authority on any question. "We will now look through the volumes of Jefferson's work and see what Mr. Jefferson had to say on this matter," Davis would announce to his audience. Comparing Grover Cleveland to Alexander Hamilton, Davis would declare that "The crowd that takes their politics from Alexander Hamilton is the crowd we have got to beat." Expounding on "Hamiltonian ideas," he would conclude with this analogy: "Jefferson opposed; so do the Populists."[1] Their mission was, in the words of Marion Butler, a search for "the principles of true Democracy represented by Thomas Jefferson and Andrew Jackson, and for the principles of true Republicanism, as represented by Abraham Lincoln. . . ."[2] Thus, the Populists looked back to an earlier age and drew on the Jefferson-Jackson tradition for both their battle cries ("Equal Rights for All, Special Privileges for None") and their philosophy of the healthy state. To the average Populist, the great contrast between his present position and his past status represented a decline in virtue; therefore, society as a whole was deteriorating because agrarian values and virtues were being displaced. In substance, much of the Populist rhetoric was an indictment of the present using the agrarian past as a model.[3]

While verbally condemning the intrusion of monopoly and its techniques of combination, the Populists, paradoxically, sought to alter the course of history through similar tactics. The political strategy according to Southern Populists, would be based on racial, class, and regional combinations cemented together through the commonality of a producer class. Inherent in Populist rhetoric was the theory of a natural harmony of interests between black and white members of the producing class. As one white Texas Populist expressed it, "They are in the ditch just like we are."[4] Of this interracial strategy, Tom Watson had asserted that "Self interest always controls."[5] In this simple classification was included also the agrarian West and urban laborers, again on the basis of interest politics.[6] In the final analysis, the Populists tried to beat the opposition at their own game, using their own tactics. Furthermore, they believed it was in the natural order of things that such a political combination would eventually win, that the moral cream of society would rise to the top. Excoriating the bitch-goddess Success as exalted by the Capitalists, prosperity was the magic word which the philosophers of Populism preached to their audiences, both black and white. The Populists felt that they had moral wealth on their side while the "opposition" had capitalistic wealth. "The People's Party," according to Marion Butler, "is distinctly a party of principle; and our principles are all that we have. We are like a woman who has nothing but her chastity; when that is gone, everything is gone."[7] The wealth of virtue, the natural primacy of the producer class, would prevail over the moneyed wealth of the opposition, according to Populist doctrine. "Hard times, then," said one popular writer,

> as well as the bankruptcies, enforced idleness, starvation, and the crime, misery, and moral degradation growing out of conditions like the present, being unnatural, not in accordance with, or the result of any natural law, must be attributed to that kind of unwise and pernicious legislation which history proves to have produced similar results in all ages of the world. It is the mission of the age to correct these errors in human legislation, to adopt and establish policies and systems, in accord with, rather than in opposition to divine law.[8]

Thus, good would "naturally" prevail over evil, right over wrong. They were the knights of right doing combat with an "unnatural" force of "mammon worshippers" which had gained ascendancy in the South (and the nation) after the Civil War. "To tell the truth," one Populist organ remarked, "we are opposed to and hate wrong—hate injustice, fight oppression and tyrany [sic], and condemn the corrupt use of money, and we propose to fight for the right. . . ."[9] The Populists believed there had been a dangerous degeneration in moral fiber as a result of the deleterious influence of this corrupt "money power." Such moral degeneration, according to the Populist platform in 1892, portended "the destruction of civilization, or the establishment of an absolute despotism."[10]

The Populist's conception of government was also closely related to his belief in a rustic concept of Emersonian self-reliance and virtue, with the development of a new political leadership based on human happiness and social democracy. His ideal would be a society in which all men, no matter what their race, would be given a chance to rise as far as their merits would take them. Thomas Nugent, lawyer, judge, and twice Populist gubernatorial candidate of Texas, had a strong faith in the improvability of man. He wanted to christianize the political order, make social Christians of men, and he wanted to use the Populist Party as a vehicle to gain these ends. Differing from many Populists, he did not expect to secure complete justice by political action or by institutional reform, although he was of the opinion that these could yield alleviation.[11] In Alabama, Joseph C. Manning, variously referred to as "the Apostle," "the Clay County Evangelist," and "Evangel Manning," constantly preaching "the gospel of human brotherhood," expressed a deep commitment to "a free ballot" and "a fair count to all parties." Not unlike Nugent, Manning had a humanitarian outlook, and he remained constant throughout his lifetime to his idealism and the expression of such democratic principles.[12]

Populism's ideological and intellectual foundations combined in political thought the idea of a social democracy, and in religion the idea of the Social Gospel—both to be demonstrated by reform activity on this earth.[13] Like many Social Gospelers, Thomas Nugent felt that the Biblical expression "Thy Kingdom Come" was in the incipient phase. Although he "never expected to live on earth to see the full day," he believed, nonetheless, that he "lived in the morning of the coming light."[14] Dr. Cyrus Thompson, president of the North Carolina Farmers' Alliance and a Populist Secretary of State, was likewise committed to the Social Gospel ideal that the contemporary church become "a manifestation of . . . divine life flowing into human history." Making no apology for his much criticized philosophy, he explained, as a Christian, that it was "un-Christly" to "disregard . . . man's daily needs until he is pauperized and unmanned." Thompson was of the opinion that "you cannot . . . render Him acceptable service save by doing, in a charitable way, service to His children here."[15] Another Populist preacher considered "the principles of the Omaha platform" to be "in perfect harmony with the ten commandments, and the application of true Christianity [i.e., Populism] in civil government." If Christ "didn't teach and practice pure socialism, he didn't teach and practice anything."[16] In a sustained critique of Southern politics a subsequent Louisiana Populist preacher was of the opinion that "the people" could not be socially and morally "wrong" and be politically right. It was, he believed, "God's will that man establish God's Kingdom"—socially, morally, religiously and politically—here on earth.[17] The Populists, then, conforming to the ethics of the Social Gospel, castigated the prevailing political and economic system for its incompatibility with Christian principles. The competitive capitalistic spirit which made men dishonest, heartless, and materially oriented created injustices while Populism, centered on the Christian state, hoped to create a new climate in which oppression of the poor would be alleviated.

Though effective in creating an awareness of poverty and the problems of modern industrialism, the Populist doctrines contained a threat of surprising naivete that reveals a serious flaw in the movement's strategy. They believed, in one sense or another and with varying emphasis on its aspects, in a moral agrarian imperative of divine sanction and a human stewardship of virtue. The Populist presidential candidate, James B. Weaver, noted that Populists "were of a religious character," like the camp meeting of old.[18] "Their earnestness," according to the leading conservative Democratic paper of Texas, "bordering on religious fanaticism, has a touch of the kind of metal that made Cromwell's round heads so terrible a force. . . . It would be supreme folly to despite and belittle a movement that is leavened with such moral stuff as this."[19] In its mind, Populism, through the tribunal of divine sanction, would be the human gyroscope that would reestablish the agrarian ideal, whose workings had been deranged by the emergence of capitalism after the Civil War.

Two of the movement's common denominators were a set of fundamentalist religious beliefs and an intensely dogmatic evangelical expression of viewpoint which tended toward combining political and religious duties. At Populist meetings, James Weaver observed, people "wept and shouted, forgave their neighbors and shook off their old party sins."[20] A Louisiana Populist organ admonished its readers that "To register [to vote] is the religious duty of every reformer."[21] In Alabama, Joseph Columbus Manning, the "Clay County Evangelist," went about the state constantly preaching "the gospel of Populism";[22] Harrison Sterling "Stump" Ashby, Manning's counterpart in Texas, possessing "the oratorical rhetoric of an evangelical revivalist," had no peer on the hustings.[23] Indeed, partisan clergymen were not reluctant to invoke religion in the name of party. One "ordained" preacher in Alabama, for example, made "a political speech" to "prove to the people that Christ was one of the third party."[24] A Tennessee Populist saw "the finger of God in every thing and ready to help the good [all] the time."[25] At an Alabama tent revival, one Populist in his enthusiastic fervor shouted "Hurrah for Kolb," the Populist gubernatorial candidate, rather than "Glory Halleluia"; the result was a break-up of the revival.[26] A North Carolina Populist stated that he "literally" believed that there was no problem "in statesmanship" for which an answer could not be found in the Bible. "Life would not be worth the struggle of maintaining it," he added, "if one calmly concluded that wrong, even in this world, could permanently keep under the right. It would destroy . . . the belief in God's government of the world." If things were left in His hands the people were sure to win "at some time."[27]

Running throughout Populist doctrines also was, in the language of Richard Hofstadter, "the dualistic version of social struggles," resulting in a simple classification of right versus wrong, moral versus immoral.[28] "A thing is right or wrong, no matter what you believe about it," a Louisiana agrarian organ asserted. "All the people in the world believing a wrong would not make it right."[29] Delineating the sharp conflict between Populist and non-Populist, Populists divided the world into two groups—the "masses" and the "classes"—and referred to the organic solidarity of the movement in achieving the agrarian philosophy. "It is a struggle," said Sockless Jerry Simpson, "between the robbers and the robbed."[30]

There are but two sides in the conflict that is being waged in this country today [declared a Populist manifesto]. On the one side are the allied hosts of monopolies, the money power, great trusts and railroad corporations, who seek the enactment of laws to benefit them and impoverish the people. On the other are the farmers, laborers, merchants, and all the other people who produce wealth and bear the burdens of taxation. . . . Between these two there is no middle ground.[31]

"We are a unit," the *Louisiana Populist* observed, "from Maine to California, having one faith, one Lord and one baptism. . . ."[32] This characteristic of Populist rhetorical style made symbols of both capitalism (i.e., immoral, wrong) and agrarianism (i.e., moral, right) and were in themselves manifestations of how the Populist ethos became transmuted into a sense of moral stewardship.

Populism took quite earnestly its own exhortations about the basic changes needed in a society in which the agrarian was perceived as being a respected and prosperous figure traditionally. "Like 'hard shell' Baptists," according to one newspaper, "they have faith in their principles, and the torture of the rack could change but very few of them."[33] The mythical idea that the agrarians were the chosen of the earth was nationwide, certainly not confined to Southern Populism; but among no other stratum of the South's population was it more pronounced than among the Populists.[34]

The very contrast between the promise of the agrarian myth and their present circumstances made Populists especially disgruntled. An Alabamian noted that his was "naturally one of the richest states in the Union" concerning farm lands, crops produced, minerals, and such. "Notwithstanding all this, we are about the poorest people on God's green earth. Why it is?"[35] Typical of this rural melodrama was a farmer with a wife and five children in Grant Parish, Louisiana; working hard during the growing season, the family, after sale of its proceeds, now "find ourselves thirty-nine dollars and fifty-four cents worse off than when we started at the beginning of the year, after consuming the fifty-seven dollars and twenty cents [mortgage] interest."[36] In his earlier years John Sparkman, later senator, interviewed an aging Alabama farmer who recalled instances in which producers had shipped huge carloads to market, only later to be presented statements indicating that money was still due for shipping charges—in addition to the total proceeds from the sale, already consumed for transportation cost. Another farmer related an instance in which a carload of horses was sent from one point to another and the proceeds from their sale was ten dollars less than enough to pay the freight cost. Another recalled that "first class" farm hands working "from dawn to dusk"—fourteen to fifteen hours a day—with forty minutes off for lunch received forty cents a day and dinner or forty-five cents if one furnished his own lunch.[37] "We are chained to the soil with long weary hours of toil before us," a Populist organ commented, "and we are to every trust and combination of gamblers in the products of our labor a legitimate prey."[38]

In counterpoint to the mythical ideal of success exalted in the New South, the agrarians were constantly frustrated and understandably despondent over the indirect relationship between individual effort and resulting compensation.[39] Jeff Wilson, a tenant character in Dorothy Scarborough's novel of cotton in the Brazos

Valley expressed the agrarian feeling of frustration pungently: "If I was to start to hell with a load of ice there'd be a freeze before I got there."[40] Paradoxically, for the Populists the dream of prosperity through agrarianism had as much attraction as ever. They were more concerned with the "unnatural constraints" placed upon them by the new capitalistic society of the Gilded Age than with the shortcomings of the ideal itself.

In a society which taught that hard work and frugal living would invariably lead to a certain degree of success, the Populists stood in stark contrast to the popular prevailing ideas of self-help. Their rigid insistence on the virtues of work, morality, and religious values accommodated itself closely to the ideal necessary for success and self-improvement.[41] Yet, as indicated above, their vigorous assertion of this ethic seemed to translate not into success but abject failure. In substance, they saw themselves as playing the game of success strictly by the rules, yet failing to achieve a significant measure of economic advancement or status. Many members of the movement understandably came to feel that their opportunities had been unnaturally restricted by some sort of conspiratorial behavior on the part of "the international money power." Ignatius Donnelly asserted in 1892 that "a vast conspiracy against mankind had been organized on two continents, and it is rapidly taking possession of the world. If not met and overthrown at once it forebodes terrible social convulsions, the destruction of civilization, or the establishment of an absolute despotism."[42] It was not enough to be aware of the existing conspiracy, it was necessary to make a concerted study of these plots in order to better recognize and defend oneself against their avaricious effects.

> Populists are not prophets, but they have studied the great conspiracies that have been and are still being formed to sap the wealth of the nations of the earth, and they have so familiarized themselves with the rise and downfall of nations, that they are able to read 'the hand-writing on the wall' as fast as the conspirators put it there.[43]

The element of conspiracy was understandably an important factor in the Populist mind; and its fantasies surely reflect the ideas of some of our own contemporaries.[44] In the case of Populism the mood was more causal than symptomatic of its harsh environment and it provides us with a concrete example of what happens when people are bewildered and insecure. However, the breaking point which perhaps distinguished Populism from its contemporaries—if only in terms of degree—was the failure to distinguish between conspiracy in history and history as conspiracy.[45] While the worst forebodings of the Populists were not realized, a perusal of their most extreme personal experiences with individual enterprise can generate an element of sympathy and understanding with their view of affairs, however untenable this view may appear on balance. It is small wonder that for a time Populism was almost a religion to the underprivileged agrarians, offering as it did comfort and joy in the present and the promise of happiness and salvation to come. Its effect was like promising water to a thirsty man in the desert.

Broadly speaking, the treatment of the Populist mind in the late nineteenth century must take into account the mood of the black man, particularly since Populism sought to coalesce both races into a single organization for reform under the aegis of a "natural harmony of interests." In short, to the Populists the blacks came to symbolize, in a major sense, parity in political competition.

That the farmers both black and white would be swayed by Populism is understandable, for it sought to prove their moral superiority and promised to improve their economic status. But the black man's party loyalty would also be colored by the increasingly hostile public mood of the period. Facing as he did as much or more of the same harsh economic problems as white agrarians, the black found his path was also strewn with many violent obstacles and personal pitfalls such as lynching, political circumscription, and segregation. And, in view of these events, Populism needed to offer some tangible inducements to the peculiar interests of a people who were increasingly the victim of rank intolerance and mob violence. Thomas E. Miller, a black representative from South Carolina, provided a superb summary to the House of Representatives on what reforms Southern black farmers needed most during this period.

> There are other things more important to us [than holding office]. First is the infernal lynch law. That is the thing we most complain of. It is a question whether when we go to work we will return or not. Second, they have little petty systems of justices who rob us of our daily toil, and we cannot get redress before the higher tribunals. Third, we work for our taskmasters, and they pay us if they please, for the courts are so constructed that Negroes have no rights if these rights wind up in dollars and cents to be paid by white task-masters. . . . Yes, gentlemen, we want office but the first and dearest rights the Negro of the South wants are the right to pay for his labor, his right to trial by jury, his right to his home, his right to know the man who lynches him will not the next day be elected by the State to a high and honorable trust, his right to know that murderers shall be convicted and not elected to high office. . . .[46]

Thus, the impetus for black support centered around four major points: economic betterment, protection of person, a share in the patronage, and actual involvement in the political process. Perhaps most crucial of these was protection of person.

The application of the New South caste system was characterized by a method of racial violence little practiced in slavery days—that of lynching. The early use of this method was not widespread, but rather it increased in intensity with the passing of the decades, reaching a peak in the 1890s during the height of the Populist revolt.[47] It has been estimated that not more than eleven or twelve blacks were lynched per year in the 1870s, but in the period from 1882 to 1889 the number averaged 149.8 per year, continuing to rise to 187.5 per year in the next decade.[48] There were 294 blacks lynched in Mississippi alone between 1888 and 1903, followed closely by Georgia with 241 for the same period. This gave these two Southern states the dubious honor of being first and second in the nation in the lynching of black Americans.[49] Reaching a peak during 1892 at the height of the

Populist revolt, the continued application of violence by whites was so severe that in 1896, a "Negro was lynched every 56 hours; few citizens, black or white, raised a voice in protest."[50]

As lynching grew in the South, blacks also faced other less fatal but equally emasculating forms of violence. An Alabama black reported that "Some of my collored [sic] friends are whip in the country very regular. They whip 2 men and 1 woman not long since and kill one man dead."[51] To anyone familiar with the region's history, this pattern of Southern race relations is too obvious to require extended comment. The sanction of violence by elected officials offered little protection through the existing political structure for blacks. Perhaps the extreme example of this attitude was South Carolina's Ben Tillman who said: "Governor as I am, I'd lead a mob to lynch a man who had ravished a white woman. . . . I justify lynching for rape, and, before Almighty God, I'm not ashamed of it."[52] A Tennessee Republican, John B. Brownlow, also condoned lynching of blacks who were "guilty" of "assaulting white women." Speaking "*like a Southern man* on the negro question," Brownlow denied any racial features of the system, adding that the Southerners lynched blacks not "*because they are Negroes but because of the crime they have committed.*" It was "the *unwritten* law of the South to lynch a brute who assaults a woman without regard to his race or color."[53] The tragedy in all this was the failure of the moral stewardship and sense of justice advocated by the Populists in their attack on the existing political order.

These elements of violence required the Negro to cultivate certain forms of protection. One segment of the black community regarded it as "the duty of the state" to "throw the law's strong arm of protection around the Negro."[54] But faced with many state officials with attitudes somewhat analogous to Tillman's, blacks soon despaired of any redress of grievances. To many black leaders, the explanation was obvious:

> Because of coveted advantages intended to be gained influential leaders among the whites of the State have either directly or indirectly advised or allowed to be taught that any treatment of the negro would tend to impress him with the white man's superior power in a conflict of force is justifiable.[55]

Bitterness was the expression of many blacks toward the federal government for its failure to intervene in their behalf. A South Carolina black minister declared:

> I hate the mean, vacillating government which, if it finds that one or a part of the citizens are not wealthy or educated, throws her back on them when they cry for redress for their grievances, and says: 'Had you staid in your right place you would not need the arm of the law; those who are murdering you and cheating you are your best friends.'[56]

But by the 1890s, the North was "tired" of being a "nurse" to the black and, despite the increased violence, he was left to the white South to do with pretty much as it pleased.[57]

Blacks were openly divided over which road would ultimately prove the most beneficial. To some the answer was simple: politics had brought ruin on the race; what was needed at this point was moral and economic elevation, and political rights would subsequently be forthcoming. A Tuscaloosa, Alabama, black preacher, the Reverend A. L. Phillips, believed that "once we have set aside all political considerations and social fears, we will find that the essence of the whole matter" would be how the two races "behave" toward each other. "Political expedients are at best," he added, "mere temporary aids."[58] The editor of the *Knoxville Gleaner,* a black, suggested that Christian education and wealth is [sic] the colored man's only savior." These two things would do more "to adjust his station" presently than any other.[59] "Take politics in small doses without any shaking," another black cautiously advised.[60] Thus, a considerable element of the South's middle-class black leadership urged Negroes to eschew politics and concentrate on economics and morality. To many proponents of this philosophy, their deteriorating situation would be alleviated by a humble plea to the better class of whites for justice which, in turn, would result in the application of Christian principles between men.[61]

But among a more militant segment of blacks the urge for political participation remained constant, although truncated. To those whites who insisted that political equality would beget social equality these blacks advocated a type of separate-but-equal doctrine, providing for political participation but allowing social separatism. A Georgia Negro, J. W. Carter, a legislative spokesman for the Colored Alliance, summed up this argument:

> We don't want social equality. All the Negro wants is protection. You white people attend to your business and let us alone. . . . The politicians and lawyers say you must keep us Negroes down. But that is not right. . . .[62]

The Reverend J. C. Price, president of Livingston College, astutely observed: "The position that political and civil equality carries with it . . . [social equality as] a consequence is contrary to the experience of all men, and especially to that of southern white men."[63] The Richmond *Planet,* one of the major black newspapers in the South, reiterated this view with the comment that "the colored people of the South have no desire for social equality" but, rather, do "favor" their "civil rights and political equality" before the law.[64] "Separate the races in everything that looks like social intermingling, but in God's name treat us fairly," a black religious organ pleaded.[65]

In their frank approbation of "social equality," middle-class blacks more often placed their emphasis on the religious and social goals of a socially separatist black bourgeoisie respectability in this life and religious salvation in the next—which morality, industry, and economy insured. Some of the more militant black middle class, such as Bishop Henry Turner of Georgia, did not believe that whites would ever grant blacks social or political equality; and, on contemplation, he was not "certain that God wants them to do it."[66] A few blacks disagreed. "If we are not striving for equality,'' John Hope said in 1896, ''in heaven's name for what are we living.''[67]

Part of the problem involved a question of semantics. To most whites, black political involvement implied black control (e.g., ''Negro domination''), whereas in the case of blacks it was used more in the sense of being able to participate in the existing political process.[68] Equally as potent a term was social equality. As Professor August Meier has observed: ''Most Negroes interpreted social equality as meaning simply intimate social relationships which they did not desire, though most whites interpreted it as meaning the abolition of segregation.''[69] The linguistic impreciseness of the two races, therefore, subjected the political ambitions of blacks to strains which seem not to have been their original purpose. Thus, political and social ideals themselves became clouded even further with ambiguities and were transformed as they were taken up by both groups and revised with the heightened tensions of the Populist revolt.

Much of the Negro's resentment and frustration centered around the increasing movement to eliminate his share of the patronage and his opportunities for political development. By the 1890s the political gulf in these areas was much wider than it had been previously. Negroes were becoming disillusioned as officeholding decreased. Indeed, many of their grievances focused on Republican federal appointment policy.

> The colored people of the South are beginning to realize with a vengeance that President Harrison has a southern policy. They say 'Ham wants pie, but he can't even get the crumbs that fall from the [Republican] table. . . .'[70]

Increasingly, officeholding and patronage for blacks on the state level also diminished. The decade of the 1890s saw white Republican resentment of black political participation reaching the critical point. In Virginia, William ''Boss Billy'' Mahone, in a summary of Republican racial policies, noted that blacks ''have been made to understand that they must take a back seat and let their white bosses and political masters run the political machine and have all the offices.''[71] Also the Republican party was in a rapid state of decline in the state, with only three Republicans left in the Virginia General Assembly by 1891—none of whom were blacks.[72] In Texas, it was suggested that the ''Republican party . . . to merit the respect of mankind must be in the hands of the [white] race.''[73] The ''white Republicans have been traitors to us,'' a Negro convention in North Carolina declared, and ''the backbone of the Republican party, got nothing'' in the way of patronage.[74] In varying degrees this story was true in the remainder of the Southern states, as the Republican party sought to make itself ''respectable'' to the region's white constituency. John Lynch, the black Mississippi congressman, spoke of the motivations behind this ''small but noisy and demonstrative class . . . comprising about fifteen percent'' of the Republican party in the South.

> What those men chiefly wanted and felt the need of for themselves and their families

was social recognition by the better elements of the white people of their respective localities. They were anxious, therefore, to bring about such a condition of things as would make it possible for them to be known as Republicans without subjecting themselves and their families to the risk of being socially ostracized by their white Democratic neighbors. And then again those men believed them, and some of them still believe or profess to believe, that Southern Democrats were and are honest and sincere in the declaration that the presence of the colored men in the Republican party prevents Southern white men from coming into it.[75]

In substance, that small group of blacks who did advocate continued political participation was in somewhat the same untenable position with the Republican party as the white agrarians were with the Democrats—they were being taken for granted and circumscribed in participation. T. Thomas Fortune, one of the foremost black leaders of the day, bitterly remarked of the two existing political parties, "none of them cares a fig for the Afro-American" and predicted that "another party may rise to finish the uncompleted work" of emancipation.[76] Gauged by the vacuity of contemporary Southern politics, the future seemed to hold promise of a willing ally for the emerging Populists if they could suppress their racial prejudice sufficiently to attract a black following. This was the challenge they faced.

V

PRINCIPLES, PREJUDICE,

AND POPULISM

There is something very engaging about the racial portrait painted by Professor Woodward of the average nineteenth century southern white Populist. "It is altogether probable," Woodward contends, "that during the brief Populist upheaval of the 'nineties Negroes and native whites achieved a greater comity of mind and harmony of political purpose than ever before *or since* in the South"[1] Portrayed as a thoroughly good man of moral philosophy, the Populist was painstakingly trying to work out his sense of right with his black counterpart in the face of overwhelming regional adversity. In him the sense of benevolence was instinctive, instantaneous, and ostensibly infallible despite regional pressures for conformity. This concept is present also in the early Tom Watson, but in him Woodward sees in addition an exaggerated moral duty of benevolence for the underdog, e.g., the Negro.[2] The implication seems clear: moral man knows right from wrong by instinct and he needs no external sense of approval if he feels an action is morally right. In fairness to Woodward, he never makes the explicit claim that this prototype is true for all Populists, although it has been hard to keep a certain facile school of liberal historians from reading this viewpoint into his pages. To these men Populism was a road not taken—a lost opportunity for racial brotherhood in the South. Consider the summation of Professor Jack Abramowitz:

> The collapse of Populism in 1896 put an end to a movement that had every chance of producing a truly emancipated South in which the Negro would have been accorded a respectable position which might have broken down hostility and suspicion between Negro and white.[3]

Wrenched out of context, the eloquence of some Populist statements is impressive and seems to be a prototype for Southern racial liberalism. Consider a salient example by Tom Watson:

> My [black] friends, this [1892] campaign will decide many things, and one of the things it will decide is whether or not your people and ours can daily meet in

harmony, and work for law, and order, and morality, and wipe out the color line, and put every man on his citizenship irrespective of color.[4]

It is relatively easy to see how a judicious selection from the rhetoric of Populism could give a moral coloration of racial equality to the movement. Upon closer inspection, however, the tenor of Southern Populism rebuts somewhat the romantic fallacy of racial equality. Perhaps the most telling examples of Populism can be found in its actions and not its rhetoric. A chain is, after all, only as strong as its weakest link.

In the initial spread of third party ideology across the South, many white farmers, acting on the conditioned reflex of white supremacy and the prejudice of their environment, believed that the Negro should be excluded; but the more farsighted, notably the leadership, recognized that the Negro, however distasteful his presence might be to the membership, represented a potent source of political power that must be utilized in order to achieve needed reform.

Recognizing the internecine strife that could result not only within the movement but within the South itself (because of white sensitivity to the race question), H. L. Loucks, the president of the Southern Alliance, expressed what was probably the sentiment of the Populist leadership when he cautioned that ''we must make reform by the ballot exceedingly slow in the Southern states where the Negro vote is an important factor.'' While venturing the opinion that ''a majority of the white men in the South believe in our principles,'' the difficulty, he predicted, would be in convincing them to vote their principles over their prejudices when the Negro was involved politically.[5]

With a philosophical shift to political realism, certain basic changes in the overt racial ideology were party foreseen and partly developed as the movement gained momentum. Due to the ideological dichotomy of a liberal and a conservative racial faction within the party, the internal psychology of the movement always suffered from a certain amount of dissension over the matter of race. Although Populism did harbor such ''libertarians'' as Tom Watson, the change in official ideology probably resulted not so much from racial liberalism as it did from the expediency of the moment.[6] If the Populists could win with the Negro, they would include him in their ranks—as long as he was a political asset. In broad terms, this philosophy can best be understood as a regional manifestation of the Populist craving for group security, notably on the economic and political level.

In formulating the official racial creed, the Populists soon realized that the basic strongholds of their political support lay in an inverse relationship to the concentration of Negro population—two general exceptions to this rule being Virginia and Tennessee;[7] therefore, in order to achieve broad control of the Southern political machinery, it was imperative to obtain the support of the Black Belt. Through sheer weight of numbers, for example, the Negro controlled a bloc of sixteen counties in Texas. Moreover, in as many as fifty Texas counties, his ballot served as the balance of power when the white vote was split.[8] In the same manner the blacks controlled sixteen counties in eastern North Carolina, and due to their numerical concentration, could serve as the determining political factor in at least thirty-two other counties within the state.[9] In varying degrees, this situation was also true of the remaining states in the South.[10]

The mind of the average white Populist was caught between the Scylla of race and the Charybdis of reform. He was faced with the realization that he must choose between conformity to his ingrained regional prejudice and his long-range desire to implement successfully his reform principles. It seemed, however, that one must come at the expense of the other. "For no matter what the Populists may think on general principles," one Virginia Democratic paper warned, "they will have to face the fact that a vote for the third party will mean a vote for Harrison and the Force Bill; a vote to bring [Black] Reconstruction horrors upon the South. . . ."[11] Perhaps the most significant obstacle the Populists faced may have been psychological. They had to choose between principle and prejudice, and the problem of race was directly involved in both cases.[12]

Since the necessary requirement of being consistent with an official ideology was oftentimes inconsistent with the Populist's inner commitment, the overt expression of racial attitudes was not always an adequate measure of the Populists' true feeling toward the Negro.[13] "The regions where Populism made its strongest appeal," Woodward reminds us, "were the very regions that found it most difficult to overcome racial feeling."[14] By taking advantage of such sentiments and dramatizing the existing racial tensions, a well disciplined party machine could effectively retard any election alliance based on the naive Populist appeal to "harmony of interest" between the races. With clarity and remarkable succinctness, Carl Carmer has captured in a short fictional passage the economic and racial cleavages that have existed in the South—cleavages which still possess some precedent and continuity in Southern politics to this day. An upland white Populist prototype in *Stars Fell on Alabama* expresses in condensed form the deep seated attitudes the Populists hoped to surmount.

> We don't like niggers in this neck o' the woods [Tom Nabors explained]. We ain't never liked 'em. I can remember my father standin' on the mountain where you can look off down toward the Black Belt an' the flat country an' sayin': 'Them black bastards is takin' the food out 'n our mouths. We oughta be down there workin' that black land but we got too much pride to work for nothin'.' They're down there sharin' the good things with the rich while good white folks in the hills have to starve.[15]

In addition, the proposed class reform movement was further blunted by the curious mixture of racism and politics which, if managed carefully by skillful politicians, could more easily result in reaction rather than reform. "I'm a Democrat, because my daddy was Democrat, and I'm g'wine to vote agin the Nigger!"[16] The interpretative problem for the historian lies in the fact that while the official creed was obvious on the surface, the represed prejudices of the order were rarely expressed in print.

Despite the necessity to suppress personal prejudices, the vicissitudes of racism did come to the surface aat times where individuals were concerned. "This is a white man's country," one Virginia Populist bluntly asserted, "and will always be controlled by whites."[17] The "People's Party in this state," according to a Louisiana Populist organ, "is a white man's party, as evidenced by its vote in every election since its organization and by the utterances of its platforms, press and speakers in this State."[18] The same paper commented further: "If you want white supremacy join the Populists [;] if you want to go into a party that acknowledges its failure to even exist without uniting with the negro, then follow the modern *so-called* Democrary."[19] It "is a condition and not mere sentiment that confronts us here in North Carolina," said L. L. Polk about the third party question. "We cannot afford to risk Negro supremacy here."[20] An Alabama Allianceman of Populist principles suddenly exploded that he was thoroughly "disgusted with all the [third party] rot carried on . . . and the effort to drag the Alliance into a third party movement that wants to affiliate with Negroes, carpetbaggers, and Republicans."[21] In Comanche County, a later Populist stronghold in West Texas, all of the region's blacks were driven out in 1886 because of the criminal acts of a black minority. A signboard was posted in DeLeon to warn all future blacks who might desire entry into the area: "Nigger, don't let the sun go down on you in this town."[22] Vocal prejudice, therefore, did lurk within the inner psychology of the movement, although it was momentarily curbed in favor of political expediency. In what might properly be called true hypocrisy, the two currents of racism and egalitarianism continued to flow side by side, eventually resulting in a fundamental split in the Populist psyche, a sort of political schizophrenia. In a cynical way, the opposition found positive pleasure in the attitudinal sublimation of the white Populists—a classical example of what the psychologist would call a reaction formation, prompted by political and economic necessity. "Mr. Scipio Africanus," according to one Louisiana Democratic organ, "ought to know that Mr. Populite loves him less than any other white man on earth, but is willing to go into a deal with him to defeat the Democratic party."[23] Harry Lincoln Johnson, a prominent black Atlanta attorney, similarly berated Populist racial efforts as a sham. "The intelligent negroes of Georgia know that there is far more hate and spleen against the negroes in the populist camp than in the democratic."[24]

If the Populists were prone to racism, it is probably no exaggeration to say that by the 1890s the black had been transmuted into a political symbol calculated to foster rather rigid notions of racial behavior for the white agrarians to live up to. The repeated use of the "nigger" theme in the region's political campaigns had exacerbated a sinister and historical white fear of Negro domination. "Nigger, nigger, nigger is its [the Democratic party's] only cry," a white North Carolina Republican shouted in his frustration over the opponents' successful appeal to race.[25] "Heavens," a Louisiana organ exclaimed in exasperation, "how we would enjoy a rest on the 'nigger' question! It seems that four-fifths of the State [newspapers] can't come out without a longwinded article . . . with the negro as their target, and what's more, they have been at it for the lord only knows how long."[26] The concept of "loyalty" to one's race had been successfully used against previous political insurgents; and the threat of "black domination" was used as a catalyst to attract most of the region's white population to the Democratic party. It was little surprise, therefore, that the distorted use of the race question was used to erode the Populist movement. By fall, 1892, Watson concluded that "the argument against the independent political movement in the South may be boiled down into one word—nigger."[27] The region was early serving notice on the white Populists to accept the Democratic party and it would give witness to the fact that they were of the region's anointed. As inheritors of the region's racist tradition, the white agrarians were troubled over the twin issues of race and reform—a reality illustrated throughout their existence in the pattern of their rhetoric.

There was a haziness in the Populist rhetoric because it was forced by practical political considerations to stop short of frankness; but there was also an uncompromising clarity in some of the less publicized actions. It remains to consider a selected few who embodied at their clearest the sublimated racial attitudes of Southern Populism. In Texas the previously discussed Thomas Nugent, twice Populist candidate for governor, did not extend his concept of the Social Gospel to the blacks.[28] "My idea," he asserted, "is that segregation as far as possible is best for the negro."[29] Consonant with this philosophy, Nugent openly supported segregation of prisons, railway cars, and schools.[30] "Cyclone" Davis, Texas Populist candidate for attorney general in 1892, clearly stated his opposition to social equality and miscegenation:

> The worst sight of social equality to be seen in this land is the sight of a sweet white girl hoeing cotton in one row and a big burley [sic] negro in the next row. Talk of social equality, when your industrial system forces a good woman's precious Anglo-Saxon girl down on a level with a burley [sic] negro in a cotton row. Oh, my God! and this in free America![31]

This passion for segregation was also demonstrated in Alabama where a "Separate But Equal Accommodation Bill" was "passed without opposition by both Democrats and Populists." "The unanimous vote on the Jim Crow seating bill of 1891," according to Sheldon Hackney, "indicates that there probably were no significant differences between the Democrats and the Populists on race relations. . . ." Furthermore, he found "no objective difference between the two parties on racial policy. . . ." In fact, he adds, "thousands of ordinary white Alabamians voted Populist without abandoning their belief in white supremacy."[32]

Equally noteworthy were the actions of Tom Watson in Georgia who, admittedly, courted the black vote. Watson's viewpoint shifted rather dramatically, however, when his stand on "nonpolitical" aspects of black rights were queried. By 1894 he supported segregation laws for public accommodations, denied favoring jury service for blacks, opposed racial equality, and took an ambivalent stand on lynching.[33] The racial consensus portrayed by Professor Woodward seems to suffer when Watson's rhetoric is compared with his actions.

A scrutiny of Watson's political career prior to 1892 indicates that he "shared the obsessions of his peers in a hatred of Reconstruction and Black aspirations and in a consistent devotion to white supremacy. Nothing in his career prior to 1890," according to Crowe, "would lead one to suspect him of racial heresy or a radical future."[34] The rabid racial sympathies of Watson's later career are well known and need not be chronicled here.[35] From this vantage point, Watson's overall career as a racial liberal seems highly questionable. If, as one historian has asserted, "Georgia Populism was Tom Watson, and Tom Watson was Georgia Populism,"[36] his career would appear to be a shallow foundation upon which to erect a prototype for Southern racial reform. A curious mixture of white supremacy and political expediency resulted in a fragile brand of white liberalism ultimately molded by pragmatism, opportunism, and caprice.

As early as 1890, the conservative element was highly visible in the Georgia agrarian revolt. In the famous legislature of 1890, dominated by the Farmers' Alliance, one of the earliest Jim Crow laws was passed; ironically, in this same assembly, these men appropriated $8,000 to create a new Negro school in Atlanta![37] Interestingly, Watson voted against state appropriations for black schools and colleges on the premise that the state was "already committed" to other costly public ventures and could not afford these outlays.[38]

The overriding influence of this agrarian element was witnessed again in 1891 when Dr. S. W. Johnson of Appling County, later a Populist candidate, introduced a bill to establish Jim Crow cars in the state. To many conservative agrarians, this was "a bill that should stand as a lasting monument to his name and statesmanship." Tom Watson's *People's Party Paper* supported the law on the basis that it would "prevent race riots" and protect blacks from "insults, etc., by rough, card playing, drunkenness, etc., in cars provided for the colored people." In a paternalistic tone, the paper concluded that "no one can fail to see the propriety and necessity for such a law."[39] Such forms of racial proscription were usually accompanied by black protest and this bill was no exception.[40] "These exhibitions of prejudice," according to the Savannah *Tribune,*

are simply an expression of hostility injected by the white farmers of the South into the great currents of passing political opinion. They represent the feeling of the agricultural class always more strongly wedded to the old ideas and less susceptible to the newer teachings of an inlarged and progressive humanity. They have their origin in an order dominated from its incipiency by a feeling of enmity to the Negro.[41]

Thus some Georgia Populists and Farmers' Alliancemen did have overt proclivities toward racism, despite the rhetorical emphasis on class consciousness and harmony of interest.

Louisiana agrarians also displayed on occasion a conspicuously racial outlook and promoted increased circumscription of the social relations between the two races. An 1890 bill which required mandatory racial segregation in railroad coaches was "with few exceptions," supported by the Farmers' Union, including its ex-president John M. Stallings. Furthermore, the Farmers' Union selected as its official state organ, the Shreveport *Weekly Caucasian*—hardly a magnetic title to attract black support.[42] How much these affected any attempts at racial coalition, particularly in the emerging Populist movement, is open to question. Such unacceptable actions probably made at best for difficulty among the blacks in distinguishing between friend and foe. However, such actions bore the impress of a general lower class white agrarian attitude about the desired relationship between Negroes and the prevailing social order.

A further manifestation of hostile Populist racial attitudes can be found in Virginia. Edmund Randolph Cocke, Populist candidate for governor in 1893, urged in 1891 the repeal of the fifteenth amendment on the assumption that "depriving the negro of suffrage . . . might have a good effect." This was, he added, "the only solution to prevent troubles."[43] Furthermore, Virginia Populists did not subscribe with enthusiasm to social mingling between the races even in political situations. In a description of a political rally, the Populists lamented that the Democrats served food for both races and they "ate side by side, shoulder to shoulder."[44] As Charles Wynes has shown, the Virginia Populists openly rejected the blacks as a political ally, and the latter generally responded by failing to attend state Populist conventions or to provide political support for the movement.[45]

Another illustration of the Populist Party's uniqueness in race relations, according to Professor Woodward, was its efforts to resuscitate the Reconstruction experiment of incorporating blacks into the political process from the bottom up. One of Woodward's most poignant statements concerns Populist efforts to implement biracial juries. "Populist officers saw to it that Negroes received such recognition as summons for jury service, which they had long been denied."[46] An examination of Woodward's evidence reveals a blanket statement of Populist actions based solely on Roscoe Martin's study of Texas Populism. Martin, in turn, relied on a hostile Texas Democratic organ which refers to a single incident of blacks being called for jury service in Nacogdoches County.[47] So central is this contention to Woodward's case for Populist uniqueness in race relations that it deserves closer examination.

A recent monograph on the Negro in Texas indicates an ambiguous pattern of jury service for blacks during the period under question. While some counties "seldom or never" summoned Negro jurymen, "several counties with large Negro populations continued to use Negro jurors until the turn of the century."[48] A comparable situation also existed in Louisiana until 1898.[49] Woodward's case on this point seems shaken if Democrats in the black belt allowed Negro participation on juries both before and after the Populist revolt. Again and again Woodward alludes to the purity of motive and action characteristic of many white Populists;[50] but his failure to recognize the existence of an opposing political order of biracial cooperation not of Populist making neutralizes somewhat the tribute he felt they deserved. This process of biracial involvement does not appear to be unique to Texas or Louisiana. In Jefferson County, Arkansas, the third ward Democrats in 1892 developed a "compromise ticket" with the blacks whereby "the Democrats be given the County Judge, one member of the Legislature, an equal division of the magistrates in every Township in the county, and . . . the sheriff appoint as many white deputies as colored."[51] In Richmond County, Georgia, a Democratic stronghold that voted against Tom Watson, it had long been an "existing practice" to have blacks on juries.[52] However, Watson denied favoring jury service for blacks in the 1894 Georgia election campaigns and attacked his opponent James Black for "promising to put negroes in the jury boxes."[53]

All in all, the record of the Populists in jury reform is not what Professor Woodward claims it to be; but neither is it a record to be read with complete contempt. If a charitable view is taken of the inevitable gap between the rhetorical aspirations of the Populists and the practical possibilities of their methods, and then extended to what they actually did achieve, the Populists were not failures. But the pattern was not Populistic alone and it is this fact that necessarily adds haziness to the Populist portrait. Thus, the overall pattern of Southern race relations was one of diversity rather than one in which any clear distinction can be drawn between Populist and non-Populist. The political order that Woodward envisaged it too rigid, too mechanical, too remote from the diversity of human nature to be considered a man-made society.

In this light, it seems necessary to examine in further detail the discrepancy between Populism in theory and Populism in practice as outlined by Woodward. He seldom allows himself the luxury of hyperbole, but on occasion he does indulge in a sentence or two in which the underlying premise has served as a historigraphical catalyst.

> Negroes were not put off with nominal duties and peripheral appointments, but were taken into the inmost councils of the party. They served with Southern whites as members of state, district, and county executive committees, and delegations to national conventions. Black and white campaigners spoke from the same platform to audiences of both races, and both had their places on official party tickets. Populist sheriffs saw to it that Negroes appeared for jury duty; and the Populist editors sought out achievements of Negroes to praise in their columns.[54]

Although he cites specific examples and ideas of black participation, Woodward's conception of Populist actions remains in the traditional white liberal mold: he associates the meaning of static biracial involvement with the democratic process, an assumption that bears investigation.

Black participation in Populist conventions varied considerably from state to state during the initial People's party gatherings in 1891–92. "You look over the large assembly and find very few of my people represented in this great movement," an angry black delegate charged at the Populist convention in Dallas.[55] In Virginia, it is unclear if any black delegates were present at all; certainly no more than one at most.[56] The Arkansas Populists had eleven blacks among the one hundred and seventy delegates in attendance.[57] The North Carolina Populist convention, according to the Wilmington *Morning Star,* had only "a few negro representatives," although over half the delegates were reportedly ex-Republicans.[58] In Georgia, the state Populist convention attracted only two blacks, although two years later black representation increased to twenty-four.[59] The high point of Negro participation in the South was reached in Louisiana where twenty-four black delegates attended the state Populist convention.[60] Alabama and Mississippi effectively circumscribed any black participation by refusing to seat Negro delegates.[61]

The number of blacks at various Populist conventions thus varied greatly but in all cases they were deprived of the substance of power. The most effective technique used by the white delegates to prevent a potential black power bloc was to assign Negro representatives as delegates for the state-at-large.[62] By failing to appoint the blacks to a particular district-at-large, the opportunity to develop a viable concentrated base of grassroots support was eliminated. This dilution served to decrease the voice of the blacks and increase that of whites who probably hoped to solicit black votes against an open display of impotent token black delegations. With whites in firm control of the reins of power, the chance of further meaningful black participation in the convention process was blunted almost entirely by the inconsequential number of Negroes at the various People's party conventions. From this vantage perhaps the major criticism of Woodward's approach and outlook is his confidence in the good intentions of the Populists by merely having black representatives on hand. In substance, blacks were little more than political eunuchs in a white harem.

The historian might see in Woodward's statements, among other things, the spirit of the Constitution making its impact on Southern race relations. However, a more pragmatic explanation seems plausible. Living in a contemporary nation very conscious of the emerging African kingdoms and instinctively receptive to reform in domestic race relations surely must have stimulated the social conscience of a transplanted Southern liberal such as Professor Woodward, who participated with Martin Luther King in the civil rights march on Montgomery, Alabama. "There we were," Woodward recalled, "walking down that highway to Montgomery. I looked over to the side of the road, and I saw the red-necks lined up, hate all over their faces, distrust and misunderstanding in their eyes. And I have to admit something. A little part of me was there with 'em."[63] In his writings, especially his collection, *The Burden of Southern History,* Woodward has particularly addressed himself to such problems of consciousness plaguing the South and the Southerner's preoccupation with guilt and the reality of evil.

In his brief assertion that "Populist editors sought out achievements of Negroes to praise in their columns," Woodward adds yet another dimension to the Populist portrait.[64] This is one of his clearest and most explicit expositions of Populist actions and, like previous statements already examined, it demonstrates the centrality of his belief in the People's Party as promoters of a liberal tradition in

Southern history. It is perhaps his highest tribute to Populism that in the face of its opponent's overwhelming preoccupation with racist allegations it had the chance to use propaganda as a weapon in its newspapers and rejected it.

Despite Woodward's contentions, however, the Populists were on occasion moved to expressions of protest toward the Negro in their newspapers. Though they harbored covert proclivities toward racism, the overt philosophy of self-interest required a conciliatory approach. The Populists grappled with this knotty problem repeatedly, swaying sometimes in the direction of racism and sometimes in the direction of reconciliation. The agitation and complaint crystallized around selected black personalities which provided a catharsis for their pent-up prejudices. Paradoxically, all of these instances revolved around social and political interaction between whites and blacks.

The brunt of these attacks was focused on Grover Cleveland and his political and social relations with certain blacks. When Cleveland invited Frederick Douglass, his white wife, and black child by a previous marriage to four different mixed social affairs at the White House, the Populists loudly proclaimed that the president was advocating "social equality" between the races. Under strong pressure from his fellow Republicans to condemn the Democratic Cleveland, Douglass nonetheless praised the president for being "brave enough when public sentiment set against me" to invite him not once "but many times" to the White House.[65] Since the condemnation of Douglass "partakes of personal character and appeals to the prejudice of race," the *National Economist* made it clear that it would not print such a story except that "numerous requests" from grassroots subscribers had demanded it.[66] This statement reveals the dualism in Populist thought between the following whose emotional preoccupation was with race and the more articulate editorship who generally exhibited a healthy skepticism toward the race issue.

Cleveland came under further attack because he had reportedly signed a bill in 1884, while governor of New York, that made provision for "mixed schools." Paradoxically, the statute concerned integration of the *black* schools in New York, providing "for the education of pupils for whom admission is sought without regard to race or color." This, the Populists charged, was "proof" that Cleveland "committed himself to both the principle and policy of 'mixed schools.' "[67] The usual pattern in Populist papers presenting this story was to print a verbatim extract of the statute, with the conclusion that this was tangible "proof" of Cleveland's integrationist attitude. "I do not believe in Grover Cleveland's plan of treating the negro," Tom Watson declared. The result of such a policy would be "eternal discord" between the races.[68]

It would be hard to overemphasize the Populist opposition to interracial association on a social basis. This oft-quoted New York statute was singled out to make this fact glaringly apparent. "Socially, I want no mixing of the races," Watson proclaimed. "It is best that both races should preserve the race integrity by staying apart." To a group of Atlanta blacks he sternly advised, "Let the whites dwell to themselves to have peace and happiness. [Populists] will not have social equality."[69] The attitude of Tom Watson and other white Populists was also summarized by a white North Carolina Populist: "We have no advocates of social equality with the Darky. All parties want their vote on a pinch. Now let the poor Negro alone."[70] H. S. Doyle, the black Georgia preacher who campaigned for Watson, cogently expressed the limitations of the biracial venture: "Mr. Watson's position was that, in politics, the color line should be wiped out. He especially emphasized the word 'politics.' His enemies misrepresented him, and claimed that he was preaching the doctrine of social equality. . . ."[71]

A third issue that received extensive press coverage during the active years of the Populist crusade was the appointment of black diplomats to what Tom Watson characterized as "white countries."[72] These pronouncements particularly centered around the proposed appointment of C. H. J. Taylor, "Cleveland's pet Democratic Negro from Kansas," as Minister to Bolivia.[73] A proponent of the "economics-before-politics" point of view, Taylor was a former United States minister to Liberia, having been appointed in 1887 by Grover Cleveland. An articulate middle-class mulatto lawyer, he had opposed the back-to-Africa element, Radical Reconstruction and urged blacks to eschew politics to prevent racial troubles.[74] A supporter of Grover Cleveland, Taylor suggested that if blacks refused "the olive branch of political peace offered by Grover Cleveland . . . then by all means disfranchise them, and that speedily."[75] Taylor's appointment to Bolivia was opposed by a faction of Republicans and his candidacy was subsequently withdrawn. He was then made Register of Deeds in Washington, D.C., where, according to a hostile Populist press, he would have "a few white girls" serving as "stenographers for his 'nigger' clerks." There is "certain to be a scramble" by Southern white "ladies" to serve as stenographers, it was charged.[76]

A similar Cleveland appointment involved Henry Clay Smith, a black from Birmingham who was made consul at Santos, Brazil. The Populists charged that the Democrats had selected a black over their "own kind," to fill a position formerly held by a white diplomat. All this, it was charged, at a time when 70,000 white Democrats desperately "needed" the president's endorsement for a diplomatic post.[77] Watson opposed such black appointees because it would break down the social barriers, thereby permitting blacks to eat, sleep, and mingle with whites.[78]

A final racial issue receiving broad coverage in the Populist press concerned a visit from a Massachusetts legislative delegation to Virginia's Governor Charles O'Ferrall. Included in the delegation was Robert Teamoh, a black. O'Ferrall staunchly asserted that he knew nothing of Teamoh's presence until the arrival of the representatives, whereupon he "merely" performed his official duties of mingling with the delegation which, of course, included the black. He reportedly "regretted the circumstances" but that was not enough for the white Populist press. But the fact remained: "he performed the act."[79] Describing the incident, Watson stated: "Teamoh was there in great shape. He drank with the proudest, ate with the most select, and wiped his distinguished lips with O'Ferrall's napkins just as if he had been at it all his life."[80]

O'Ferrall's contention that he was unaware of Teamoh's presence in the delegation appears to have been manufactured *ex post facto* for public consumption once the incident received unfavorable notice. The Virginia delegation included John Mitchell, Jr., Negro editor of the Richmond *Planet* who arrived with the mayor of his city. Mitchell was ostensibly included in the local entourage as a social companion for the visiting black, and dined at the governor's mansion with Teamoh.[81] [A]ll stretched companionable legs under the same mahogany,'' Watson asserted, "and forgot the toils of political war in a feast of brotherly love."[82] Ridiculing the episode with racial sarcasm, Watson added: "Mitchell saw, ate, and drank along with the Massachusetts delegation, the Governor and the Governor's wife, *just as natural as if he was a human being,* and Governor O'Ferrall hasn't found it out as yet."[83]

The pattern of thought developed in this essay has by no means exhausted the collection of racial events surrounding Populism; common sense has indicated the limits of its application.[84] However, it has been sufficient hopefully to stir the historiographical dust surrounding the portrait of Populist racial attitudes laid down earlier by Professor Woodward. If we judge the actions of the past by our own present sympathies, it becomes impossible to examine without disapprobation some of the statements and actions of nineteenth century Populists. But there was a maturity to Populism, even in hours of peril, that testifies in part to the profound truth of Woodward's liberal concept of the movement. It did not, for example, often make blanket indictments of blacks as did its opponents but concentrated largely on specific personalities and events. In these incidents, Populist actions were not totally irrational acts of racism but, on examination, had a logical basis in fact. The attack on C. H. J. Taylor stands as a classical case in point. Although a Populist candidate for the Kansas legislature in 1892, Taylor labeled Jay Gould, one of the Populists' major opponents "as great a benefactor and philanthropist as the world has even seen."[85] In addition, Taylor was a staunch defender of the Democrat Grover Cleveland, a figure the Populists regarded as their political nemesis. Denouncing the Populists as "shabby, shiftless" and not "as good as any kind of negro," Taylor responded to the defeat of the Alabama Populist gubernatorial candidate, Reuben Kolb, with obvious pleasure.[86] Such sentiments certainly helped prompt later Populist outbursts against Taylor, and provided a rational basis for Populist actions. Purity of motive cannot overlook the practicalities of political life—even for a reform party. It would be a mistake, then, to attribute Populist attacks on particular black personalities solely as rabid appeals to race prejudice alone. Put in a less pleasant way, the exigencies of the age demanded that Populists yield to political expediency.

But on balance the pattern of actions Woodward has outlined was not Populistic alone. The political and social views conceived by Woodward are too rigid, too sharply delineated and are by their very nature intellectually precarious if not factually untenable. It would be a mistake to equate white Populist support of black political participation beyond the perspective of immediate class interest and reform. To be sure, Populism would not pass the current tests for racial militancy and liberalism and nowhere did it approach the millennium in race relations, even at its height, that its defenders imply.

We may now pass to another aspect of Populist thinking, the biracial philosophy. It was the Populists' supreme achievement to formulate a philosophy in which political tolerance of blacks had become an essential part of the reform compromise. But insofar as any sort of social leveling such as egalitarianism was a fundamental of Populist thinking, it violently rejected the concept of social liberty and the equality of men of different races to associate in perfect fellowship. Every one of the previously examined incidents aptly illustrates this point. The sincerity of white Populist convictions on this point seems unimpeachable: political equality could never beget social equality; it would be an ''unnatural'' function of the social order. If anything, Populist adherents—particularly at the grassroots level—were more vehement on this point than their opponents. Perhaps the rabid attacks of their opponents also exacerbated this tendency in Populist actions, making it into a sort of defensive mechanism.

To sum up the racial philosophy of Populism is not simple. The following might be tentatively offered: the reformer cooperates biracially in a class sense during the political process insofar as it makes his movement more effective in the struggle against the established order. However, he is antagonistic to ''social equality'' and helps suppress such ''unnatural'' egalitarian qualities as being harmful to the welfare of both races. It remains now to turn to the application of this philosophy to local political affairs.

VI

THEORY AND PRACTICE OF POPULISM:

THE ATLANTIC SEABOARD STATES

Populism illustrates as well as any movement in American history the truth of the adage that politics makes strange bedfellows. According to Populist doctrine, black and white alike must be brought to an awareness of their identity of interest; indeed the promotion of this idea took on the urgency of a cause. The fact that the proposal could be seriously raised before such old antagonists was symptomatic of how bad things were. Actual conditions, of course, forced a compromise and the ideal vis-a-vis politics varied from state to state. This chapter seeks to identify and describe these diverging patterns of Populism—both of a political and philosophical nature—in the seaboard states of Virginia, North and South Carolina, and Georgia—classic examples with which to illustrate this political concept and its uneven application. This discussion is concerned, therefore, not merely with the formal and conspicuous revelations of political conduct but with the characterization of a philosophical plan of action which not only reflects but helps explain these developments. A subsequent chapter will examine these conditions in the Gulf Coast states.

Centered in those areas where racial antagonisms were strongest, Populism was imprisoned in a rigid set of intellectual shackles forged out of its own racial climate. This strain of thought was undoubtedly an important factor in molding the conservative agrarian mind, but there was a further dimension to the Populist formla for success. Indeed, we have seen how the exponents of Populism, intent upon striking a proper coalition between an individual's occupational and political calling, were willing to cross racial, regional, and class lines in order to create a political party which would be of value in reestablishing the agrarian moral and political order. A troublesome byproduct of this political strategy was the extent to which conflicting white attitudes toward the blacks were constantly being called into question. On the one hand the Populists were willing to grant the Negro limited political equality; but, conversely, social contact during political intercourse caused confusion and perplexity about the deeper implications of their party's actions as an unwitting instrument of social change. Indeed, the Bourbon opponents of Populism went so far as to argue on occasion that poverty was actually a better alternative for the regon than a division of the Caucasian race.

To be sure, extensive social intercourse is not crucial for a political movement, but all such movements are nevertheless marked by a degree of group activity.[1] Consequently the Populist appeal to potential members and sympathizers through an organized campaign would of necessity create a certain amount of association with blacks. Although complete uniformity or consensus is never achieved in any such movement, there remained beyond the initial gathering of a simple Populist following the nagging problem of retaining a close-knit membership which could function without dissipating its energies through interracial conflict. The challenge of an interracial coalition was perhaps more acute in the untutored thought of the common agrarian than in the more cultivated philosophy of the leadership. The taunts and jeers of political adversaries, exploiting the sensitive issue of "social equality," were a provocation that put the movement on the defensive from the very outset.

Populism grappled with this problem repeatedly, swaying sometimes in the direction of conciliation and sometimes in the direction of unmitigated, emotional racism. Insofar as the Populists can be said to have solved this dilemma, the leadership sought to create an artificial personality for the movement in order to restrain the antiblack tendencies of its following. The appeal to the membership was simple: the process was one of political necessity and self-interest. As a minority party, Populism desperately needed votes and the disaffected blacks, however disagreeable their presence might be to the membership, represented a potential source of much-needed strength.

The official racial ideology, its interpretations, and its application to the Populist racial dilemma were formulated by the movement's leadership. It was Tom Watson who served as the official racial interpreter of the order. Watson was capable of being a philosopher, yet even more perhaps than his practical-minded followers, he had an instinct for the practicalities necessary for political reform. Postulating the basic Darwinian premise that "self interest always controls," Watson in an 1892 article in the *Arena,* set forth the official ideology to be used in consolidating the poor black and white agrarian class.[2] The polemics of the Negro question, he argued, had been resorted to for so long by both major parties "until they have constructed as perfect a [political] 'slot machine' as the world ever saw." In summary, a polarization founded on the basis of race had created conditioned political responses on the part of the South's electorate. On the basis of this campaign issue, Watson lamented, "We have a solid South itself, a solid black vote [Republican] against the solid white [Democrat]."

Because of "the sharp and unreasoning political divisions" maintained by this issue, "a new party was necessary" to break this rigid pattern of thought control. But how could Populism entice the traditionally Republican Negro into voting with the poor white farmer who despised him? "Their every material interest is identical," Watson replied.[3] Therefore, "granting to him the same selfishness common to us all . . . would he not act from that motive just as the white man has done?" Watson's underlying political philosophy was perhaps best revealed in his viewpoint as to what would motivate the average voter. Only a foolish optimist, he believed, would deny the dark realities of personal interest at the bottom of all human nature, regardless of color.

> Gratitude may fail; so may sympathy and friendship and generosity and patriotism; but in the long run, self interest *always* controls. Let it once appear plainly that it is to the interest of a colored man to vote with the white man and he will do it. Let it plainly appear that it is to the interest of the white man that the vote of the Negro should [and must] supplement his own, and the question of having that ballot freely cast and fairly counted, becomes vital to the white man. He will see that it is done.[4]

While the Populists reacted favorably to a policy of Negro suffrage, they nevertheless viewed their black counterpart as an inferior social ally. Like many of its contemporaries, Populism associated the meaning of American democracy with a narrow parochial interpretation of the prevailing ethnic and social order. "Anglo Saxons, whether Populist or patrician," Richard Hofstadter tells us, "found it difficult to accept other peoples on terms of equality or trust. Others were objects to be manipulated—benevolently, it was often said, but none the less firmly."[5] Populist reactions to the formulation of the new political ethic with blacks were as diverse as the criticisms of American life which had provoked them, but their agreement on the basic rejection of the ideal of equality between the races was near consensus. Reflecting the prejudices of their culture, they subordinated such intangible conceptions of natural rights and virtue to the more immediate interest of practical politics. "The question of social equality," Tom Watson constantly emphasized, "does not enter into the calculation at all. That is a thing each citizen decides for himself."[6] As a body, the white Populists, if not socially solid, were at any rate inchoate. The opposition, however, had made the question of racial equality into an obsequious political issue: if the Negro was granted political independence, the Democrats charged, the Populists would be going beyond the limits of public acceptance in social equality.

Due to the harping tactics of the opposition, the Populists were forced to assume the burden of ideological defense against an emotional social issue. The Populists desperately denied any ideas of condescension beyond immediate recognition of the Negro's political rights; yet their basic defense was always a denial—political equality did not beget social equality. "Let's stop running campaigns in North Carolina by abusing the Negro," one Populist angrily retorted to these charges. "We have no advocates of social equality with the Darky. All parties want their vote in a pinch. Now let the poor Negro alone."[7] While the two races shared a sense of economic desperation and urgency for reform, social integration, even if it had been desired, would have been difficult, if not impossible, because of Southern values and inbred prejudice.

Clearly, then, the Populist appeal was to the economic and political—not the social—instincts of the Negro. This more practical philosophy, they believed, would provide a great personal impetus toward political improvements in the

South and would eventually provide incalculable economic and political benefits to both races. If the Negro would find it difficult to agree with this viewpoint, the Populists further contended, there was little to quarrel with concerning his economic dependence on the whites. In a regional perspective, the rank-and-file Negro farmer, such as the tenant and sharecropper, suffered from the effects of being employed by a white agrarian debtor class. Therefore, a Texas Populist concluded, "what is good for the plain, white people of the South is good for the Negro. Whatever destroys the prosperity of the white producers of wealth, in the South, will [further] enslave the Negro. . . ."[8] When "a law oppresses a white Georgia farmer," said W. L. Peek, the Populist gubernatorial candidate in Georgia, "the colored farmer just behind him suffers also."[9] In essence, the Populists pointed out that it was the white race which employed the black farmer in the South, and it was necessary to bring about certain political reforms before economic benefits would follow for either race. "The time has come," said one white farmer, "for the whites to explain the truth to the blacks, and let them know that, while it is a white man's country, we propose to do them justice and give them a chance. . . ." If "logic" dictated the black race's actions, then "they will gladly follow" with political support.[10] As political accommodation became more marked in the 1880s, a significant segment of the black community, particularly in the South where the full implications of incurring white displeasure were becoming more pointed, came to espouse such ideas of economic improvement through subordination to white influence. John B. Rayner, probably the most prominent black leader in the Populist movement, believed such a program of racial accommodation as offered by the Populist party was a viable solution to the race question. His advice to blacks was simple: "The only rights we Negroes will ever enjoy will be the rights the southern white man gives us. Vote the People's Party ticket; we will get better wages for our work and we will have better times in the South."[11]

It is largely against the background of increasing racial hostility that the political actions of both blacks and whites must be considered. The recrudescence of the agrarian protest tradition in the 1890s had ushered in an effective sycophantic defensive posture of white solidarity championed by the Democratic party. Another invigorating ingredient that caused a shift in the force and direction of black politics during this period was the change from a positive to a negative attitude on the part of a sizable segment of the Republican party.[12] In a desperate attempt to find some solution to what appeared to be a hopeless political situation, many middle-class Negro leaders such as Booker T. Washington, expressing the desire to essay a compromise or accommodationist position with the rich and powerful, attempted to maintain friendly relations with the South's established white leadership. Naturally, the acceptance of Tom Watson's "self-interest" philosophy was largely determined by these conditions and by the extent to which Populists, in contrast to their opponents, could deliver on their promises to blacks. In view of all these circumstances, state branches of the Populist party differed in their open alignment with the Negro, some expressing affinity with the blacks and others insisting on their identification with whites only. In the following pages we will trace the political alignments and discuss black identification with the Populist cause in the various seaboard states.

In Virginia, the Populists generally sought to disassociate themselves from the Negro and his ballot; the black man, in turn, long steeped in personal and political prejudice, understandably did not respond to the principles of the third party.[13] J. H. C. Beverly, formerly an Alliance leader and a Populist, said of the Virginia Negro:

> The Negroes to some extent voted for the Populist if there was no Republican candidate, but they always voted the Republican ticket if there was one. The Negroes were very unreliable, their promises amounted to nothing. They could be bought for money or whiskey. Major Mann Page told me of an amazing experience. A Negro leader had promised to support him and did not. Page reprimanded him, and he replied, 'Major Page, don't you know that God made the Negro for sale to the highest bidder?'[14]

At the outset of the Populist revolt in Virginia, there was an attempt to organize blacks on the precinct level. Votes of any persuasion or color were needed to offer a credible challenge to the Democrats. In the summer of 1892, Charles Pierson, editor of the *Virginia Sun* and Populist state committee chairman, urged each precinct committee to "have one or more colored citizens on it to look after the colored vote."[15] By fall, 1892, the Virginia Populists, probably as a result of the increasing militancy of Democratic opinion, shifted to a policy of organizing segregated Negro Populist clubs. The procedure was simple: seek out the most influential black in the community, secure him as a convert, and then proceed to build grassroots support from this point.[16]

In their denunciation of Populist efforts to organize the blacks, the Democrats, as always, raised the old political remedy of "Negro domination," warning the white population of the state that "every vote cast in the South for the third party will be a Republican vote by proxy, tending to encourage the Negro to another effort for supremacy."[17] These volatile charges received added impetus with the development of a "cult of the Confederacy" under the aegis of the Democratic party.[18] This blind devotion to the "Lost Cause," bolstered by the racial issue, laid a firm foundation for the absolute and unanimous loyalty demanded of the white voters to the state's Democratic organization—an obstacle which the Populists failed to surmount, either psychologically or politically.

A factor that further reinforced the issue of party and race solidarity in Virginia politics was the infamous presence of William "Boss Billy" Mahone. Through a clique of black preachers, bought Negro votes, and corrupt elections, Mahone, a Republican, had made his presence thoroughly distasteful to the Democratic element in the state.[19] Although he had suffered a substantial loss of power and prestige by 1890, Mahone nevertheless retained a base of power in Virginia politics until his death in 1895. To the third party movement in the state his presence was very significant, since white opinion had come to hold that "the man blessed with a white cuticle is false [to his race] if he does not in this emergency cooperate with the Democratic party."[20] As one newspaper expressed it, "The party . . . is the very life of Virginia."[21] In the Virginia of the 1890s, voting Democratic was not as much a matter of politics as it was a test of race loyalty. Ironically, it was this very gap between white and black that made it impossible for Populism to be acceptable to both groups.

Faced with this situation, informed Populists had, by 1893, given up the notion of soliciting the Negro vote and sought rather to dispel the belief that they desired the support of the black man. John Mitchell, Jr., the black editor of the Richmond *Planet* observed in the 1893 gubernatorial campaign that "the colored people were practically ignored by the Populists." If the white Populists wished to attract black voters, Mitchell added, then its "platform must furnish strong inducements" to the Negro.[22] After 1893, however, there were few serious efforts to bring blacks into the party. To be tagged as "the party of the Negro" would prove, Populists came to believe, more of a liability than an asset. Yet, while white economic advancement, self-help, and reform were paramount in Populist ideology, some observers believed they saw an underlying hint of political amalgamation with the Negro. In the mind of the white population, the ever present apprehensiveness about reviving Black Mahoneism was such that the fears of the voters were intensified, further driving an ideological cleavage between the two races. Taking note of these conditions, Sheldon has concluded that "the election of 1892 made apparent once more the fact that economic issues must remain subordinate to the racial problems . . . so long as the Negro was a potential factor in [Virginia] politics."[23]

Philosophies of racial chauvinism and political solidarity, however, were but part of a larger complex of problems facing Virginia Populism. The Democrats, determined to retain their hard earned supremacy, still employed the corrupt methods of Readjuster days in order to insure their claim to victory. The *Virginia Sun,* the official Populist organ of the state, lamented that "never were such bacchanalia of corruption and terrorism" seen as in the 1892 campaign in Virginia.[24] Especially notable were the fraudulent nature of the voting practices. The Populists had "no doubt at all" that they had been deprived of victory in at least four congressional districts by the Democrats who went "through precinct after precinct" and threw out the Populist returns.[25] "Devotion to fraud and perjury," the Richmond *Times* declared of this period, "was set as the standards of the Democratic faith . . . as if, forsooth, principle and not principle were one and the same thing."[26] The *Times* further claimed that fraud and arbitrary action by local Democratic election officials resulted in the entire vote of 31 of 98 voting precincts in the fourth district, which voted Populist, being thrown out in the congressional election of 1894.[27] The Democratic governor frankly admitted in 1895 that previously "there had been much confusion and disorder at the voting places and that large sums of money had been used in every election to corrupt voters by all political parties, and men's ballots had been purchased like stocks in the market. . . ."[28]

The gubernatorial election of 1893 represented the "last, almost desperate bid for state control" by the Virginia Populists—an attempt to blend the state's heterogeneous white elements into a workable political machine.[29] In that summer, the Negro's totally indifferent attitude toward the party was made conspicuously clear to all when not a single black member attended the gubernatorial nominating convention![30] Even those Democrats who had loudly lambasted the Populists with the Negro question regarded this absence with surprise, inasmuch as all party conventions usually contained a few Negroes.

The racial attitude of Edmond Randolph Cocke, selected as the Populist gubernatorial candidate, had been made clear as early as 1891 when he suggested that Congress repeal the Fifteenth Amendment, since "the only solution to prevent troubles . . . is to disfranchise the Negro."[31]

Although the Populists attempted to disassociate themselves from Republicanism, the Negro, and Mahone, the loose lip of "Boss Billy" succeeded in placing the two parties in the same camp—at least in the mind of the white electorate. Since the Republicans decided not to nominate a ticket in 1893, Mahone's open admiration of the Populist platform, distasteful to both Republicans and Populists, merely confirmed the suspicions of many whites and added flames to the already heightened political atmosphere. In the minds of the whites, this confirmed a long held belief that "the Republican party in Virginia is the snake and the Populist Party is the toad just about swallowed already."[32] The fear that a Populist-Republican fusion would return Mahone to power, and with him the despised Negro, was a strategic position to hold; for with it, the Democrats could cut the ground of white support from under the Populists.

It was, unfortunately, under such conditions that the National Populist movement chose to attach considerable import to the election, intending to point out to the nation that it could win in a state that had traditionally served as a political leader in the South. While the state movement suffered from a shortage of money, there is evidence that ample operating funds for the campaign were furnished by the National Committee, out-of-state sources, and Western silver interests. Now in desperation for support, the Populists proceeded to "beat the bushes" for political discontents who could provide them with votes.[33]

A factor that should have been in the Populists' favor was the state's rising agricultural problems, accentuated by the Panic of 1893. While Virginia was suffering less than many of her sister states, the material change in the state's economy was becoming obvious by the fall of 1893. By the following spring conditions had reached the point where Negro votes "could be concerned at half price." In the fall election the Democrats took advantage of the Negro's destitute condition and "for a consideration," purchased his vote.[34]

The usual method of buying votes was through a coterie of corrupt leaders or preachers whose influence over their following, particularly in rural areas, approached something akin to thought control. This grassroots solidarity behind black leadership, even in the face of commercial activity, must have engendered a certain degree of envy among white Populist leaders whose stress on collective action was not shared evenly by all members of the producer class. The pattern of corruption normally involved the payment of a sum of money, "fifteen, twenty and sometimes fifty dollars or more," for the delivery of a certain number of votes in a district.[35] "The negro vote, like the cotton crop," according to one white observer, "is always on the market, to be sold to the highest bidder. . . . The negro is for sale today as much as ever."[36] Since the Democrats as a rule were more prosperous, they were able to exert undue influence on local election machinery through devious means. Indeed, Populist emphasis on moral sentiment and class development as a concomitant to political activity encouraged disillusionment with some Negroes for thus debasing the election machinery. To the Populists, these actions were detrimental to the blacks' own self-interest and were not in consonance with the "imminent conflict" between capital and labor.

When the 1893 election was over, not only had Charles T. O'Ferrall, the Democratic candidate, emerged the victor, but he had won by the largest majority of any gubernatorial candidate in the history of the state![37] After this crushing defeat, the Populist cause, not only in Virginia but in the South as well, had suffered an irreparable blow.

An analysis of the election has revealed that the white Republicans split their vote almost equally between the Democratic and the Populist parties. In the Negro's case, it appears that nearly two-thirds of the eligible voters boycotted the polls, with a sizeable portion of the remainder "voting" for the Democrats. It would appear therefore, that the failure of the Negro to support the Populists' cause cost them the election.[38]

Economic expediency as well as political despair had prompted the blacks to revise somewhat their traditional policy of voting with the Republicans. With the failure of the Republican party to make any nominations for either the General Assembly or the gubernatorial office in 1893, the Negro was left pretty much at the disposal of the party in power—in this case, the Democrats. Any attempt by the blacks to give tangible expression to their views through their own candidates had been eliminated by the removal of the last blacks from the State Senate in 1891—the first time since 1867 when members of the Negro race were not represented.[39] In turn, the successful Democratic exploitation of the racial issue had forced the Populists to stop short of soliciting black support. It is one of the ironic burdens of Southern history that Democratic appeals to the racial question resulted in the subsequent inclusion of large numbers of blacks under the Democratic banner—under the ensign of a party which had appealed to the baser instincts of both races and had helped to create the unfavorable sentiment which doomed black progress in the South. One conclusion and only one can come from a study of such black actions: economic expediency and political despair had forced the Negro, poor in both spirit and finances, to support his own worst enemies. The Negro Democratic League of Virginia expressed this attitude when it advised blacks to vote with "that class of white people that own and control everything."[40] Although Democrats had made bold use of the race issue against their opponents, they were not yet willing to forfeit such a bloc of voters, no matter what their color. As a result, "large numbers of Negroes turned to the Democrats in furtherance of what appeared to be their best interests."[41]

Although the Virginia Populist movement was never strong, it was a mere shadow of its former self by 1896. What vitality remained was slowly sapped by the Democrats with the following tactics: "First denounce it, then accept its platform, and then force the party out of existence."[42]

Whether the movement's failure to encourage Negro participation would have prevented its untimely decline seems doubtful in light of the political chauvinism and ideological separation accompanying its ascension. With the death of Mahone in 1895, the impending threat—at least in the mind of the Virginia electorate—so long feared was past; but paradoxically, so was Virginia Populism.

To what extent the decline of the Republican party in the South directly influenced Negro defection to the Populist cause is difficult to evaluate, although in North Carolina, at least, party disunity and abuse over the racial issue probably drove a number of Republicans into the Populist ranks as early as 1892.[43] While this internal feud might have caused some black Republicans to defect, the large majority retained their dogged loyalty to the Republican party, partly because of the prospect of social ostracism—and this, ironically, from members of their own race.[44] Since the white North Carolina Populists were as a rule "avowedly anti-Negro,"[45] and they did not anticipate or solicit the black vote in some cases,[46] it is unlikely that the party ever received much support from the black community in North Carolina.

The North Carolina Negro's consistent loyalty to the Republican party, despite the abuse he suffered from many of its white members, is one of the complex phenomena of the state's history. This development sheds some light on how the expressed ideas of the articulate and prominent members of higher social and political groups, in this case the Republicans, can hold sway over the thought of the untutored masses. Observing this state of mind in the black community, a white North Carolina judge recalled that during this period the Negroes "exercised no choice at all" in their votes but "voted precisely as automatons" under the tutelage of the Republican party.[47] The white Populists were not unaware of this current in the larger stream of Negro thought. In an early analysis of the various types of voters within the state, the *Progressive Farmer,* in a rather cynical tone, speaks of the "voter of rather dark skin" who has been branded "straight ticket R. P. [Republican Party]" in several places. Around this voter's neck was fastened "a party collar" to which was attached a "chain," a link of which was passed through the Negro's nose with a white Republican leading him about and vigorously applying the "party lash" to his body—which was covered with "a bloody shirt" that had not been washed in years.[48] Four years later another white Populist wrote, in words suggestive of the earlier statement, that "The Negro is as close under the repub. as ever, voting against his own interest as well as oours. This state of affairs has no future. . . ."[49] All in all, black sympathies for the Republican party as a vehicle for political protest failed to result in increased rights for the Negro race.

With the rise of the third party in North Carolina, the Democrats, in typical fashion, attempted to solidify the white population around the old rallying cry of "white supremacy" and "Negro domination."[50] The possibility of fusion between the Populist and Republican elements in 1894 was not lost on the Democrats who planned to duplicate their 1892 victory in any way possible—even if it meant the open solicitation of Negro votes. With the white vote split, all camps soon recognized the political value of the Negro and proceeded to court him with equal vigor.

Showered with racial epithets in 1892, the Populists eagerly seized this later opportunity to ridicule the Democratic opposition about its predilection for Negro votes. They took obvious pleasure in pointing out that the Democrats no longer referred to "the coons" and "the brutes" but spoke benignly of "our colored brethren" in their campaign speeches. Also, the Democrats made open appeals to Negro leaders and candidates, hoping thereby to deprive the Republican and Populist Party—which had fused—of the Negro vote. The Populists charged, probably truthfully, that the Democrats planned to "kill off" politically these Negro candidates once they received the benefit of the black vote.[51]

While doubtless exaggerated, the underlying Southern Democratic attitude toward the Negro was sarcastically portrayed by the *Progressive Farmer* in a post-election parody of the opposition's political naivete. In a humorous exchange between two "courthouse politicians" ("R" representing the Populist viewpoint and "B" the Democratic attitude), the paper unwittingly revealed a prototype of fixed political principles and pragmatism in Southern politics. The Democrat opens the conversation by lamenting that "the nigger voted ergin us" in the 1894 election, sadly concluding that "it iz a downrite disgrace ter be beat by nigger votes."

R says—'But it is entirely honorable to beat the other side with the help of Negro
         votes.'
B says—'But of course it is. If enough niggers had voted with us Dymakrats ter beat
         you fellers it would hev bin awl rite, but I dont like ter get beat by folks what
         ain's got no souls.'
R says—'Certainly you dont. In your estimation, no one, white nor black has a soul
         unless he voted the Democratic ticket.'
B says—'Oh yes. The colored folks whut voted the dymakratic ticket hes souls, but
         them whut voted for the cooperative Fusion ticket haint got enny souls.'[52]

With their relentless emphasis on success, the Fusionists viewed it as both normal and natural that the Democrats would exert maximal political influence by invoking fraud and corruption against them. As early as January, 1894, perhaps more in satire than in earnest, the *Caucasian,* in anticipation of this problem, offered a "prize" of $25 for the best method of insuring a fair and honest election that fall.[53] If the Democrats could not secure the Negro vote, the Fusionists loudly proclaimed, they would suppress it; a Democratic organ, the Charlotte *News and Observer*, countered with the indignant defensive reply that "In a few Negro counties, it may be that the Negro vote has sometimes been partially suppressed, but this has never occurred in more than eight or ten counties and it is a base slander [for the Fusionists] to charge otherwise."[54] It is difficult to judge the degree of political corruption from the charges in the literature. Following the election of 1894, however, the Populists charged that the Democrats had stolen 40,000 votes and had still lost the election.[55] In spite of claims to the contrary, it cannot validly be said that "there is no reason to think that there was wide-spread fraud" in the 1894 election.[56]

Beyond the utterances of men active in political life, the charge of corrupt election practices found continued expression in the political life of the Populist party. Viewing the situation from the vantage point of the 1896 election, another Populist added that there were some "localities" in North Carolina where elections were "reasonably fair" but "taking the state as a whole" there had not been "a fair state election in over twenty years."[57] The Democrats, "by some hook or crook . . . will get the legislature" a disgusted correspondent from Farmville informed the Populist leader Marion Butler.[58] From Mecklenburg County came reports of "a most tremendous fight against fraud and rascality."[59] The "cry of 'nigger' " was the "cowardly subterfuge" being used by the local Democrats "to deceive men into voting for a party with a record as black as hell." In the Charlotte area, after "many voters were unjustly erased from the Registration books and our election box broke up," Democrats moved in and "reorganized" the election machinery, excluding Populist votes in the recounting process.[60] Walter R. Henry, a lawyer and Populist candidate from Mecklenburg discovered a Democratic plan to keep blacks "from the ballot box" by intimidating or arresting the "two or three hundred negroes" who had registered to vote but had not paid their taxes—which was "a misdemeanor." The blacks, who would likely be unable to pay the fine, would either "run away to avoid arrest" or else be incarcerated during the election process. These votes were "important" to the Populist victory in that area but it was nonetheless reported that "the negroes [were] sent to jail on frivolous charges."[61] From the sixth district came similar reports by an angry Populist candidate who had lost to the Democrats because of election fraud. "Whenever a man gets to *stealing*, whether it be *bonds* or *ballots*, he has gotten as low as a human being can get." Such actions

> make my cheek blush with shame when I think that *Southern white men* have sink [sic]*so low* as to steal votes. Before the war the 'nigger' stole from the 'old master' but since the war old master, the *high-toned and honorable gentleman*, has gone to stealing from the 'nigger.' Oh! What a fall was that!![62]

The Republicans, long accustomed to working with the black voter, took it for granted that the stimulation and development of the Negro vote would require certain concessions, such as Negro candidates on the ticket. In Alamance County, for example, where blacks constituted "the majority of the Rep. party," the Negro made clear his demands: "They want recognition—a County Com.—magistrates and jurors."[63] While the Populists inwardly opposed the Negro as an officeholder, they overtly agreed, nonetheless, to this unpleasant prospect for the purpose of gaining political ascendancy. But it was more difficult to keep the rank-and-file in line when the Negro was so intimately involved. One former Democrat who became a Populist did not "imagine" that his future "political affiliations" were "to be governed by a party [Republican] who in my own state is three fourths black. . . ." To the Populist following, association with a party which "set forth and passed [resolutions] in Negro school houses in the dead hours of night" was not a pleasant thought.[64] From Alamance County came comments from other disgruntled Populists. "If to vote for [Daniel] Russell and a Republican Legislature is to bring the negro into the front in political prominence, the Alamance Pops don't want [it.]."[65] Heartened by the prospects of victory, however, the bulk of the Populists steadfastly maintained their silence, although they obstinately refused to give any public endorsements of the Negro candidates on the ticket.[66]

Populists who formulated the coalition ticket with the Republicans shared few basic principles or party traditions with their allies. Republicans generally favored sound money, the gold standard, a protective tariff, banking legislation, and other legislation partial to the business community. Populism wanted government ownership of railroads, telephone and telegraph companies, and free and unlimited coinage of silver—policies almost diametrically opposed to the principles of the Republican party.[67] This situation would seem to give further credibility to the old adage that politics make strange bedfellows.

Since the Fusionist ticket represented two distinct political philosophies based on expediency, it is hardly surprising that this dubious relationship harbored a certain amount of dissent and antagonism. The example of Andrew D. Cowles, a white Republic leader from Iredell County, stands as a case in point.[68] Cowles, who strongly opposed fusion on the grounds that it would lead to an erosion of Republican principles, expressed his belief that

> . . . There is not a plank in our platform on which the Populist Party would stand, and not one in theirs on which a Republican should stand. *Expediency is the only bond of union.* I have tried to reconcile it with conscience and principle. I can't do it. Being as I am, Republican to the core, I can't be a Populist even skin deep. . . .[69]

Such expediency on the part of both parties, however distasteful, was more a matter of necessity than choice. "I have always thought that the natural alliance was between Dems. and Pops in the fight," a Populist observed, but the Democrats "force us to fight them."[70] Yet the advocacy of principles over expediency was the campaign sentiment espoused for the continuation of this unholy alliance. "Everyone must admit that such a fusion for such common interests is not only legitimate but of the highest importance," a Populist campaign pamphlet asserted. Populists and Republicans must in good faith "unite to secure a free ballot and a fair count."[71]

The absence of clear-cut issues, the difficulty of uniting with old enemies, and the surfacing of the racial issue—all served to create a state of apathy among the voters, particularly in regard to national questions. "I have never seen so much indifference" from "the voters in my life so near a Presidential election," a correspondent reported from the Piedmont area. If there was "any real difference" between the three parties it was that "the Rep. are in better shape than either of the other parties."[72] A Farmville Populist also observed that "our people are surely lacking in enthusiasm" over the national ticket.[73] The voters were further confused by the statewide deviations on the local level. In the Newton area a Populist leader cried out in dismay and utter confusion: "I am confronted in my Disct. with Republican-Populist fusion in some counties and Democratic-Populist fusion in others[;] it seems that a great many [voters] look no further than their local [conditions]." An analysis of the situation revealed that "This state of affairs exist to some extent all over the state"—and so it seemed.[74] In Rockingham County it was reported that "we have fused with the Democrats [and] some of our Pops have kicked against it and wanted to fuse with the Republicans. But I think it will be all right."[75] The Populist gubernatorial candidate observed from the coastal area that "Our folks have up to date generally fused with the Republicans. . . ."[76] In the La Grange area, however, the Republicans had expressed reservations about fusing with the Populists.[77] Much of this shifting around was due to parochial loyalties but much of it was a desperate attempt to find some relief at the local level. In the following months such a state of affairs made a concerted statewide campaign almost impossible for the Fusionist ticket.

Under such circumstances the Negro was as much the victim of varied interests and shifting emphasis as his white counterpart. The Negro's deteriorating status angered him and was making his vote an uncertain quantity and hard to control— even under the discipline and tenacity of the Republican leadership who were normally able to exert significant influence over the course of black support in the Tar Heel state.

By the 1890s, elements of middle-class black leadership were openly flirting with the Democrats "to procure a job or to attempt to gain favor with the white community."[78] Always tactful, this group sought to cultivate the sources of power as a means of redressing personal or racial grievances. The "best thing for the colored people to do," according to the Baptist minister Garland H. White, "is to unite with the governing class of white people in this section who are Democrats whom we have to depend upon in emergency."[79] A spokesman far more prominent nationally and locally, President J. C. Price of Livingstone College, Salisbury, believed that blacks "would do well to harmonize with that element . . . even at the sacrifice of nonessentials" as much "as is consistent with the instincts of mankind. . . ."[80] These expressions show clearly the pervasiveness of the white Democratic power structure on the party loyalty of middle-class blacks who were, in turn, increasingly seeking a conciliatory policy with the white South.

Understandably, many blacks were uncertain whether the animus of Populists toward the Negro would allow any common ground from which to launch a campaign against the Democrats. To compound the dilemma, the blacks, like the whites, were also driven by factionalism over local issues, personalities, and the neat separation of state and federal issues consequent upon the fusion maneuver. Blacks in the sixth district were "split all to pieces" over "free silver" although "4 to 1 say they will vote for silver" and support the Populists over the Republicans in the event fusion failed to materialize.[81] In the Burgaw area, Populists were certain they could "divide the negro vote with the republicans in this county from president down to say nothing of the gains we shall make from the democratic ranks."[82]

A goodly number of Negroes—not only in the Tar Heel state but elsewhere as well—were split in their selection of "the Great Commoner," William Jennings Bryan, as the Populist presidential candidate. (Bryan, though not a Populist, was closely associated with the movement as its official candidate in 1896.) On closer examination, the reason for this division becomes clear when Bryan's attitudes on race relations are surveyed. He shared a contradiction with the Populists: his much-vaunted talk about "letting the people rule" and "defense of human rights" did not always square with his actions toward blacks and other minorities.[83] In the matter of Negro education, Bryan, during his first term in Congress, had developed a substantial middle-class black following through his promotion of educational opportunities "for the race." This support centered around his "generosity of heart and earnest eloquence" in supporting an 1892 bill proposed by Henry Cheatham, a Negro Congressman from North Carolina, "to aid in the establishment and temporary support of common schools." Inasmuch as it was "designed particularly to promote the interest of the colored people of the South," blacks particularly wanted the bill passed. Although Bryan gave the proposal his "best" efforts "from first to last," white Republican opposition ultimately defeated the measure.[84] Conversely, in discussing the Negro's political rights, Bryan used the cliches of the day about disavowing "social equality" and the "excesses of the black legislatures" during Reconstruction.[85] Generous and broadminded in some respects, Bryan, like the white Populists, was not unique in failing to square his attitudes toward race relations with his rhetorical emphasis on "letting the people rule." In this regard his position was consistent, for he had said "essentially the same things at the turn of the century that he was saying in the 1920s."[86] His advocacy of limited political rights for Negroes understandably did not result in blacks voluntarily supporting him in large numbers. North Carolina Populists had come to believe that "we will get very few negro votes for him unless we can get some money from the national committee."[87] Essentially, blacks support would rest upon profit rather than principle.

It seems ironic that in the face of such disunity the Populist gubernatorial candidate, W. A. Guthrie, could optimistically contend in early October that

"Democratic leaders now see inevitable defeat in the State staring them in the face."[88] Despite all the inconsistencies, the twistings and turnings during the campaign, Guthrie had summed up the situation perceptively. Discouraged as they were by the trend of events, the voters still supported the Fusionists and their program in their eagerness to overturn somehow the seemingly irresistible Democratic hegemony. Here, then, was an example of collective effort based upon class solidarity and self help. But the illogical coalition was already being subjected to strains and as a result of a mass exploitation of the racial issue, would disappear by the turn of the century.

Sweeping their opposition before them, the Fusionist ticket, both in 1894 and 1896, enjoyed a remarkable political success in North Carolina.[89] While the Populists enjoyed the benefits of black voting power along with their Republican allies, it is doubtful that the election results can be interpreted as a widespread defection of blacks from Republican insulation to a consciousness of Populist principle. A close examination of the local election results in 1896 reveals the continued perseverance of blacks to the Republican party. Although Populists and Republicans had fused in support of a slate of legislative and congressional candidates, each party had kept its own separate nominees for auditor, lieutenant governor, and governor. Although the total state vote was the largest on record at that time, Populist candidates carried only Sampson County and lost 16,000 of the 1892 votes to Democrats and Republicans. The Republican gubernatorial candidate, Daniel L. Russell, carried 44 of the state's 96 counties. In the 1896 election, 59,000 more Republicans voted than had voted four years earlier; a substantial part of this increase was due to the added support of blacks in the eastern area.[90] In substance, the blacks were never very enthusiastic about the prospect of fusion and the election results are simply a manifestation of this feeling. Paradoxically, the Republican Russell had on several occasions heaped abuse on the Negro and a goodly number of black leaders had voiced their objections to his candidacy.[91] Yet, in the final analysis, blacks espoused the Republican cause—although aware of its inconsistencies—in order to insure its success. The Negro had responded not to a new set of principles but to an old code of party prejudice. "It appears that the [North Carolina] Negroes committed political suicide," Helen Edmonds has concluded, "by continually supporting the Republican party."[92]

A central theme in Populist philosophy was that "a free ballot and a fair count" would first be necessary before "the people" could attain their objective of economic reform at the ballot box. This necessity of initially reforming the election machinery was reinforced by, and in turn strengthened by, the widely held philosophy of advancement through class solidarity and the subsequent use of this power in politics to undermine "the money power." Discouraged as they were by the examples of gross election fraud, it is not surprising that the North Carolina Populists sought to minimize corruption in the state's political system. In the 1892 state platform, the People's Party included a plank to "deplore the corrupting use of money in elections as tending to degrade manhood and to corrupt the ballot-box, and . . . to subvert the rights of the people at the ballot box."[93]

In 1894 the platform carried an even stronger and more extensive statement about corrupt election methods "concocted and executed by the Democratic machine of this state."[94] With the advent of the 1896 election "a free ballot and a fair count was yet more to be desired than free silver." It was "the main issue." Free silver was merely "drink and lifeblood" of the Party but "the privilege of a vote and that vote being counted was greater still."[95] In the final analysis, North Carolina Populists were never able to reform adequately the election process, particularly at the local level, and as such, were unable to champion their own interests politically.

South Carolina presented a slightly different picture from either Virginia or North Carolina, primarily due to the influence of the quasi-Populist, Ben Tillman.[96] The triumph of the Tillman machine in the election of 1890 was destined to put an end to the overt Populist ideology of catering to the Negro vote out of self-interest. In his first term inaugural address of 1890, Tillman made clear the dominant ideological position he would follow toward the Negro. Even though "we come as reformers," he said "this administration represents the triumph of [white] Democracy and [white] supremacy over [Negro] mongrelism and anarchy." While there "never was any just reason why the white man and the black man of South Carolina should not live together in peace," it must be recognized by all whites that "the intelligent exercise of the right of suffrage is as yet beyond the capacity of the vast majority of colored men."[97] It was soon clear to all that this new force of the common man, working within the acceptable Democratic Party, shared a reciprocal relationship between the covert Populist racial ideology and the inimical hostility of the white agrarian class toward the Negro.

The Tillman machine, once established, had for all practical purposes negated the broad policy of class and self-interest that had justified a temporary withdrawal of race prejudice in other states. Yet in the mind of the Populists, there was a lingering class consciousness which extended beyond Tillman's dominant ideological expression of racism. While the Democratic Party served as the core of political orientation in South Carolina, there was behind this tactful facade a conviction on the part of the minority Populists that in numbers there is strength. The attitude of white Populism toward the Negro is exemplified by J. W. Bowden, the Populist manager of South Carolina, who wrote in words suggestive of an official statement:

> We are not [openly] considering the negro. This is a question the negroes will have to settle for themselves. I have reason to believe that thousands of them will not go with the Republicans any longer. Especially do I believe this will be the case among the Colored Alliance.[98]

Thus, while the Populists soft-pedaled their overt interest in the Negro vote, there was an undercurrent of awareness that indicated a certain tendency to reinforce class advantage. This indicates that underneath the dominant Tillman philosophy, the realities of class interest were still such as to encourage the use of the Negro vote in order to consolidate better personal position.

As for the prediction that the Negro might support the Populist Party, the evidence again indicates that he generally remained loyal to the Republican party, clinging to a psychological dependence built up over the years.[99] The fact that many Negroes could still look to the Republican Party for their salvation—despite the rising element of "Lily Whiteism"—shows how well they had absorbed the regnant ideological myth of a liberating Republicanism.[100]

The political outlook of the South Carolina Colored Alliance is in large part epitomized by the actions of George Washington Murray, "the Republican Black Eagle." By "no means a bad-looking colored man," Murray was described as having a "cannon-ball head" and a hue as black as "the ace of spades." While enjoying a close association with the Colored Farmers' Alliance, he rose from the Republican ranks and was elected to Congress in 1892 as a representative of "the toiling and producing millions, who are neither gold bugs or silver bugs." Despite the abuse he suffered, Murray remained in the Republican Party, serving as the last Negro Congressman from South Carolina.[101]

Since the South Carolina Populists carefully sheltered their enthusiasm for class solidarity and the Negro continued his general allegiance to Republicanism, it seems highly doubtful that the fast declining Populist party enjoyed much fruit from the black vote. Moreover, the Colored Alliance went into a state of decline in 1891, and from all appearances, had probably disappeared by 1893.[102]

Up to this point it has been something of a paradox to parallel the overt ideology and the inner commitment of the Populist movement toward the Negro. In Georgia, however, it is possible to detect a tincture of positive ideological affirmation which can be traced through the early days of the movement's rise to its ignominious decline in the late 1890s. "To the colored man the People's Party in Georgia," one correspondent correctly asserted, "is largely what the Republican Party was to him in this nation thirty years ago."[103] From the very first, Populist ideological proclivities were inconsistent with the Democratic racial policy, which made few efforts to conceal an obvious anti-Negro bias. While temperamentally conservative racially, the white Democrats could not understand, and therefore would not forgive, the actions of members who deserted their ranks to join a party that openly trafficked with the Negro.

Of those who adopted the policy of common class grievances, few, if any, were more respected by the Negro than the charismatic Tom Watson. The ideological foundation of the state's racial philosophy was essentially the work of this one individual. Moreover, the influence of his personal charisma on the Negro cannot be ignored when evaluating the various political forces that attempted to promote an ideological cohesion among the state's black population. Watson early became the strongest advocate of a pragmatic but realistic racial policy encompassing five essential considerations aimed at benefitting both races at the expense of neither. By promoting his program, based upon reform and stimulating the passion for personal progress, Watson prophesied that "the People's Party will settle the race question."

First, by enacting the Australian ballot system. Second, by offering to white and black a rallying point which is free from the odium of former discords and strifes. Third, by presenting a platform immensely beneficial to both races and injurious to neither. Fourth, by making it to the *interest* of both races to act together for the success of the platform. Fifth, by making it to the *interest of* the colored man to have the same patriotic zeal for the welfare of the South that the whites possess.[104]

It was, then, out of an eventual consolidation of the two races on a platform of self-interest that Georgia Populism would hopefully be welded into a strong cohesive political force. As a fledgling party, Populism needed every vote it could muster to defeat the Democrats—a fact which did not go unnoticed by the blacks. "The People's Party," one Negro newspaper noted, has "from the very *necessities* of the situation . . . delivered the colored voter in Georgia from political bondage."[105] Since the Democrats branded everything hostile to them as pro-Negro they served, in an indirect manner, as one of the best propagandists for Populism among the Negro masses. In addition, the assimilation of a faction of discontented Republicans, along with such minor Negro leaders as W. H. Doyle and John Mack, provided other positive forces to attract the black vote.[106] Perhaps the best known Negro leader who worked for the Populist cause in Georgia was the Reverend Doyle, who was active in Watson's campaigns, making sixty-three speeches in 1892.[107]

As Democratic hostility became more intense in the 1892 campaign, the heightened racial consciousness caused by hostile propaganda required a further explanation about Populist solicitation of black support. "Why cannot the cause of one [race] be made the cause of both?" Tom Watson inquired of the white community. "Why should not a colored farmer feel the same need of relief as the white farmer? Why is not the colored tenant open to the conviction that he is in the same boat as the white tenant . . . .?" Watson, voicing the feelings of many white Populists, could "see no reason why I am less a white man—true to my color, my rights, my principles—simply because black people are convinced that our platform is a fair one and will vote for me on it."[108] By emphasizing the philosophy of self-interest, the Populists created a defense mechanism that would not only stimulate but defend the sentiment of common class grievances.

The Populist argument—articulated by Tom Watson—that the two races were logically bound together by economic ties and self-interest was not unique in Southern history. In Georgia, Sidney Lanier was calling for a united front between black and white farmers as early as 1880. Predicting the "obliteration of the color line," and its subsequent political implications, Lanier's argument of class consciousness and self-interest had foreshadowed the general philosophy of Populist propagandists by over a decade.[109] The epochal Populist campaigns of the 1890s appear to be sadly miscast in terms of racial uniqueness. Rather, Populist sentiments of class consciousness appear to be the culmination of a philosophy which grew upon a tradition that had existed for at least a decade before the birth of Southern Populism.[110]

That the Georgia Populists, especially Watson, were making an open appeal for the Negro vote was obvious from the very outset of the party. "I want to say," the Populist gubernatorial candidate, W. L. Peek, said of the political implications of this policy, "that the nigger has been in [Georgia] politics since the war and will be there until the last trump[et] has sounded. The only trouble in this case is that [the Democrats] think [the Populists] will use the Negro vote."[111] Using the 1892 People's party convention in Atlanta as a platform to make these remarks, Peek, in a dramatic incident which served not only as a test of his political courage, but of his determination to solicit the black vote, allowed John Mack, the Negro Populist leader, to second his nomination for governor.[112]

On the surface such expressions of Populist racial sentiment appear laudable; but the true measure of this policy was the extent to which it was applied and hence strengthened the Populist organization in Georgia by attracting black votes. Above and beyond its rhetoric, a careful scrutiny of Populist policies provides ample reasons for blacks to distrust Populist overtures. An examination of the 1892 ticket has indicated "a total absence" of blacks from the list of Populist candidates. Furthermore, only "two lonely and isolated blacks" were present at the state Populist convention in Atlanta.[113] Finally, the traditional anti-Negro sentiments of most Populists did much to heighten the suspicions of blacks. Fostered on the tradition of poor white race-baiting which had existed at least two decades before the birth of Georgia Populism, many Populist candidates, according to W. H. Styles, a black Republican senatorial aspirant, "were in the front rank when that army of oppression came against the negro."[114] The sudden outburst of Populist "egalitarian" rhetoric understandably was not sufficient to alleviate black suspicions of past hostilities.

Generally outspoken against proposals for fusion, Georgia Populists ostensibly missed a grand opportunity in 1892 to attract a large mass of Negro voters by failing to make greater efforts to enlist Republican support. In this they failed to broaden their voter appeal. Even after the Republican convention had refused to nominate its own candidates, Tom Watson rejected unequivocally any fusion proposal. "My policy is for a straightout fight. I whip the other fellow or he whips me. . . . [N]o republican must vote for me under the impression that I am heading for the republican camp."[115] This aspect of Populist strategy in Georgia suggests the nature of one of the difficulties faced by many third party movements—the failure to broaden their base of support to include a constituency whose appeals are inconsistent with a set of dogmatic reform principles.

Despite the flurry of Populist rhetoric preceding the election, the traditions that clustered around state and local election practices were not suddenly transformed. "The size of the colored vote for a particular candidate might depend primarily upon the personal popularity of that man with the Negroes and upon his record in matters relating to the colored people, regardless of his political label," writes a modern authority on Georgia politics.[116] In this respect, Georgia blacks differed somewhat from the mass of Negro voters in most other Southern states. Furthermore, under such circumstances, the notorious anti-Negro records of some Populist leaders offered few prospects of soliciting Negro votes.[117]

In the last months of the campaign, a small group of prominent black leaders found the record of the Democratic gubernatorial candidate, William J. Northen, more appealing on racial matters than that of Peek, the Populist nominee. Even before the state Republican convention decided in August not to nominate a slate of candidates, "Northen Clubs" were being formed by blacks. It was Pledger, the black Atlanta attorney, who spearheaded this campaign among the articulate Negro leadership which would, in turn, enlist the support of the black masses. Following the Republican decision, a group of black delegates, most of whom were members of the State Central Committee, openly endorsed Northen.[118] "We . . . prefer in the campaign to follow the plan mapped out by Hon. W. A. Pledger and vote for Governor W. J. Northen."[119] In the face of this endorsement, Pledger predicted that Northen would be re-elected by a majority of 40,000.[120] The key portions of Northen's record which captured the black imagination concerned added educational appropriations, promise of an anti-lynching bill, and a strong anti-lynching stand.[121] Working within the established power structure, Northen would well be able to deliver on his promises to the blacks—if he so desired.[122] In turn, the Populists were seeking to establish a base of power and could do little more than make promises. Politically, blacks have been pragmatic in their ideologies with regard to eliminating discrimination.[123]

The Democrats were not slow in taking steps against the new political party; the old pattern of using various forms of fraud and corruption was repeated. The spirit of Populist protest was stifled under the guise of white supremacy, the fear of a second Reconstruction, and, ironically, the corrupt and venal use of the Negro vote; bribery, corruption, fraud, and violence, in turn, negated the rebellious Negro's response to Populist principle over party loyalty. At least fifteen blacks and several whites were killed during the election.[125] According to Professor E. Merton Coulter, a careful historian of the Georgia scene,

> the election throughout the state was a pathetic example of the venality that often accompanies the rule by the people. Negro voters were bought and sold like merchandise and herded to the polls like so many cattle. They were fed at barbecues and made drunk and *penned* up to prevent them from voting if they could not be otherwise controlled. Most of them who voted were in the hands of the Democrats.[126]

That even the Populist philosophy of self-interest did not generally override Negro venality and white corruption is aptly exemplified through the conspicuous example provided by a black Populist from Zeigler, Georgia. Unable to restrain his indignation, he lamented that the "price of Negroes had depreciated in the last 40 years." Even though he had "personally" sold for $1500 in the 1840s, he saw one Negro in the 1892 election "bought" for a glass of cider, a second for a "two-for-a-nickel" cigar, and a third for a pint of peanuts! With the price a vote should command, it was obvious, he concluded, derisively, that the Negroes "are holding themselves too cheap." Available in bountiful supply, black votes generally sold from three dollars to ten dollars, the price advancing as the election neared its end. One Democratic faction, further driving home the injustices suffered at the hands of venal Negroes, openly boasted of purchasing 1,100 black votes to defeat the Populists.[127]

Perhaps the degree to which corruption occurred in the 1892 election is best illustrated by the case of the Augusta district. Out of an area that possessed a total voting population of 11,466, the district's total vote was 12,558! Investigation revealed that Negroes, transported from South Carolina in four-horse wagon-loads, had added appreciably to the overall total. One Democrat later admitted to dressing black women as men, filling them with liquor, and voting them through-out the Augusta area.[128] "Lying, red whiskey, and counterfeit bills . . . have ran [sic] the thing over us" one white Populist painfully concluded.[129] The *People's Party Paper* provides an incisive criticism of the political techniques used by the Democrats and the inability of the Populists to overcome such lawlessness.

> The leaders and newspapers of the Democratic party have touched a depth of infamy in this campaign which is almost incredible. They have intimidated the voter, assaulted the voter, murdered the voter. They have bought votes, forced votes and stolen votes. They have incited lawless men to a frenzy which threatens anarchy. They have organized bands of hoodlums of both high and low degrees to insult our speakers, silence our speakers, rotten-egg our speakers, and put lives in danger.[130]

Like the Populists, President Harrison was unable to overcome his loathing of Democratic election practices in Georgia and other Southern states. Learning of the widespread fraud, Harrison asserted that "I have washed my hands of the south. It is a land of rebels and traitors who care nothing for the sanctity of the ballot, and will never be in favor of making an active campaign down there until we can place bayonets at the polls."[131]

The Democrats also resorted to the use of the highly sensitive "Force Bill" issue, loudly predicting "Negro domination" and the revisitation of a second Reconstruction upon the South if the whites split their vote. The "Force Bill," according to one Populist, had prevented three-fourths of the white Democrats from defecting to the Populist camp.[132] While this claim is obviously exaggerated, many whites doubtless did refrain from splitting their vote when the disturbing memories of Reconstruction days were revived.

The Georgia election of 1894 proved, if anything, even more corrupt and venal than its predecessor; few elections illustrate so vividly the fraudulent nature of Southern politics. "In this election," Coulter tells us, "the Negro vote was so corrupted as to make an unbearable stench to all men in both parties."[133] Arnett has described it as "the most exciting as well as the most degrading election since the overthrow of the 'carpet-bag' government."[134]

While the Democrats had, in general, retained control of the political machinery in 1892, it was evident that a concerted effort would be necessary to retain their power two years later. In order to head off the Populist challenge in the state, the

Democrats selected more and better men to represent them on the local level. In addition, an effort was made to undermine local Populists organizations by wooing their abler men back into the Democratic party.[135]

During the 1894 campaign, Democratic leaders agitated frantically for the Negro to pledge his support to his "personal and political friend[s]" in the party.[136] On the other hand, they continued to voice considerable campaign rhetoric about "Negro domination" if the Populists were allowed into the political circle. Their underlying motive was to garner both the black and white vote by holding to both clusters of racial emphasis—or parts of both—until after the election, and then to shift back to the characteristic white supremacy orientation of the party. Both disenchantment and expediency caused the Populists to wax bitter toward their Democratic opposition's maneuvering, since in the main, their racial ideologies were poles apart.[137] In moments of despair, Populists were moved to acrimonious and virulent criticism of the Negro when he became an unwitting instrument for perfidious politicians. Expressing a tone of derisive futility, the *People's Party Paper* concluded that "a Negro lost his African origin if he voted right [Democratic] and took on the scent of the rose-geranium if he could chatter Democratic gibberish. A Democratic ballot made [them] color blind and a Democratic speech from ebony lips lent sweetness to the desert air."[138] If reform drives were paramount in the movement's political ideology, the sweeping corruption of 1894 merely reinforced the increasing prejudice toward the Negro.

With little or no abatement, the same kind of corruption and venality were practiced as in the preceding election. In the "terrible tenth" district, one Democratic candidate repeatedly received 3,000 votes from 500 Negroes "who practiced this fraud" for ten cents a vote![139] "I think that the stench from the 10th District will fill our nostrils for a generation to come," one Georgian said. "It will be held up to the nation for decades to come as proof positive of the fraud and violence of Southern elections."[140] In Dalton, it was somberly reported that "the Negroes went solidly against us on account of bribes mainly."[141] Another constituent was "perfectly outraged" at the "simply monstrous" frauds in Richmond and Hancock counties. If the "reported vote" of 15,000 from Richmond County was correct, he asserted with astute acumen, the population would be 105,000. But "in my opinion" there were not "over 2,000 legally qualified voters" in the whole county, despite the approximate total of 15,000 votes.[142] "We had to do it!" contended one prominent Democrat. "Those d——— Populists would have ruined this country."[143]

Of course, there was a basic problem underlying much of the corruption that did not escape the most astute contemporaries, including many Populists who sympathized with the Negro. The black man's faith in the class denominator of Populist ideology was frequently negated by white Democratic control of the rank-and-file Negro's vote. In the 1892 election, for example, it was reported that the black was "bulldozed, intimidated, driven from the polls, and in some instances, shot for attempting to exercise the right of citizenship."[144] White employers, who were in the main Democrats, would oftentimes threaten to "turn the Negroes off the place'' if they did not vote Democratic.[145] Negroes were also considered incapable of voting competently without some restraints—an inherited popular suspicion held over from the early days of Reconstruction when blacks were identified as slavish tools of carpetbagger governments. More than any other group, the Negro, member of a perennial debtor class, was subjected to economic and physical coercion that literally compelled him to conform to Southern white majority opinion—notably, Southern white *Democratic* opinion.[146] The obvious result of such actions was not only to make a mockery of public elections, but to give expression to Democratic demands for unilateral conformity to the principles that the party deemed as representative of Southern politics.

Under the cover of national indifference, political standards, not only in Georgia but in the rest of the South, had gone by the board, or were so flagrantly violated in the name of white supremacy that they ceased to be binding. Since Populism and the race issue aroused the Democrats much more than the enervated endeavors of a dying Republicanism, the white Populists were forced, as we have seen, into dissipating much of their reform energy toward fighting the corruption of the opposition, thereby taking an inactive defensive stand. By the mid-1890s it could truthfully be concluded:

> . . . Heretofore the Negro has been the man against whom the frauds of the South have been directed. Now it is the white [Populist]. If when white man proposes to divide in that section of the country which has for years been called 'the solid South' the same frauds are resorted to continue this [white] solidarity, and the North yields to it, then we must expect that solidarity to endure through time.[147]

The challenge the Populists presented to the political status quo in the seaboard states represented the spirit of an agrarian class seeking an identity of interest with the blacks. Self-interest was adopted as a rallying cry because it appealed to groups as diverse as the white agrarians and downtrodden blacks. But the neutrality of its supposed detachment from prejudice failed to come into play. Populism had started with the hope and promise of reform, but its purported sense of class consciousness failed to emerge for several reasons. Foremost, Populists were generally deprived of the black vote as a result of corruption and because of the traditional loyalty of the black masses to the Republican party.

Secondly, one of the outcomes of the Populist campaigns, from Virginia to Georgia, was the awkward choice taken by more and more blacks—particularly the middle class—of voting Democratic as a result of their instinct for preservation and self-interest. In Georgia, a state sometimes portrayed as the archetype of the Populist biracial experiment, blacks supported such Democratic nominees as Northen because of their past record of accomplishments for the Negro race.

Although Populism actively promoted the illusion of biracial interest, it was unable to translate its preachments into practice; it was not merely a spokesman for the powerless but shared this same failing politically. In contrast, the established Democrats had the ability to provide a stabilizing function, however repressive, on the prevailing order. To the black man, accommodation was a viable alternative to violence. Tom Watson had articulated the Populist philosophy of self-interest, but ultimately maintained that the political good which benefits the individual ("self-interest always controls") is greater than the interest which benefits the class. It follows that the blacks' accommodation to the Democratic order was quite consistent with this philosophy. Put in a less pleasant way, the hostile spirit of the age demanded that they yield to political expediency.

In the Atlantic seaboard states, many blacks who ostensibly should have shared the economic values of Populism often rejected the Populists' facile class expression of self-interest, even when unrestrained. This further supports the view that blacks found the values of the rank-and-file white Populists antagonistic to Negro interests. In North Carolina, for example, the open display of loyalty between blacks and the Republican party was substantial. It is revealing of the relationship between the two races that it was often the blacks who demonstrated a lack of sympathy for fusion between Republicans and Populists. The old inspirational tradition of Republican association with emancipation continued to run strongly in the mind of the black masses, even at a time when such a body of beliefs was on the wane politically. It is important to remember also that in this period the Republican party appeared increasingly as one of the great subverters of blacks' rights. Conversely, this Negro loyalty served only to provoke Populist antagonisms as they observed blacks as a source of assistance to the political forces that were frustrating them. Such a body of dogmatic party loyalty severely strained the expression of class loyalty by Populists and in this way, perhaps, served to exacerbate racial resentment.

There was, of course, a reactionary potential in the Populist myth. This came into full glare in South Carolina particularly, where the forces of tradition were violently antagonistic toward Populism as a symbol of radical social upheaval. In the presence of such prescriptive forces, Populism generally enjoined in its literature the principle of biracial class consciousness and did not cultivate widely blacks as sources of voting potential. In Virginia and South Carolina, the Populist party was, in racial terms, conservative.

The failure of the Populists to solicit or enlist the support of blacks, particularly the leadership, foreshadowed the gradual disappearance of the party in the Atlantic seaboard South. It remains to study the nature of the difficulties faced by the Populists in the Gulf Coast South.

VII

THEORY AND PRACTICE OF POPULISM:

THE GULF COAST SOUTH

More than elsewhere in the South, criticism of the prevailing order in the Gulf Coast states had been stifled by the forces of conservatism. Perhaps it may have been merely a matter of degree. Yet in this area political passions of earlier third party movements had slowly lost their virulence in the face of overwhelming Democratic adversity; but what is paramount, what colors and affects all else in the 1890s, was the emergence of Populism in the face of such enervating disapprobation. It is the burden of this chapter to examine the Populist challenge to the established order in the three major third party strongholds of the Gulf Coast area—Alabama, Louisiana, and Texas—and to shed some light upon the conflicts which emerged as a beleaguered people sought to achieve some measure of desirable reform.

The reasons for the emergence of Populism in such a hostile climate are not clear. Perhaps the answer lies in the atavistic nature of the conflict. According to a former Alabama governor, "The origin of the Populist movement in Alabama was the low price of farm produce and poverty of the people. They were fighting and did not know where to strike."[1] Judged in terms of its rhetoric—producer vs. consumer, or if you will, the money power against the people—Populism suggested that it was attempting to impose a class solution on a prevailing economic problem. Compared with other radical movements in he postbellum South, Populism must rate as a major eruption of unbridled hostility between a largely agrarian population and a more mature industrial Bourbon group. The significance of this rustic challenge to the priestly class was not lost on the Alabama historian, William Garrott Brown, a contemporary observer of this tumultuous period in the Gulf Coast South. "I call that particular change a revolution," he recalled, "and I would use a stronger term if there were one; for no other political movement—not that of 1776, not that of 1860–1861—ever altered Southern life so profoundly."[2] To another historian, the tenuous connection linking theory and action was race, since in the final analysis, "the negro, more than any other factor, was responsible for the Populist party in Alabama. Economic questions fell into the background."[3]

What we begin to see in Gulf Coast Populism, at least in Alabama, was the conscious shadowing of a kind of class order, not one solely of economic making but one that evolved out of the political and geographical order of things. Running throughout the period was the cry of "black belt domination" and "fraud" by the "machine bosses." The growing interest in political reform provides an incisive explanation of the causes of Populism in the state and the difficulties it faced. "Running throughout Alabama Populism was," according to two modern analysts, "a trend of free ballot and fair count, perhaps the central theme."[4] The Alabama "political evangelist," Joseph C. Manning, "was so thoroughly imbued with his mission that he concentrates every energy in promulgating ballot reform and doctrines." Manning was "confident" that "an honest election is of paramount importance" to "the southern man." Reuben Kolb, Alabama Populist leader and twice gubernatorial candidate, contended that "honest elections" were "the paramount issue" in the state's campaigns.[5] His reasoning was abundantly clear: "Until a fair and honest election is assured, no [economic] reforms, however needed can be instituted. . . ."[6] Economics was, therefore, of necessity subordinated to the more pressing question of election reform. So central was this question than an essential difference between Populism in the Gulf Coast and the Atlantic seaboard states was a more complete exposition of political over economic reform in the former.

In Alabama, postbellum sectional bitterness between the northern hill country and the black belt crystallized around the turbulent Reconstruction period. The complaint of the "poor whites" centered around the charge that the counties in North Alabama had "rescued" the black belt from "Negro domination" during Reconstruction but that the poor whites, in turn, had failed to receive their fair share of political influence.[7] The sectional basis was thus laid early and, in the face of economic discontent and declining prices, the transition toward organized political effort as a means of ameliorating the distress will become clearer as the story develops. In the years following the constitution of 1875, race was a strong adhesive power for white political solidarity, but sectional and economic griev- ances came to the surface at times in the form of Republican, Greenback, and independent candidates. These efforts were, in large measure, unsuccessful be- cause the tenet of white supremacy, despite the chronic condition of grinding poverty, was exaggerated during these campaigns.[8] Race was a potent weapon in the Bourbon arsenal, for it obsessed the agrarian mind with its threatened woes, real or imaginary, of graft, corruption, social equality, and ignorance; with its use the Bourbons dissipated earlier third party efforts and sustained their dominant position. Nevertheless, while earlier political revolts were largely failures, Populism was strongly conditioned by the radical third party tradition of its predecessors.

With rising economic discontent among farmers, the time and conditions were right in the 'nineties for the disruption of Alabama politics. According to Albert Goodwyn, Populist congressman and gubernatorial candidate, the "farmers" developed the Alliance "for the purpose of ascertaining the cause of such abnormal [economic] conditions, and to find a remedy for them. After much discussion they concluded that these conditions were *political,*" with the result being the formation of the Populist party.[9] The conversion of the white farmers to a point where they would support a third party was not easily accomplished. Democratic casuistry once again overcame strenuous objections from the agrarian community. The transition from the old party was so painful in Alabama that a discontented faction sought refuge in a third party variant called "Jeffersonian Democrats." Despite legitimate grievances, the hold of the Democratic party on the white mind was still such that a complete political cleft proved too proscriptive for amicable adjustments. Although the Jeffersonians voted with the Populists and were, "in effect," Populists, they never merged with the smaller party.[10]

The gubernatorial election of 1892 was particularly significant since it represented the first major election around which the Alabama reform element could rally. The Democratic incumbent Thomas G. Jones was seeking reelection and he was opposed by the Jeffersonian candidate Reuben F. Kolb, former commissioner of agriculture and successful pioneer in scientific agriculture.[11] The realignment resulted in a campaign that was particularly virulent—a fact recognized by the state's historians. "The resulting contest for the nominations and then for governor," according to Sheldon Hackney, "was probably the most scurrilous on record in Alabama."[12] The state "had never witnessed a more acrimonious or exciting campaign," Rogers has written.[13] The schism in politics resulted in a state of turmoil which shortly polarized the populace. Charles Summersell, a student of this canvas writes:

> Electioneering in 1892 was rough. Speakers were booed down. Preachers who differed with their communities were sometimes fired. Merchants lost business after political arguments. It was reported that Guntersville lost about $8,000.00 in business when Kolb supporters in Marshall County adopted the slogan "Down with the Town Clique." Friends and close relatives disputed and parted company, and boycotts and social ostracism were weapons in the fray. In Athens Jones was hanged in effigy. P. G. Bowman of Jefferson was preaching a doctrine of "ballot, bayonet, and blood."[14]

In this highly emotional campaign both parties openly sought the black vote. Seen in retrospect, Reuben Kolb, the most prominent of the Alabama reformers, presents a somewhat paradoxical attitude toward the blacks. As an active "redeemer" during Reconstruction, he had reportedly bragged about "suppressing Negro votes," but once the "white voters . . . repudiated him" in later years he "turn[ed] with open arms" to the blacks whom he had earlier "spurned." Furthermore, Kolb was an apostle of "white supremacy."[15] In January 1892, before he had broken with the Democrats, the *Huntsville Gazette,* a Negro newspaper, contended that in a recent speech in that city Kolb had "exhibited a sense of intolerance and hatred to the black man."[16] By July, however, he sought Negro speakers to proclaim him from the hustings during his campaign. At

Talladega, his audience listened to a black speaker for over an hour; at Greenville he was followed on the platform by Ike Carter, a local Negro.[17] At Gordon in Henry County, Kolb and a black third speaker, L. W. McManaway, were unable to speak due to agitators hurling eggs at them.[18] Kolb also had two blacks, "Professor Cooper" and Lewis Bostick, on the campaign trail flashing "what it takes to make the mare go."[19] The problem of interpreting Kolb's actions is made even more vexing by his eagerness for Negro votes on one hand and his reluctance on the other hand to admit blacks to the party organization.[20] As a further indication of political attitudes, not a single Negro Populist candidate was offered by the party in 1892.[21] In his attitude towards blacks as candidates and participants in the party organization, Kolb differed little from other Southern Populist leaders.[22]

The 1892 platform of the Jeffersonian Democrats contained a "Negro plank" designed to attract the black vote:

> We favor the protection of the colored race in their *political* rights, and should afford them encouragement and aid in the attainment of a higher civilization and citizenship, so that through the means of kindness, better understanding and more satisfactory condition may exist between the races.[23]

To drive home further their appeal, the Jeffersonians focused critical attention on the thirteenth plank of the Democratic platform:

> We favor the passage of such election laws as will better secure the government of the State in the hands of the intelligent and the virtuous, and will enable every elector to cast his ballot secretly and without fear of restraint.[24]

Clearly, the Jeffersonian-Populists were making a strong appeal for the black vote. In addition to principles, Populists did on occasion employ limited economic inducements to get black votes, usually paying up to $1 per vote. Since this sum was equal to two days' wages for a field hand, the Populists were to some extent successful, but extreme poverty and Democratic control of the election machinery was an immense disadvantage.[25]

The Democrats made open appeals for the Negro vote in much the same manner as the Populists. In his acceptance speech Jones stressed the need for harmony between the races.[26] Both candidates maintained clubs for black and white supporters of their respective parties.[27] Like Kolb, Jones also had his share of black speakers and purchased votes. Dr. C. N. Dorsett, a black Republican from Montgomery, publicly endorsed Jones as did a number of prominent Negroes from the city of Mobile and the counties of Elmore, Pike, Lee, and Russell.[28] In substance, both parties sought with few distinctions to harvest black votes yet maintain a basic commitment to white supremacy and social inequality.

On August 1, Thomas Jones was reelected governor with 126,959 votes to Kolb's 115,552.[29] The charges of election fraud were rampant—some accusations palpably false and others of substance.[30] Indeed, scholars are still divided over who won the 1892 Alabama gubernatorial election. Hackney believes Kolb "would have won in a fair election in 1892"; Rogers "seems certain" that Kolb was "legitimately elected but counted out."[31] Clark's figures "do not bear out this conclusion."[32] Probably the most honest conclusion was presented by Summersell, who believes that it is still not possible to give a yes or no answer to the question, "Was Kolb counted out"?[33] As a result of unmitigated fraud, the dilemma is probably unsolvable; yet it is significant that the election revealed an old pattern of intrastate sectionalism. An analysis of the returns has indicated that Kolb's support was strongest in the white hill country of North Alabama, whereas Jones received more Negro votes than Kolb in the black belt.[34] Thus, the voting pattern was along traditional geographical lines of hill country vs. black belt. It has been estimated that Kolb would have been elected by a majority of 17,000 without the black vote received by Jones.[35] Black belt counties cast an incredible portion of Negro ballots—70 percent in Dallas County, 87 percent in Wilcox County, and so on. Overall, of those counties with a two to one black majority, Kolb carried only Macon County where Tuskegee Institute and Booker T. Washington were located; there is no tangible evidence, however, of activity on Washington's part.[36] The 1892 election proved to be the turning point of Alabama Populism, and by 1894 the movement was already on the decline in the state.[37]

The failure to win the 1892 election was so demoralizing that it was difficult to pick up the pieces and reassemble them for the next campaign. These were crucial years for the Jeffersonian-Populists, for they needed desperately to retain their organization in order to counteract the anxieties of poor whites who were in danger of moving away from third party doctrines. The situation was further complicated by the stigma attached to third partyites as traitors to the ideals of white supremacy. Paradoxically, the Democrats had managed to secure a landslide margin in the black belt counties, yet transfer to the Jeffersonian-Populists the stigma of racial treason! This had the dual effect of identifying the Democrats as a white man's party while serving notice that a Populist victory would have the same "negative" consequences on Alabama politics as had black reconstruction. Caught up in the image of scalawags, many whites felt completely out of step emotionally and were reluctant to oppose Democratic wishes when it involved "cooperation" with blacks and Republicans.[38]

As the 1894 election approached, there was a significant parallel in the pattern of provocation, the "Democrats" again appealing to the same old potent racial patriotism of "saving" the state, a ritualistic feature of Alabama politics since Reconstruction. The conglomerate of reformers met in February and renominated Reuben Kolb as the combined candidate of the Jeffersonian-Populist party. Like most other states in the 'nineties, Alabama was involved in a factional dispute between the Lily Whites and the Black and Tans within the Republican party. In substance, the diversion was a struggle over black or white control of the party. Since 1888, the Lily White faction had been led by Dr. Robert "Bob" A. Moseley, Jr. Moseley's groups generally favored cooperation with independent parties and the Populists in particular. The Black and Tan faction was led by

William "Bill" Stevens, a black barber from Anniston, who favored a straight-out Republican ticket. Stevens had been a black leader during Reconstruction, and in subsequent years had allied himself with Independents, Greenbackers, and the Alabama State Labor Party. He had developed a reputation as a somewhat unsavory character and opportunist whose loyalty was purchasable. Such a reputation made the Populists suspicious of his moves. Stevens was suspicious of the Populists, doubting their promises of political equality with blacks.[39] With the 1894 convention, the political situation had crystallized into one of open hostility between Stevens and the Populists. As Stevens attempted to enter the Jeffersonian-Populist convention, he was unceremoniously ousted by force. In turn, he led the Black and Tan faction against endorsement of Kolb and threw his support to William C. Oates, the "one-armed hero" of the Civil War who was nominated as the Democratic gubernatorial candidate. Many other middle-class black politicians, teachers, lawyers, ministers, and editors subsequently gathered around Stevens and endorsed Oates.[40] In turn Populists ridiculed Stevens:

O did you see Billy Skaggs, upon his toe,
Lift Billy Stevens through the Wigwam [hotel] doe;
O, did you see Bill Oates in big alarm,
Lift Billy Stevens under his arm.[41]

In addition to receiving Lily White Republican support, Kolb approached the Republicans for a much needed campaign contribution. The Democratic organs picked up this venture and gave it wide prominence as anti-Kolb propaganda. It is impossible to tell how much money Kolb received from the Republican party, inasmuch as Republican papers tended to maximize the figure ($50,000) while Populists tended to downplay the amount received ($5,000).[42]

Acutely aware of their experience with fraud in 1892, the Kolb supporters made a "free vote and an honest count" their foremost demand in 1894.[43] Closely connected was the question of the Negro vote. "On one point all agree," William Skaggs concluded, "and that is that the ballot has been a curse rather than a blessing to the Negro."[44] To bring about an end to election corruption the Jeffersonians had proposed on two occasions, once in 1892 and again in the spring of 1893, that a white Democratic primary be established. On both occasions, the Democrats refused the offer.[45] To counteract this, the third partyites made an open appeal to the blacks to "stay away from the polls." Moseley circulated a petition in the black belt urging Negroes not to register. Skaggs claimed that "less than one percent of those of voting age actually registered." A Democratic organ claimed that not more than 20 percent of Alabama blacks registered, while a Jeffersonian paper advised the Negroes that "the best thing" they could do "in the coming registration and election is to keep hands off and let the white voters settle the matter themselves."[46]

All of these actions, however, were to no avail. In the Black Belt sections, Negroes were added to the registration lists and voted when they were not even near the polling place on election day;[47] furthermore, dead blacks and fictitious names were added to the lists.[48] Other votes were simply stolen. In Tuscaloosa County, for example, ballot boxes from Blocker's beat, a strong Populist section of the county, contained no ballots whatever when they were opened.[49] The Democratic explanation for such corruption was that it was "more humane to manipulate the ballot against the Negro than to use brute force to drive him away from the polling place."[50] In substance, fraud was a more viable alternative than violence and indeed regarded as less harmful morally than the open application of brute force.

In view of such tactics, it is not surprising that Kolb lost the 1894 election. The vote was 109,160 for Oates; 83,394 for Kolb.[51] The intrasectional parallel between Jones' 1892 vote and Oates' was readily apparent. It was the overwhelming lopsided black belt vote in favor of Oates that insured his victory. Politically impotent, Kolb could do little more than urge the formation of "honest election leagues" to insure that such fraudulent methods would not be employed in the future.[52]

As indicated earlier, 1892 marked the climax of Populism in Alabama and subsequent campaigns were a repetition of fraud and the ills of the "people" against the "black belt" and the "machine."[53] In the case of the Negro, the third partyites were placed in a peculiar position. On one hand, they believed strongly in the sanctity of the ballot for all people; on the other hand, continued Negro "participation" insured their inability to win control of the state government. This problem was not only moral, it was political. To some Populists, the disfranchisement of the black man represented a reform of the electoral process.[54] A continued theme throughout this period was the need for a constitutional convention to settle the question. Consider the opinions of one agrarian organ:

> There is but little doubt now that there will be a Constitutional Convention. The last election has convinced all that a large proportion of the Negro vote is purchasable, and that much of the opposition to their disfranchisement will cease. The only thing in the way is how to do it without disfranchising a large number of whites. Purchasable votes mean that the dollar and not the man is to rule, and we think a law should be made disfranchising all who sell or buy votes. We would not object to a Constitutional Convention, if we could have a fair election in choosing delegates. . . .[55]

Running throughout this argument also was an appeal for white unity. Even though "the classes" are divided "by the accident of fortune," a Jeffersonian newspaper added that "they are still bound by the same pure blood." There was also strong opposition to disfranchising any whites through a constitutional convention. "No disfranchisement except for crime of a single white man must be tolerated."[56] The third partyites also wanted to prevent the subsequent "setting up of one class of whites over the other class and pulling down another class to the level of the negro. . . ." They adamantly believed that a convention should "save all [whites] or save none."[57] According to I. L. Brock, a Populist editor, "the Populists always were willing and ready for the negro to be disfranchised if it could be done without disfranchising the white man."[58] Such prominent Populist leaders as Reuben Kolb, Joseph Manning, and William Skaggs came slowly to an acceptance of disfranchisement. Indeed, a significant portion of the third partyites had by the mid-1890s come to believe that "we are not bound to count the negro in the horoscope." The black man was "now recognized" as a "nuisance" to "honest endeavor" and to "hard won achievement"—a "peril" to "civilization." He "will be disposed of at an early day as an abnormal political force broke loose from its moorings and careening through the land without license."[59] One proposed manner of "disposal" was through the setting aside of a separate state for the exclusive use of the Negro. As early as 1894, the Alabama Populists had endorsed such a scheme in their convention. Emigration also seemed to many impoverished blacks their only salvation from white economic, political, and social militancy. A contingent of Alabama blacks had already chosen Mexico as the site of their new nation.[60] Populist endorsement probably added some encouragement to such unlikely ventures.

The increasingly hostile tone of race relations during this period insured that some steps would be taken to eliminate the black vote—be it disfranchisement or some less likely proposal such as deportation. The long discussed constitutional convention became a reality in Alabama in 1901, and with its inception came the almost complete elimination of Negro voting. Following the convention the racial differential in voting was marked. By 1906 only 2 percent (3,654) of adult male Negroes were registered to vote; conversely, 83 percent (205,278) of the whites were registered. These figures would remain pretty much the same until the black voter drives of recent years.[61] Politically, the blacks' role had been largely played out by the turn of the century, yet the counterrevolution was brittle and evanescent for the third partyites; Populism had become an abortive crusade. True, the party still persisted, but the potential for any spectacular political assault had long since been eliminated; and, insofar as the term "Populist" was used, it had become oblique and insidious—a confession of defeat rather than a potent threat.

In the 'nineties came reinforcements for these Alabama heretics from another Gulf Coast state, Louisiana. Many of the same problems which mystified a generation of Alabama farmers were familiar, even elementary, to Louisiana Populists, and it is not unimaginable that citizens of the Pelican State read the Alabama third party organs in which these tortured experiences were traced. Louisiana Populists did not need to. The doctrines of election reform and vote fraud could easily be documented by third partyites who saw the same malaise inherent in the Louisiana system. Whatever the explanation, the facts are incontrovertible.

Profound as was the Populist revulsion from a corrupt biracial political order, Louisiana's racial complexion revealed a curious disparity in black voter registration in comparison to its neighbor states. Indeed, Negro voter registration outnumbered the whites up to 1890, although the two races were roughly equivalent in population.[62] Although there was considerable coercion, discrimination, and political manipulation, blacks still voted to a much greater degree than is often recognized. A formal system of race relations had not as yet been established, and blacks still retained enough organization and leadership to force politicians to come to terms with them.[63] Since Negro registration was abnormally high, this was also a further incentive for whites to seek black support. "Everybody wanted" the black vote "and everybody was soliciting it," a contemporary recalled.[64] A factor which also allowed the Negro to retain a significant role in Louisiana politics was his ability to divide his vote. The state's Republican party, often stereotyped as the party of the Negro, rarely received over 50 percent of the black vote; furthermore, even this percentage of black commitment was on the decline by the late 'eighties.[65] As a result, white factions openly vied for Negro support.

Upper-class conservatives in Louisiana rarely practiced the subtle philosophy of *noblesse oblige* that other aristocrats in the post-Reconstruction South used to attract Negro support.[66] When necessary, a crude application of violence, directly involving the white conservatives, effectively accomplished the same purpose in the end. Less violent methods were also equally applicable, and were equally emasculating. The Bourbons largely controlled the election machinery and, when necessary, stuffed ballot boxes and employed intimidation and violence to secure votes for the Democratic ticket. For whatever combination of reasons, the Bourbons could claim " 'lots' of Democratic voters throughout the state."[67] Between these two competing white factions the Populists would need to launch a vigorous campaign to capture the black vote which still held the balance of power during the 1890s. Such a campaign was the key to destroying the power of the dominant conservatives, assuming that Negroes would be allowed to vote unmolested and that they could be persuaded to support the agrarians.

Populism had entered Louisiana by the summer of 1891. The small white farmers of the northwestern parishes had been particularly receptive to the Populist doctrines.[68] These rustics regarded themselves as the true inheritors of the Jefferson-Jackson tradition—as men with a deep passion for patriotism and justice who had been beset in recent years by an unscrupulous "class" of politicians. Corrupt machines, established by these same politicians, had subjected the farmers to programs not designed to satisfy agrarian grievances. According to one portrait, nine-tenths of Louisiana Populists were "true American citizens of Caucasian blood." Furthermore, "many" had fought in the Mexican War and "nearly all" who were old enough were "good confederate soldiers"; moreover, "until a few years ago they were enthusiastic Democrats." Although Populists still regarded the black man with the same trepidation as before, they did not fear a repetiton of the "excesses" of Black Reconstruction—and understandably so from their perspective. During "the dark days of Radicalism," when the lowland parishes were "in the hands of negroes," it was these same men who had, ironically, "helped to redeem the state" from the same groups they were now accused of aiding in a political seizure of the state! "If it had not been for the white men in the South who are now Populists, the Republicans would indeed now have 'black heels on white necks.' ''[69] Composed of the "little one to five bale farmers" in North Louisiana, the movement was strongly marked with the Baptist religion and an overwhelming sense of history in highly personal terms.[70]

The inefficacy of the existing political structure had resulted in a degree of agrarian frustration which had become the focus of political activity. The catalyst for Populism in Louisiana was a People's party convention held on October 2, 1891, at Alexandria. Seventy-eight delegates from seventeen parishes attended, including Isaac Keys and another black Allianceman from the state's Colored Alliance.[71] On October 3, the party presented a campaign "Address to the People of the State of Louisiana People's Party . . . Irrespective of Class, Color, or Past Political Affiliation." This first platform made a strong appeal to capture black votes from the Republicans.

> You colored men . . . you must now realize that there is no hope of any further *material* benefit to you in the Republican party, and that if you remain in it you will continue to be hewers of wood and drawers of water in the future as you have been in the past.[72]

Aware that black votes alone were insufficient to accomplish a political revolution, the People's Party platform included a plank designed to test the power of white supremacy on the mind of Louisianians, a factor which had largely rendered past movements ineffective. Pointing out the unproductive results of "uninterrupted Democratic rule" in the state, third partyites contended that

> The spectre of negro supremacy has been used to keep you in the toils of the scheming machine politicians as effectively as the vodou [sic] is employed to terrify the credulous negroes themselves.[73]

The party made a strong appeal to its members to assert their rights against conservative domination and "not let the scarecrow of Negro domination longer drive them to the Democratic wigwam."[74] No nominations were made at the Alexandria meeting. These would come later in February.

Meeting again in Alexandria, the nominating convention had increased to 171 delegates, of which twenty-four were blacks. Significantly, two Negroes, Charles A. Roxborough and L. D. Laurent, were placed in nomination for the office of state treasurer.[75] Both were well known Negro leaders in the state and their endorsement would probably insure a degree of black support for the new party. A long-time leader in the Louisiana Colored Alliance, Laurent had been a delegate to the Ocala meeting in December 1890 and had been designated to attend the St. Louis convention in February and the Omaha meeting in July 1892. As early as the Ocala meeting he had backed the proposal for a third party.[76] During the summer of 1890, Roxborough had resigned from the Republican party, labeling it as an organization dedicated to "white supremacy." Paradoxically, in his letter of resignation, he had hinted that the blacks might support the Democrats although, like the Republicans, they were oriented "towards that same goal—white supremacy."[77] In either case the choice was not bright for the Negro. The endorsement of these black leaders undoubtedly helped the Populists present a more serious challenge to the Bourbons. Both Roxborough and Laurent withdrew their names, however, on the premise that "it was not the proper time" for black political candidates in Louisiana. As befitting their station within the black community, both men were subsequently placed on the Populist State Executive Committee.[78] Conscious of the critical role Negroes would play in the forthcoming electons, the Populists presently added an even stronger plank in their bid for black voters. Strangely reminiscent of Tom Watson's philosophy that "self interest always controls," this statement clearly established a biracial class character to their challenge of the Bourbon power structure.

> We declare emphatically that the interests of the white and colored races in the South are identical, and that both would suffer unless the disputed control of our government were assured to the intelligent and educated portion of the population.
>
> Legislation beneficial to the white man must, at the same time, be beneficial to the colored man.
>
> Equal justice and fairness must be accorded to each, and no sweeping legislation should be allowed bearing unjustly on either.[79]

Robert L. Tannehill was nominated as the Populist gubernatorial candidate for 1892. Almost completely unknown outside of Winn Parish, Tannehill, like most of the other obscure members of the ticket, was destined to failure. Opposed by the Democratic gubernatorial reform candidate, Murphy J. Foster, and Samuel D. McEnery, the Lottery candidate, Tannehill was buried under a landslide, receiving only 6 percent (9,804) of the state vote. Foster won with a sizable majority of 79,388 votes.[80]

All candidates, save Foster, claimed—and with some justification, it seems—that gross frauds had been committed. In the fifth district, an area containing the highest concentration of black population in the state, corruption was widespread. Furthermore, it was reported that the "infernal row" within the Democratic party had "destroyed all interest in life—has poisoned social enjoyment." Warring factions throughout the district were throwing out ballots, be they "spurious" or whatever. There was a genuine "fear" that "bloodshed" would result. "Whether it is due to the climate, or to the many races that make up our population, I do not know," a U.S. Marshall noted, "but it is a fact that Louisianans never seem to understand when they have had enough of fighting."[81]

By 1894, certain trends which would undermine black political strength had begun to emerge. Prominent among these was a proposed change in the suffrage laws. According to the constitution of 1874, "no qualification of any kind for suffrage or office, nor any restraint upon the same, on account of race, color, or previous condition of servitude shall be made by law."[82] Rather than attempt a new constitution, the Democratic legislature of 1894 passed a bill, to be offered to the voters in the 1896 state election, which would restrict the franchise to any adult male who "shall be able to read the Constitution of the state in his mother tongue, or shall be a bona fide owner of property . . . assessed to him at a cash valuation of not less than $200." A subtle provision attached to this bill allowed, upon endorsement by the voters, the legislature to rewrite the existing suffrage amendment in the 1874 constitution without voter approval.[83] Populists strongly opposed this particular measure but, in turn, strongly endorsed some type of effective ballot reform. They were acutely aware that the Bourbons were maintaining themselves in power through the corrupt venal use of black votes. Consider the major complaint widely lodged against the 1894 congressional elections: according to the *Louisiana Populist,*

> . . . in all the hill parishes where the white people are in the majority, the Populists polled big majorities, but in the river parishes where the Negroes were in the majority the Democrats succeeded in maintaining white supremacy (?) with the Negro votes.[84]

The Democrats were amazingly candid about their dishonesty, openly advertising as attested by the frank comment of a leading North Louisiana daily their plans to manipulate the election machinery:

> It is the religious duty of Democrats to rob Populists and Republicans of their votes whenever and wherever the opportunity presents itself and any failure to do so will be a violation of true Louisiana Democratic teaching. The Populists and Republicans are our legitimate political prey. Rob them! You bet! What are we here for?[85]

To the Populists, the question of ballot reform had become by 1894 necessary to the party's survival. Indeed the subject shortly took on a militancy that allowed no middle ground.

> The war of ballots will be between Populists and Plutocrats. The Populists will have for allies all honest silverites, prohibitionists and socialists; while the plutocrats will be divided into Democrats, or Southern Plutocrats and Republicans, or Northern Plutocrats. . . . It will be a mighty contest between manhood and money—between principles and policy, between freedom and slavery.
> There can be no neutrality upon this grave and important question. Those who are not in favor of honest elections are in favor of corrupt elections.[86]

In addition to the more pressing matter of political survival, the third partyites endowed the franchise with a remarkable degree of sanctity: "The ballot box is our highest legal authority."[87]

As a matter of necessity, ballot reform was moved to the forefront of the political struggle. There is a strong parallel here between the situation in Alabama and in the Pelican state. Expediency and self-interest ruled the Populists, and under such extreme pressures from the opposition the third party was forced to readjust its priorities. Political reform must precede economic reform. Following the 1894 congressional elections a major third party organ commented that now "this movement is as much a ballot reform move as a silver move."[88] The crucial point was that the party would achieve no other reforms until ballot reform was instituted. "Until we get this we are simply and only political slaves working for the master of election machinery."[89] This particular strain in Populist thought did not abate but rather increased with the passage of time. The same theme again surfaced at the People's party state convention at Alexandria on January 8, 1896. The party made a firm appeal for "a perfectly honest and a fair election" to be conducted in the state's forthcoming campaigns. To allow each citizen to "cast his ballot freely and secretly and the vote . . . be fairly counted as they are actually cast" was of the utmost importance. "This is the supreme issue in this campaign. . . ." The Populists still denounced the proposed Democratic suffrage amendment, believing that it would not "purify and elevate the ballot box" as claimed, but rather disfranchise "large masses of worthy citizens."[90] The use of an educational qualification was also opposed as a move "tending toward the aristocratic form of government."[91] If such measures were passed it was not unlikely that they would be used to exclude large numbers of poor whites and blacks.

The Populists regarded themselves as the true "white man's party" since, in the main, it was the Democrats who manipulated the Negro franchise during elections.

> The People's Party in this state is a white man's party, as evidenced by its vote in every election since its organization, and by the utterances of its platform, press and speakers in this state.[92]

The third partyites believed that the "money power" through coercion and venality "want to extend their dominion over the people as the slave power did over the blacks."[93] In the face of such omens, it is understandable that Populists preferred "a white man's government and a white man's party," although this did not mean that "the negro should not be allowed to help choose officers." Their major objection was to a party that "must" depend on the black parishes, through the use of fraud and venality, for its election success.[94]

By 1894 the shift in Populist attitudes toward the black voter had begun to crystallize. By this time Populists in the Fourth district had proposed a white primary to the Democrats, who subsequently had rejected the measure as did the Republicans in the Third district. To the third partyites, the reason for the Bourbon opposition to the measure was crystal clear: it was "because they wanted to use the Negro." Indeed it had "become very convenient in the Southern states to have a *black belt* to rely upon, that never fails to roll up a big majority in favor of white supremacy." Paradoxically, the Democrats who manipulated the suffrage were "unceasing" in their cries of "negro domination" against the Populists—an indictment skillfully used as a subterfuge to continue the pattern of fraud. "This old cry of negro domination is kept up by scheming politicians as a pretext to stuff ballot boxes."[95] Believing strongly in the sanctity of the ballot for all groups the third partyites found it a painful problem, but one that required a defensive posture if the party was to survive. The obvious obstacle was the black vote and the answer suggested—at least by some Populists—was the white primary, which would *"legally* and *honorably* free the country from the negro vote."[96]

In 1896 the Populists again decided to "throw down the gauntlet to the Democrats by inviting them into a white primary." The Bourbons must now "accept or shoulder all the blame for fraudulent elections." Again, the Democrats refused for much the same reasons as before. By these actions, declared the Populists, "the Democratic party is no longer a party of white supremacy."[97] The election process, they contended, had become little more than a "farce." They deplored "this condition of damnable corruption" which allowed "the politicans and place hunters" to "count negro votes that were never cast nor ever existed." The "rule" in the "black parishes" was "to count the negro—not to vote him."[98] To aid their cause further the Bourbons reportedly

> . . . made open and secret deals with the negro and brought him into primaries and conventions and caucases, they have him in office and on their ticket. Not only so, but they deal only with the corrupt and purchasable element of the negro.

In turn, Louisiana Populists averred that they would not stoop to such tactics. By 1896 their position on working with the Negro was abundantly clear.

> The Populists have NEVER at any time or place, appointed or empowered any committee man or set of men to see, negotiate or confer with any negro committee, convention or individual, and all these things have the Democrats done at specified times and places, and they cannot or will not deny it.[99]

It was actions such as those which accelerated the disfranchisement movement. Admittedly seeking Negro votes initially, many Populists had by now shifted their attitudes completely. This polarization was later recalled by a man who had helped resolve the suffrage dilemma.

> The riot of 1868 was white against black—that of 1895 and 1896 was white men against white man, for the negro vote. One side said, "He should not vote. If he does, we go under." The other side said, "He must vote. He will save us."[100]

Other groups were likewise now eager to eliminate the Negro from the political scene. By 1895 the Lily White element had seized control of the Louisiana Republican party and were seeking to undermine the blacks' power.[101] Furthermore, the stiff competition for Negro votes by the two white factions had increased the prices demanded. In short, it was becoming too expensive even for the more affluent Bourbons to buy up a Negro majority.[102] Living in an age when wages generally ranged between seventy cents to one dollar a day for "first class" black laborers, Negroes who accepted Democratic bribes probably did so more from efforts to redress economic grievances than as acts of demonstrated faith in the Bourbons.[103]

The culmination of the white ''counterrevolution'' was reached in the constitutional convention of 1898. The new constitution required a voter to demonstrate the ability to read and write or to possess property of not less than $300 in value. For illiterate, propertyless blacks, the stipulation was fatal. The so-called ''grandfather clause,'' which limited voting to individuals, or their descendants, who had voted prior to 1867, provided a loophole for the less affluent white Populists, yet largely eliminated the Negro.[104] In view of their negative experiences with the black vote, Populist approval of the disfranchisement process is not difficult to comprehend.[105]

To counteract the loss of black votes, the Bourbons put to best use their remaining constitutional advantages. Principal among these was the use of population—in this case the disfranchised Negroes—to determine representation in nominating conventions and in the legislature.[106] Populists strongly opposed this Bourbon tactic and spoke out loudly for its restructuring.

> Verily the ''nigger'' is to remain an important factor in Louisiana politics. He is to be disfranchised but his white neighbors will now make use of him in naming candidates of every political party, instead of using them in the election. The black belt can control the policy of every political party in this state and therefore cannot be much interested as to which party wins.[107]

This advantage would remain with the Bourbons, however, until it was abolished in 1906.[108]

The effect of the educational and literacy qualifications on black registration was marked and sharp. During the period 1890 to 1900, Negro registrants dropped from 127,923 to 5,320. White registrants also decreased but not nearly as sharply, with 126,884 in 1890 as opposed to 125,437 in 1900.[109] Perhaps the most immediate effect of the constitutional provision was the increase in voting power for the upland areas where Populism was strongest. Six alluvial parishes of Red River, Caddo, Concordia, Tensas, Madison, and East Carroll—long standing Democratic strongholds—dropped from 28,498 registrants in 1896 to 5,453 in 1900. In turn the Populist parishes had dropped from 27,702 voters in 1890 to 16,043 by 1896; yet, they were able to outvote the alluvial parishes by 3–1, whereas previously the situation had substantially increased their political power, and were now in a much better position to outvote the Bourbon strongholds which contained a large black population. With this state of affairs there was little need for white men to divide on party lines; Populists slowly returned to the Democratic fold.

By the end of the century, it was clear that Negroes were pretty much beyond the pale of political expression in Louisiana politics. The accelerating effect of disfranchisement was explicitly manifested in national elections: 130,344 Negroes were registered for the 1896 election, with black registrants representing a majority in twenty-six parishes; by 1900, two years after the constitutional convention, no parishes had a majority of Negro registrants, and there were only 5,320 blacks registered state-wide. During a four-year period, Negro registration had dropped 96 percent.[111] This limitation became even more severe in the twentieth century. No blacks were on the voting lists of 45 of the 64 parishes in the state by 1944. Of the few remaining Negro registrants during this modern period, approximately three-fourths were concentrated in Baton Rouge and New Orleans.[112]

As a result of the cleavages during the Populist revolt, the Negro had become the common enemy, the black herring which was causing continued division between the whites. There was a need, therefore, for a return to political stability, and disfranchisement accomplished this. "In effect," Dethloff and Jones have written in their analysis of race relations in Louisiana, "disfranchisement, aside from its racial implications, was a political compromise."[113] While the ensuing compromise never resulted in concensus, the decline of Populism ushered in a period of relative calm which endured in Louisiana politics until more recent years.

Third party doctrines, so authoritatively propagated by the high priests of the faith, were brash intruders in the domain of Texas politics. Populism emerged in the face of competing Democratic and Republican parties not so much because of its superior organization as because of its superior relevance and utility. Before its appearance, discontented agrarian elements had coalesced around the Progressive Democratic governor James S. Hogg, who attracted a varied and impressive backing in the farming regions of central, east, and north Texas. Overthrowing the Bourbons in 1890, Hogg subsequently became a storm center between Democratic reactionaries and radical alliancemen. Disaffected alliance leaders criticized the governor for being "too conservative" on such issues as the legal rate of interest, free textbooks, and the subtreasury plan.[114] This growing dissatisfaction led to the emergence of the Populist Party in Texas.

Given this situation, a third party convention was scheduled for August 17–18, 1891, during the annual session of the Farmers' Alliance in Dallas. Two blacks, Henry Jennings of Collins County and R. H. Hayes of Tarrant, were elected members of the State Executive Committee.[115] Following this a state People's Party convention assembled in Fort Worth on February 9, 1892.[116] The question of political fellowship with Negroes immediately came to the surface during the first day's session. A black delegate from Grayson County, "Watson," addressed the delegates in a speech mixed with humility and anger.

> I hope it is no embarrassment to you for a colored man to stand before you. I am an emancipated slave of this state. I was emancipated in 1865 and it is now useless to tell you my interest is yours and yours mine. You look over this large assembly and find very few of my people represented in this great movement. It is recognized that the Negro holds the balance of power, and the democrats and republicans are trying to hold him down. You should remember that those parties intend to keep the Negro out of this reform movement if they can, and when you bring up your old war-horses you are putting tools into the democratic and republican hands to help keep the Negro out of your movement.[117]

Efforts at organizing blacks at the grassroots level had been made since the Dallas meeting; they appear fairly substantial for a six-month period of time. Several Negro Populist Clubs had been formed. Henry Jennings, the black state committeeman reported that he "had organized many people's party colored clubs in Texas and had branded them." From south Texas came reports that "the colored people are coming into the new party in squads and companies. They have third party speakers and are organizing colored clubs." Speakers from the Colored Alliance were also addressing rallies in several counties.[118] In Gonzales County, about one-third of the Populists were black and six of its nineteen delegates to the convention were Negroes. These membership drives symbolized in part little more than illusionary efforts of participatory democracy—for Populists expressed little inclination to support black candidates.[119] The Negro's role was to be that of an organizer and supporter rather than candidate.

Texas Populists were not satisfied with their current successes at the local level, and rightly so, for Governor Hogg and the Democratic party had recently shifted to the left to absorb more of the disaffected farmers. Prominent among Hogg's efforts was a plank that supported free coinage of silver—a vexing subject that had strong Populist support not only in Texas but in the national party.[120] Yet the tide of disgruntled farmers leaving the Democratic party was not stemmed, due in part to the energetic recruiting efforts of the third partyites in the rural areas. By May it was reported that "so many Hogg democrats are going into the third party that he will be left in the primaries."[121] The governor's conciliatory efforts were too little and too late to blunt the Populist organizational activity.

A state nominating convention subsequently selected candidates for state office. The gubernatorial nomination went to Judge Thomas L. Nugent, a former Democrat and Confederate officer, described by an opposition newspaper as "a quiet, self-contained, intellectual and scholarly man and an accomplished lawyer" whose candidacy would add "dignity and moral elevation to the campaign."[122] Nugent had a strong faith in the improvability of man. He wanted to socialize Christianity, make social Christians of men, and he wanted to use the Populist party to these ends. According to his biographer, he was "a political expression of the social gospel movement." Nugent differed from many of his fellow Populists in that he did not expect to secure complete justice by political action or by institutional reform, although he was convinced that these could afford alleviation.[123]

Like many Populists, Nugent represented something of a paradox. A sensitive, religious man, with a strong humanitarian spirit, he separated the Negro from his strong sense of Christian charity. "My idea," he asserted, "is that segregation, as far as possible, is best for the Negro."[124] Nugent was a vigorous supporter of segregation in railway cars and in schools where blacks should be "prevented by law from close association with white people."[125] He also wanted to extend segregation into the prison system on the premise that the Negro's supervision of his own penal system would provide valuable training.[126] Like other Populists previously examined, Nugent vigorously opposed social equality between the races, believing that it was unattainable.[127] His opinions on this matter were buttressed by James H. "Cyclone" Davis, the Populist candidate for Attorney General, and Davis further suggested that one of the prime motives for reforming the American economy was to prevent white women from being forced into "hoeing cotton" beside "a big burley Negro."[128]

The Texas Populist party was largely unsuccessful in 1892, winning only eight seats in the legislature, and running in third place behind the other two major parties.[129] Hogg easily won the gubernatorial election, receiving 43.7 percent (190,486) of the vote.[130] During the bitter struggle, Hogg made a strong bid for the Negro vote while the Populists relied heavily on the Colored Alliance to turn out that vote. The third partyites also made no overtures for Republican support—an omission which further retarded their Negro support.[131]

It seems reasonably clear that Hogg received the lion's share of the black vote. Like W. H. Northen, his gubernatorial counterpart in Georgia, he was favored by blacks even though he headed the party of white supremacy. The reason was probably related to his record of honesty and fairness to blacks. Like Northen, he particularly made a strong stand against mob action.

> Now, I have gone this far, when mobs have become too strong in the State for the local officers to cope with them. I have quelled them by the strong arm of the law without conferring with anybody. I have suppressed more than one mob too. Did you ever hear of an influential and wealthy man being killed by a mob? Let a humble negro or a poor white man commit some crime and a gang of enterprising and wild and wooly fellows will swing him to a tree without a trial.[132]

Hogg's comments on equal law enforcement were not idle boasts. He subsequently placed "rewards over the heads of all these criminals [lynchers], and propose[d] to let them stay there as long as I hold the office of Governor."[133] He also granted "numerous" pardons and commuted the sentences of Negro offenders.[134] His biographer has

> . . . found this theme of abhorrence of mob violence throughout Hogg's addresses and writing, as part of his fundamental concern with and insistence on law enforcement and justice for all manner of man.[135]

Hogg's case was further strengthened by the support of such black leaders as David Abner, Jr., president of Guadalupe College at Seguin, W. O. Lewis, Negro attorney from Denison, John Anderson, and a host of others.[136] There seems to be massive evidence to document the fact that Hogg received a substantial portion of the black vote in 1892. It also appears that this support was not based largely on fraud and coercion.[137] Populists, in turn, had little appeal to either Mexicans or blacks and depended for their success on areas largely devoid of Negro population.[138]

It was readily apparent from the result of the election that the attraction of black leadership would be a key factor in the future success of the Populists. It was at this point that the third partyites managed to convert the portly John B. Rayner, a former Negro Republican, to serve as a grassroots organizer and stump speaker.[139] With the aid of "a corps of colored assistants," Rayner roamed from one end of the state to the other preaching the doctrine of Populism to the black man.[140] His speaking schedule was arduous, for he filled three engagements for every one of the white Populist speakers. The necessity of having Negro speakers in the black community was readily recognized. H. S. P. "Stump" Ashby, chairman of the State Executive Committee, recognized that Rayner was "the most useful speaker [we] can employ to implant our principles among the colored voters." As Ashby indicated, "the work I want Rayner to do no white man can do."[141]

Rayner's career reads almost like that of an evangelist crusader. His enthusiasm and ability to endure hardship was remarkable. His salary was minimal, often nonexistent; at one point he was so destitute that he did not have money enough to buy postage stamps.[142] Rayner was later credited with converting at least 25,000 blacks to Texas Populism, and as a reward for his diligent work, he was appointed to the state Executive Committee in 1895.[143]

Rayner found fertile ground for his doctrines, for political discontent within the Texas Republican party reached new heights during the 'nineties. By 1888, Lily White Clubs were being formed in opposition to the Negro's participation in the party.[144] In Texas, as in most other Southern states during this period, the Republican party was slowly dividing over the "Negro question"—a rift manifested openly at the state Republican convention at San Antonio in September 1890. The black faction, according to one correspondent, thought they "have got dem white folks where the hair is short."[145] However, this elation was short-lived, because of political maneuvering on the convention floor by the Lily White faction which subsequently managed to nominate their own candidate.[146]

This was merely the beginning of a long series of defeats for black Republicans. By 1894, the Lily Whites proposed setting up an independent Negro republic for blacks.[147] Segregation should not only be along party but geographical lines. By 1896, Norris Wright Cuney, black leader of the Negro element, had lost his place in the party and the suppression of blacks was even more dramatic.[148] With this change of fortune, the Negro was open to solicitation from the parties. As previously indicated, a large element of the black community had supported James Hogg, the Democrat, in both 1890 and 1892. How much of this is attributable to his personal magnetism is difficult to say; but in any case he was a decided asset to the party, especially where Negro support was concerned. By 1894, Norris Wright Cuney advocated fusion between the Populists and the black Republicans, perhaps less as a result of sympathy with Populist principles than, in the words of Cuney's daughter, "the combined vote of the two parties [which] was far greater than that of the Democrats."[149] During the 1892 election, Cuney had opposed fusion with both the Democrats and the Populists, but the Populists in particular.

I objected to Mr. Nugent because he is in line with Mr. Hogg; but a few steps removed toward socialism and communism—for instance, the Government ownership of railroads and the subtreasury. His principles seek to undermine our whole system of business, which has existed for years, and under which our country has become great and strong, and made itself the foremost among the nations of the world.[150]

Four years later, Cuney still opposed fusion with the Populists although in practice he was not averse to fusion with other political parties.[151] It was during this period that his leadership was being challenged, and reconciliation with the Lily Whites was being advocated. With Cuney's demise, new black leaders were committed to fusion with the Populists.[152] A faction of the black Republicans under the aegis of William "Gooseneck Bill" McDonald continued to oppose fusion for much the same reason as Cuney: because of the fundamental philosophical difference between Republicanism and Populism.[153] By this point it made little difference, for Texas Populism underwent a marked decline after 1896.[154] This drop in electoral interest can be largely attributed to Democratic appropriation of Populist policies.[155] There was never a high degree of incompatibility between the Populists and the Progressive Democracy ushered in by Hogg in 1890.[156]

The effect of Texas Populism on black suffrage represents a somewhat different picture from Louisiana and Alabama. In the latter states, black electoral participation took a drop after the effects of disfranchising conventions. It was not until 1902 that a constitutional amendment enacted a poll tax in Texas. According to Rice's *Negro in Texas*, " 'Black Populism' eventually led to the adoption of the poll tax and the white Democratic primary."[157] Yet blacks were effectively disfranchised and a substantial portion of the white voters had begun to boycott the polls long before this.[158]

Perhaps the explanation lies partly in the limited number of qualified black voters in the state—approximately 20 to 30 percent of the total. After 1896, blacks were never a real threat to white supremacy unless fusion was effected with other parties.[159] In substance, the Negro was ineffective and his "apathy," coupled with white violence when necessary, neutralized his influence. The Negro vote remained larger in the city than in the country and on occasion did prove of value to parties of disputation. Political "indifference" occurred largely in the rural districts although there were local variations. It appears that the base of power for blacks was largely in the cities following the agrarian revolt.[160] Populism had been a potent influence in the formation of election alignments in Texas and it propelled the Negro to the fore in politics. However, the campaigns in Texas were mild in comparison, and the issue of race was never as sharp as in other states.

Populism's legislative impact in Texas was minor during the 'nineties for the party had not elected enough members to effect change. The state's ethnic diversity complicated the situation and, despite strong efforts, Populists never attracted significant support from blacks, Mexicans, Germans, businessmen, or prosperous farmers.[161] Moreover, improved economic conditions after 1896 worked against Populism as a protest party. Politically, most returned to the Democratic party and several former Populists were elected as legislators.[162]

President Lyndon Johnson, sometimes seen as a Progressive Democrat, may in reality have become a neo-Populist—representing one of the threads of Texas Populism that ran into the 1960s. His grandfather had been a Populist and he acknowledged that his "father and grandfather handed down to him a philosophy of life."[163]

The Populist challenge in the Gulf Coast South differed in some respects from the Atlantic Coast variety. One prominent difference, particularly in Alabama and Louisiana, was the overriding demand for ballot reform. Populism here had started out with economic issues being prominent, but it soon became clear that reform would not be effected at the ballot box with the amount of corruption and fraud existing. By 1894, economics had been relegated to a subordinate theme. Afterward, the Populists placed great stress on suffrage change: political reform must precede economic reform, for without this no party which sought to work through the established election system could be effective. The nemesis during these campaigns was the Negro and his vote which was being manipulated by the Bourbons. This problem was cleared away with disfranchisement conventions; but, ironically, Populism had been slowly eroded by the completion of the disfranchising process.

The Texas pattern was complicated by the existence of a progressive Democratic party which constantly incorporated Populist issues into its platform. Concurrently, progressive Democrats such as James Hogg received substantial portions of the black vote due to their liberal record on race relations. Also, Populism was unable to attract a substantial following of Negro leadership to promote its program in the black community. The few converts it did gain, such as John Rayner, were overburdened and underpaid. The picture was further complicated by black Republican leaders who did not endorse fusion with the Populists until the party was disintegrating.

With these studies of Populism in the Atlantic and Gulf Coast states completed, we shall turn to a profile of Populism: a discussion of the current literature on the subject, a quantitative analysis of the movement, and an evaluation of its impact on the racial and electoral process during its ascendancy.

VIII

THE POPULIST PROFILE

Since the estimates of Populist character and composition by C. Vann Woodward in the 1950s, Populist historiography has been enriched by a spate of monographs and articles. It would be well to analyze the current crop in an effort to explain and interpret the direction of the literature and sort out fresh trends and findings. By consulting these recent works, steeped in primary research and major secondary resources, we are able to focus more sharply on the local political structure and operational methods of Populism. This will, in turn, allow us to move to an extended discussion of the similarities and differences between the various states and, with additional quantitative analysis, construct an updated profile.

It was Woodward who was the real pioneer and formative scholar of Southern Populism, and his influence is readily apparent in later studies. Fresh as is Woodward's analytical interpretation of the unique role of Southern Populism, functionally his works may best have served as models for other scholarly examinations of the subject, particularly on the local level. Following his explorations, other scholars have added new information, and a survey of this new historiography invites comparison with some of Woodward's earlier more provocative conclusions.

Woodward portrayed "typical" Southern Populist leaders as "men of substantial landed property, successful farmers and planters, and withal literate, informed, and capable citizens." This class, he contended, had previously found its way to political office, usually as Democrats, and were often articulate members of the community.[1] How accurate is this characterization? Detailed compilation of biographical data on the state and local level offers an opportunity to evaluate this standard interpretation of the Populist leadership.

A recent analysis of 126 Populist leaders in Texas indicates that farmers provided "about half" of the major leadership, "attorneys, one fourth, and businessmen, editors, teachers, skilled laborers, ministers, and doctors the remainder." Only 20 percent were native Texans although "most" were from the South. Approximately one-third had held office as Democrats, but only a small fraction had been major Democratic leaders. The average age was forty-eight, with ranges from twenty to seventy-eight. In comparison, Texas Democratic leaders averaged "slightly" younger, and about 30 percent were Texas-born. About half were attorneys and, in contrast to the Populists, had "somewhat more" experience in the upper levels of government. Texas Populism did not represent a progression of the same men from the earlier Grange and Greenback parties.[2] This fact would indicate that such figures who held rural oriented views may have become Populists as a result of their frustrated ambitions in the Democratic party.

A comparable analysis of Alabama Populist leadership supports these findings. Of nine Populist legislators, only one was a "planter," but five listed themselves as "farmers." Of the Democratic leadership, 50 percent (18) were judges or lawyers. A much higher percentage of the Democrats were officers during the Civil War. In comparison, none of the Populists were college graduates; moreover, they were, in general, recruited from a lower social class. "The common denominator among the upper echelon of Populist leaders," Professor Sheldon Hackney has concluded, "was restless aspiration linked to experience with failure."[3]

One of the most revealing examples of this "restless aspiration" was William Hodge Kitchen, a disgruntled North Carolina Democrat who, combining conservatism and opportunism, sought an alternative line of development to extend his influence and satisfy his hopes for a political career. Referred to by Jonathan Daniels as the "original advocate of white supremacy and the father of that expression," Kitchen represented the type of leadership that on occasion prevented Populists from coming to grips with the racial problems, they faced.[4] Exemplifying a principal devotion to self-interest over class reform, the case of Kitchen illustrates why blacks were not totally committed to the Populist program and leadership. Political sentiments voiced by such leaders bespoke a discontent with the existing order, but the proposed remedy often was for a greater appreciation of their own abilities.

It is relatively easy to see in Populist leadership—as in all people—the utilitarian principle that he who best serves his own end is thus able to make his maximum contribution to the greatest happiness of the greatest number. The fusion of reform and self-aggrandizement is complete in Populism; but the reform motive, which is always the saving grace, does not suffer by the merging of self-interest and altruism. Consequently, Populism was not motivated solely by altruism and seems sadly miscast as a citadel of human equality and natural rights. It should not be forgotten that it was Tom Watson who remarked that "Self interest always controls."[5] In this characterization, Populism provides the perfect synthesis of morality and self-interest. Thus, Woodward's earlier analysis of Populist leadership has failed to withstand completely the test of quantification and more in-depth study.

With few exceptions, such as Hackney's recent monograph on Alabama Populism,[6] works on the movement have followed a pattern of non-quantitative analysis. Populism needs fresh examinations by the case method, using election returns, census data, and other available material to arrive at challenging new

interpretations. The works created by most historians are based on such artifacts of'
the past as manuscripts, newspapers, and the like. The main scholarly technique
devised and employed by historians is documentation, using "written" evidence
and employing the language and logic of the individual as the unit for analysis. In
turn, this "individual" evidence is combined in such a way as to provide a total
picture of a particular situation. Woodward's approach is largely based on this
method and his thesis is rendered more palatable by his skill in weaving the
language of his individual subjects into his narrative.

The danger with this method is that it suffers from a common tendency to accept
the logic and language of the participants and, in turn, to make synonymous the
creed and the deed. If Hofstadter is correct in his assertion that Populists were
paranoid and conspiracy-minded, the inherent danger of accepting such biased
observations and language for factual analysis is readily apparent and is sufficient
reason in itself to develop additional research techniques for evaluation of the
movement.[7] Anyone embarking on an examination of Populism probably should
employ some statistical research methods as a check on the more palatable
distortion of human fallibility and error. The remainder of this chapter will attempt
to extrapolate from the statistical data (see the Appendix) some of the general
behavior patterns of Populism.[8]

Perhaps a few words of caution should be injected at this point. The acquisition
of reliable data is a basic need for any sort of quantitative study. Yet it must be
recognized immediately that no matter how complete the collection of statistical
data on Populism, major difficulties in analysis arise inevitably from the improvident, corrupt, and unreliable character of Southern politics during the period under
examination. Democrats never really gave the apostles of Populism their political
blessing and sent them on their unfettered way. Unaccustomed to losing elections,
the Democratic party met the threat to its hegemony with intimidation, bribery,
and widespread fraud. Exceptions existed and the situation differed from time to
time with adjoining counties in the same state, yet as states deviated from the
pattern of Democratic hegemony, corruption and fraud were generally developed
to the proportion necessary to win. The consequences of these variations in
election fraud among the various states often reduce analysis of the results to the
realm of art rather than scientific measurement.

It is difficult to judge the degree of corruption from the charges in the literature
but a few examples of the character of Southern politics will illustrate the cruder
nature of the practices during this era. As previously noted, frequency and degree
of election fraud were closely associated with differences in the voter balance
between Democrats and Populists. Corruption in states such as Tennessee, Arkansas, and Mississippi where Populism was never a major threat was minimal, at
least in comparison with major Populist strongholds such as Georgia, Louisiana,
and Alabama.[9] Yet the former states manifested in accentuated form the corrupt
strain that ran throughout the South—even where Populism was a politically
impoverished rival.

In Tennessee "a corrupt county court and a few self constituted bosses," according to one Populist, had prevented the party "from getting a fair Election in the western division of my state." The result was that "the will of the majority had been trodden underfoot" by the Democratic bosses. The "paramount issue" was "the American franchise viz a free ballot and an honest count."[10] Such corrupt practices had their general origin in obedience to the priestly conservative class during Reconstruction, but as regional politics grew in complexity, and hence in heterogeneity and definite form with the passage of time, the code of fraud that had developed to defeat blacks during Reconstruction had ceased and the pattern often became one of open callousness practiced against native white Southern opponents. "I ask if there is a member of this floor who will pretend to deny that nine ballot boxes were stolen from the clerk's office in . . . [Pulaski] county," the Speaker of the Arkansas house of Representatives inquired in 1889. A Pulaski delegate indignantly denied the charge. "Only six were stolen," he maintained. "Very well, I stand corrected," the speaker replied. "Only six ballot boxes and poll books were stolen from . . . the county in which stands the capitol of the beloved Arkansas."[11] In some states, such corrupt practices achieved at times a measure of sadistic humor in the method employed. "With mock solemnity," a modern authority on Mississippi politics has written, "newspapers reported that boxes containing anti-Democratic majorities had been eaten by mules or horses."[12] In nearby Alabama during the same period, there were "numerous instances" of "dead Negroes and faithful hounds" voting against the Populists.[13] Such incidents are frequent in the annals of Populism, and these few cases in point have by no means represented the most flagrant examples.[14] One conclusion and only one can come from a study of such incidents: the election machinery did not work because, in one sense or another and with varying emphasis on its aspects, the contestants for power did not count the ballots as cast. To seek precise statistical patterns from such data would be to chase an impossible will-o-the-wisp. That much is philosophy; the rest is politics.

Reaching valid conclusions with such unreliable election data inevitably introduces problems of method. Consequently, I have supplemented the raw statistical material for interpreting the election results with my acquaintance with the documentary data. Moreover, this method has involved insofar as applicable the findings of recent scholarly inquiries. This approach gives an uncommonly broad but tenable view of the process and practices of the interracial role of Southern Populism.

Populism was never strong politically in areas of high concentration of black skin and black dirt. From a statistical standpoint, there was a high inverse relationship between third party successes at the polls and Negro population. There were some major exceptions: in Tennessee, Populism was strongest in the middle and western sections where blacks were concentrated in greater numbers. Yet the state was relatively unimportant in the overall pattern of Populist politics, never achieving a movement of any magnitude. Moreover, blacks never played a prominent role in Tennessee's own Populism and rarely gave it much support, probably as a result of their increasingly circumscribed political role.[15] There was also a decided lack of Populist appeal to black voters. Finally, the third party never brought about a large scale fusion venture with the Republicans as was the case in North Carolina; for the state as a whole little was done—or attempted—along these lines.

In North Carolina, Populism managed to secure a major base of operations in the eastern coastal area where blacks were numerous. The percentage of the Populist vote in black belt counties correlated highly with the percentage of Negro population—an atypical situation for the South as a whole.[16] Fusion politics, particularly in 1894 and 1896, blurred the pattern in North Carolina, and it is difficult to calculate how much success Populists would have had in attracting Negro support unilaterally. The manuscript evidence examined lends itself to no definite conclusions.

The real key to Populist successes in attracting black support can be found at the local level. Negroes who did vote for the Populists tended to vote in greater numbers in state and local elections. Conversely, on the national level blacks tended to vote for Republican candidates.[17] In the 1892 election, Weaver, the Populist presidential candidate, tended to run weaker in areas of high black concentration than did the Populist gubernatorial candidates. How much this was due to the Republican patronage system and the influence of the black leadership on its following is difficult to gauge.

With the maturation of Populism, Negroes tended to vote less for the movement as it advanced chronologically. Judged from the primary materials examined, it appears that the third party made greater efforts toward racial cooperation with the Negro in 1892 than it did later. As the movement gained momentum and the Bourbons concentrated on defeating the Populists through the corrupt use of the Negro vote, the white Populists could not wipe away the bitterness over the fact that they were being defeated by a class ally—at least in their eyes. The result was a slow shifting to a philosophy that argued for ''fair elections and a free count.'' This change in strategy logically meant a mounting dissatisfaction with black influence in election matters. In brief, the shift of thought in Populist racial philosophy was accompanied by a concurrent shift in black support.

Populism tended to receive fewer black votes in the Gulf Coast states than in the Atlantic seaboard area. The highest negative correlations between black population and Populist vote, for example, were found in the deep South states of Alabama, Mississippi, and Louisiana. A probable cause can be found in the wholesale frauds practiced; from the sources examined, it is clear that the greatest excesses of voter manipulation were found in these states. In this light the crucial test of Populist attraction of black votes is almost impossible to judge. Viewed on a subjective basis, however, Populists seemed less successful, as a general rule, in attracting Negro support in the Gulf Coast than in the Atlantic seaboard area.

Populism made much of its class strategy of combining farm and city laborers, and black and white farmers within the South into a viable political alliance.[18] Using statistics to assess this vaunted claim, one could easily conclude that the overall appeal was largely a failure, for none of these variables received high positive correlations. Of all the elections evaluated, only in Tennessee and Alabama in the 1894 gubernatorial elections were there any positive correlations between urban population (towns of 2,500 or more) and Populist vote. In these elections, the correlations were insignificant, being .03 in Alabama and .04 in Tennessee. The same was also true for the presidential election of 1892. Only in Alabama was there any positive correlation (.13) between urban population and Populist presidential vote. Conversely, Harrison, the Republican candidate, received in 1888 a much greater correlation between blacks, urban population, and farm ownership than did Weaver, the Populist candidate in 1892. This can perhaps best be attributed to a basic difference in interests between blacks, urban areas, and third parties. In brief, Populism sought higher prices for its products, while conversely, increases in prices meant greater costs for the urbanite. In the case of the black, his emphasis was on higher wages for his labor—a stress which was antagonistic to the small white farmer who could scarcely afford higher wages for black tenants. By definition, the goals of the respective groups were fundamentally different. At bottom, this exposes the fallacious assumption that political coalitions can be built and sustained on the basis of sentimental appeals to class consciousness. If "self interest always controls," as Tom Watson had said earlier, it is significant to note that each group always had its own interests in mind. These conflicts of interest would seem to offer significant lessons for black people in the context of present day America who seek such coalitions with urban white liberal groups who must view the scene through drastically different lens.[19] It remains not to make an interpretive summary of Populist actions during the period and tally up the balance sheet.

IX

THE BALANCE SHEET

Southern history has witnessed a long line of third parties—from the Greenbackers to the American Independent Party of George Wallace. Usually, all of these have achieved some notable successes at the state level. Their decline came about not so much because of voter rejection—since any party of substance must withstand defeat, but because they were cut off from the national patronage system under the domination of the two major parties.[1] In this context, Populism was no exception for it was not only a spokesman for the powerless but suffered the same failing politically. Populism was essentially a political defense mechanism of the disinherited; despairing of substantial return through the established parties, the agrarians turned their backs, very reluctantly, on the political system which had denied them benefits and looked to its disavowal by "the people" in a cataclysm which would exalt the agrarian, moral, and underprivileged and cast down the rich and powerful "money power."

The Populists were caught in the unsettling posture of being both inside and outside the regional ideology—passionately committed to it, yet by that very passion inevitably alienated from it to some degree. Thus, they found themselves at one and the same time inside and outside of the region's racial values, trying desperately to strike a balance between the roles of conformist and critic. But the journey out of the old ideology into the new had a certain gnawing insidiousness about it, an inevitable inner ambivalence between the collective racial experiences of the past and of the present. As a result of their political heresy, Populism's elected officers became outcasts within the very system through which they were trying to work, with no perquisites of party seniority and patronage. The lack of patronage to serve as outlets for ambitious followers acted also as an enervating weakness at the grassroots level. What better proof that a thread of frustrated political ambition existed in the Populist movement than in several instances prominent Populist leaders eventually moved off into one of the other major parties? This political realignment also seems true of the electorate. Leaders such as Watson, Kolb, and Butler continued their careers in the Republican and Democratic parties. Populism could offer few inducements beyond principle to leaders, black or white, and was, therefore, insisting upon a political alliance and mode of appeal that largely precluded accessibility to patronage or, in the case of blacks, protection of person. Furthermore, black Southern leaders were suspicious of the earlier bitterness manifested toward their race by many of the same men who subsequently opted for a class alliance. Given this limited opportunity system, coupled with a gnawing ambivalence about the role of blacks who had reentered politics as the balance of political power, Populism seemed doomed to an ig- nominious defeat.

A much more negative and phlegmatic restraint upon the advance of Populism came from the fanaticism of the Bourbon class. The conservatives shared few of the third party's convictions for Negro political rights, and saw the security of their own position being threatened by a combination of lower class whites and blacks. Out of their own political maneuvers, Bourbons developed a defense of white supremacy using black votes. The observation of these events was enough to discourage even the most stout of heart. Populists shifted to a tone of hard-boiled realism and called for a drastic reform of the election process. Some third partyites now came to regard the blacks as one of the forces that were challenging the moral legitimacy of their proposed new order. The logical response was a competitive style of race relations which downplayed the proposed program of class measures brought on by the pinch of economic pressures. This shift in attitude was accom- panied by a corresponding shift in black support—all of which signalled the discontinuity of Populist class feeling with the Negro.

Populism started with the rhetorical assumption that there could be no progress until there was a consciousness of class interests. A people must know what it is reasonable to want, and then seek to achieve it through concentrated political effort. Yet, the great majority of Populists, black and white, had their aspirations shaped by a society that placed great confidence in a program of self-help. Reared on this tradition, it is not surprising that the movement was largely a refurbishing of the Protestant ethic. At bottom, Farmers' Alliance and Populist rhetoric repre- sents an agrarian translation of the traditional Protestant conception of wealth through work and virtue. With great admiration, they referred back to the days of Jefferson and Jackson as their ideal of economic organization. The Populist's view of government was also closely related to his belief in a rustic concept of Emersonian self-reliance and virtue, with the development of a new political leadership based on human happiness and social democracy. Its intellectual and ideological foundations combined, in religious thought the idea of the social gospel, and in politics the idea of a social democracy. Its stated ideal would be a society in which all people, no matter what their race, would be given a chance politically to rise as far as their merits would take them. In theory, theirs was to be a monolithic coalition of special class interests recognizing no race or regional boundaries. The inherent danger of Populist rhetoric was that it ruthlessly over- simplified all groups into either "producers" or "consumers" on the basis of economic grievances—the classic struggle of the have's against the have-not's or, rather, the have-not-enough's. These bold simplifications overlooked the more abstruse and difficult problem of people of all races—namely the social and sentimental responses that often determine personal needs. The distinctive sociological ingredients of equality are more often honored in the breach than in fact, especially in a bourgeois capitalistic society such as America. It remains to admit that self-interest, which the Populists hoped to use to usher in a new order of race relations, was a more competitive encroachment than class measures in the New South.

The existence of intrarace Negro class prejudice was a factor Populists seem to have overlooked almost completely. In many ways the black class structure was more difficult to comprehend, more protean, and prone to greater political problems than the white community. Although existing prior to emancipation, the Negro class structure was largely a postbellum phenomenon still largely channeled through a light-skinned leadership and the Negro church. Frederick Douglass was acutely aware of the class-color problem within the black community. "While the rank and file of our race," he lamented, "quote the doctrine of human equality, they are often among the first to deny it in practice."[2] Furthermore, the misery which Populism hoped to use to reconcile poor blacks and whites was often muted by an equally passionate racial hatred. In both the abstract and in person the enmity that existed between the poor of both races was captured in a song known to blacks throughout the South:

> My name's Sam, I don't give a dam; I'd rather
> be a nigger than a poor white man.[3]

The blacks, like the whites, were not immune to the racist traditions that clustered around their historical experience. With this liability, the South's characteristic vice of racial adversity easily undercut any sort of colorblind equalitarianism.

In its appeal to both poor blacks and whites, Populism did provide something of a common class and political denominator for those who felt ignored and bypassed. It appears that the mass of the blacks who supported Populism were the rural poor, caught like their white counterparts in the chasm of economic despair. The arrogant elitism of the black middle class, concentrated in urban areas, largely precluded them from supporting a party of the humble, earthy, sweaty common man. Indeed the observations of W. E. B. DuBois reflected the orientation of middle-class blacks. Speaking of Populism, he denied that "the conclusions of ages of conscientious research are to be cast away in a moment just because some long beard from the wild woolly west wants to shirk paying his just debts."[4] To DuBois, "The Populists as a third party movement beginning during this time [the 1890s] did not impress me."[5] Frederick Douglass likewise expressed little enthusiasm for Populism and for the most part, entirely ignored the movement.[6] It is hardly surprising, therefore, that Populism attracted so few black leaders in the South. This feeling of antipathy was further compounded by strong Negro loyalty to national Republican candidates and the awkward choice of more and more black leaders openly supporting intrastate Democratic candidates to promote local sources of strength and stable race relations—a role the Populists were particularly ill equipped to handle.

In practice, Populist racial attitudes took two distinct strains: economic and political reform and social inequality. The two often overlapped, and the crossing of racial lines created a feeling of ambivalence, a confusion about patterns of race relations. This ambivalence was severely strained by the emotional outcry of the conservatives against the coalition. On one hand, Populism implied a class coalition with the producer class, including the Negro; on the other, it suggested an unyielding social inequality of the races, a kind of folk malevolence. Socially, the Populists believed in a fixed inequality of status between the races with moral and intellectual capabilities at its center. The second strain, involving political relationships, contained many contradictions and complexities depending upon both the state and the individual involved; but the dominant white group, recognizing the necessity of some concessions to the blacks in order to enhance their own political role, provided a limited political equality necessary to accommodate a racial coalition based on class alignment—arrayed in the solution of economic disorders. The purported catalyst was "self-interest" which would cut across racial lines and bring about a class defense calculated to better one's own status and economic condition. In other words, the Populists, in challenging the South's political traditions, were forced to imagine an alternate line of racial development that to them, whether ethically, politically, or economically, seemed more realistic. In this essay at a coherent and systematic racial philosophy which only intermittently held the attention and passions of Southerners—black and white— in this very attempt, many white Populists, such as Tom Watson, later became not only staunch advocates of traditional racist mores but critics of the very values they sought earlier to implement.

At the outset, the Populists put major stress on economic reform brought about through changes at the ballot box. It soon became apparent, however, that political reform would be necessary before economic reform could be achieved. As the movement progressed, the principle of ballot reform received wider audience and was promoted to a position of equal importance with economics. Indeed, one of the distinctions between Western and Southern Populism was the latter's greater emphasis on political reform. As a result, a few Populists came to regard the Negro as the tool of the "money power" rather than a class ally and subsequently regarded elimination of his vote as a reform. "Purchasable [black] votes mean that the dollar and not the man is to rule," a Louisiana organ concluded, "and we think a law should be made disfranchising all who sell or buy votes."[7] Far from being inconsistent with their principles, these Populists viewed this strategy as a natural realignment of moral and class interests, one to which the region must accommodate itself if the political structure was to be consistent with the principles of Jefferson and Jackson.

The challenge venality presented to the ideology of Populism created a major psychic crisis acutely felt on all levels. In fact, the association of venality with political rewards threatened to turn the moralistic political standards of Populism upside down. Every election examined during this period was symptomatic of the breakdown of political standards in Southern politics. Unable to master a coherent defense against these infectious trends, Populism became cynical about the linkage of virtue and political success. It deplored the widespread corruption of the vote through pressure and pecuniary reward and, in turn, could not recover from the Democratic use of the racial issue. Yet, one must remember that the promotion of Populism took on the urgency of a crusade. Populists saw themselves as active combatants in the struggle for human dignity, fighting to preserve moral agrarian traditions which they believed were being undermined by the Democrats. Such strong impulses of idealism and moral indignation, once blunted, often harbor an equal or stronger impetus for reaction.

Some Populists such as Joseph P. Manning of Alabama, endured the bitterness and brutal campaigning to the end with all the courage and determination of Sisyphus or Prometheus. Others such as Tom Watson finally broke under the distortions, invective, corruption, and violence and became openly embittered and obsessed with race hatred. The contrast was sharp. There was a time in Watson's early career when blacks would crowd about him, touch his garments with reverence, and go home and tell their families, "I seen him today. I seen him and heard him talk and touched his clothes." Yet, in his later years his abuse and bitterness toward the Negro bordered on the pathological.

Both blacks and whites had supplied reasons for some of the prejudices which enslaved Populism. The white Redeemers, having early encouraged dishonest election procedures, found themselves obliged to continue with the worst products of it in order to survive politically. The injustices and evils of the system, so plainly seen and condemned by the Populists affected attitudes toward the Negro because of the central role blacks played in the system. Consider the brazen steal in Richmond County, Georgia where Tom Watson was counted out. "I remember," one inhabitant of the area recalled, "seeing the wagonloads of Negroes brought into the wagon yards, the equivalent of our parking lots, the night before the election. There was whisky there for them, and all night many drank, sang and fought. But the next morning they were herded to the polls and openly paid in cash, a dollar bill for each man as he handed in his ballot."[8] The Populists who had befriended the blacks and had been demanding that honest election processes be honored were understandably affronted by such actions—which occurred on a wide scale through the South. Populist conclusions were not, of course, exact or even perhaps totally rational; the truth was more complex and multifaceted than the Negro's outward appearance of accepting such corrupt practices. Yet, such sights affected the Populist conscience and attitudes and produced a racial bitterness which some saw as retribution, and others saw as ironic.

Against this backdrop of concern over morals and materialism, Populism helped bring forth a consciousness of one of the region's most pregnant dictums, the separate-but-equal philosophy, of Booker T. Washington. No one prior to Washington's famous Atlanta Exposition speech in September, 1895, had been able to articulate this dimension of the Southern race system very precisely, and Populism was no exception. Southerners seized upon Washington's philosophy and inverted it with the most far-reaching implications. Yet Washington had merely reinforced the doctrine that Southern Populists had been proposing all along. According to Tom Watson, Washington's plea for vocational education, economic progress, and political accommodation represented "the same opinions as to the Negro question which we were handed down for uttering in 1892."[9] Watson regarded the Tuskegee philosophy of thrift, industry, and encouraging blacks to "cast down your bucket" in the South "as mighty sound doctrine."[10] An Alabama Populist paper likewise endorsed Washington's idea of maintaining a separate "social character" but working together on matters of "material welfare." This was, the Populists agreed, "a solution [to] the race issue." The organ further contended that "the Populists are simply making a practical application of this sentiment."[11] Washington's philosophy of black vocational education largely reflected also what both Populists and non-Populists believed it ought to be. "Make Booker T. Washington manager of negro schools and give him a long tether," an Alabamian suggested. "He would revolutionize our ideas."[12] Populism, then, was a link which connected the ascetic virtues of the Protestant ethic with the Washingtonian belief in social separation of the races. This continuity may be likened to a single thread that stretched across the whole of the Populist biracial experience.

It is one of the ironies of Southern history that Washington's proposals on the race question enhanced his influence as a black spokesman while similar utterances from white Populists were received as revolutionary acts of regional defiance. Both Washington's followers and the Populists had sought to inject a spirit of biracial compromise, but the South cynically brutalized both. Already at a tactical disadvantage, both groups were fated to forfeit their ideals to the point where further compromise meant surrender. Unfortunately, the swelling forces of racism ultimately rendered both philosophies impotent.

EPILOGUE:
FOOTNOTES FROM OUR TIME

The Populist themes that touched such a popular chord in the nineteenth century have persisted to the present day and are shared by several participants of recent Southern political life. Notable among these individuals are such disparate personalities as Lester Maddox and George Wallace, Lyndon Johnson and Jimmy Carter. It should be emphasized that we are still dealing with a dichotomy—a "conservative" and a "liberal" outlook—in modern populism, as in the nineteenth century variety. George Wallace and Jimmy Carter more clearly personify and articulate the lines of cleavage in modern populism than do most of their counterparts, Wallace being the "conservative" and Carter the "liberal," although both men present a picture full of contradictions and changes.[1]

There are some suggestive similarities between the constituencies of the "conservative populism" of Wallace and those of the "liberal populism" of Carter. The Wallace majority has its analogue in the army of the alienated—the blue collar worker, the elderly, the service industry workers—but with few members of minority groups, in contrast to Carter. In Alabama, however, both Wallace and his wife, Lurleen, also governor of Alabama in 1967-68, paradoxically have received significant support from blacks in their gubernatorial races. The 1974 Alabama gubernatorial race is often pointed to as an example of strong black support for Wallace, and indeed it was, despite denials by his critics. However, the black Wallace voters in 1974 came from the rural areas where some local black politicians endorsed Wallace largely for patronage or state aid. In urban areas where the bulk of the black population lives, Wallace received less than 10% of the black vote.[2]

Wallace's commitment to his "conservative populism" has come at a high cost to him. Like the Populists of old, Wallace has been vilified and harassed in his campaigns and has survived an attempted assassination which left him permanently crippled. "We have been heckled, we have been stoned, we have tried to bring a message to the American people," his wife Lurleen recalled of their efforts.[3] Indeed, his gruelling campaigns have come as close to recreating the vilification and hostility experienced by the nineteenth century Populists as any of those of prominent figures in recent Southern history. It is painfully evident that Wallace loves the South; and it is perhaps for this reason that, among Southerners, he has never been completely repudiated. Nationally his appeal among "the working men and women" still haunts the Democratic Party establishment.

Many of the perspectives common to the nineteenth century Populists are still prevalent in today's variety: coalition politics; concern over a burgeoning, federal power structure; anxiety over declining moral prudence, and a disproportionate distribution of power between "haves" and "have nots" or, in the nineteenth century Populist formulation, the "producers" versus the "non-producers."

Perhaps their approach to coalition politics is among the more popular impulses of the modern "liberal" populists, particularly since the New Deal and the Democratic Party's acquisition of the emerging black voter. The roots of the situation lie in the ethnic, racial, and religious makeup of the Democratic Party. First, the Republican Party has not proved to be an effective institutional channel for the expression of the neo-populist position and its constituencies. As of 1976, all the major ethnic and religious groups, except the white Protestants, identify overwhelmingly with the Democratic Party, both nationally and regionally. Approximately 60 percent of the Catholics in the United States, 70 percent of the Jews, and 90 percent of the blacks call themselves Democrats. Even white Protestants divide almost equally between the Democratic and Republican Parties nationally, with each party getting approximately 40 percent. Further, 42 percent of Americans identify themselves as Democrats, while only 21 percent admit to their Republicanism. Because of this factor alone, the normal Democratic vote is basically made up of "have not" groups.

What we are seeing on the current political scene, with the election of a Southern President, Jimmy Carter, a born-again Christian, is not as new or impossible as it may have first appeared. Carter may represent a relatively benign and gentle version of the Populist's evangelical conception of virtue, and he propitiously capitalized on the neo-populist's last ditch hope and plaintive cry for honesty, morality, and simplicity in public life through the election of honest, moral, and simple leaders. Ostensibly, the end result was to accomplish what the nineteenth century Southern Populists had sought to accomplish but failed to achieve. Indeed, Carter admitted that his acceptance speech before the Democratic Convention in New York was in part inspired by a Populist heritage. By dropping such phrases he has invoked all the legends and saints of the Southern Populists, called forth the hoary ghost of Tom Watson and the credo of the biracial legend. In view of his assertion it is incumbent to examine the Southern electorate's support of Carter.

The black vote in the eleven states of the old South in 1976 played a significant role in carrying the region for President Carter. First, let us review some of the highlights in the voter characteristics of the Negro in the modern South. There are, as of 1976, approximately four million registered black voters in the South. Of this number, 70% voted in the 1976 presidential election, an extremely high turnout among a group of people who have not voted in large numbers. In those precincts in which blacks represented over 90 percent of the registered voters, Carter secured between 90-98 percent of the black vote. The large urban centers voted for Carter as well as the rural areas. In Mississippi, Louisiana, and Texas blacks proved to be the deciding factor, the "swing vote," which carried the states for Carter. Approximately 92% of the black vote in the South as a whole went to Carter.[4]

In contrast, approximately 45% of the Caucasian vote in the South as a whole went to Carter. The Southern white vote for Carter was predominantly Baptist, blue collar, and relatively poor economically. Broken down by local or regional units, the voter distribution did not always follow the traditional nineteenth century Populist voting pattern as discussed earlier.[5] However, the result was to accomplish what the Populists had sought but failed to achieve.

It was Andrew Young, a young black Congregationalist minister, who did more than any other individual to persuade blacks to vote for Carter; and Young is the only person in America to whom President Carter has openly acknowledged a political debt. Tom Watson owed the Reverend W. H. Doyle, the black minister who made sixty-three speeches for him in 1892, a debt that was roughly analogous to the one Carter owes Young.

Carter's own life can be similarly compared to Young's. Carter grew up with mostly black playmates in the hamlet of Plains, Georgia, whose most eminent citizen was a black bishop of the African Methodist Episcopal Church. Young, who was born in New Orleans, grew up with mostly white playmates, few of whose parents were as respected or as well-off as his own father, a dentist. Partially as a result of these experiences, both men brought a much more sophisticated perspective to bear on interracial cooperation than did many of their counterparts.

Carter has in some respects paid back the political debt he owes to the black community. Consider the following salient examples: Andrew Young was made Ambassador to the United Nations, despite the fact that he planned and participated in a protest demonstration in 1967 against the Viet Nam War in front of the United Nations building. Furthermore, he is the first black in the job. President Carter further appointed Patricia Roberts Harris, the first black woman to hold Cabinet rank, as head of the Department of Housing and Urban Development. At this stage of his fledgling administration, therefore, Carter's appointments have reflected a biracial tone which is unprecedented. Hopefully, this brief sketch will remind readers that the populist biracial philosophy, whatever its original or present motivations, seems to have visibly returned from the wilderness where it has wandered for some decades after the fierce regional struggles of the last decades of the nineteenth century. But populism has reconquered only a small part of the influence and impact it had on Southern life in the nineteenth century, when theirs was an open voice calling for a working alliance between the two races. What is more important, of course, is the Populist legacy to all Southerners, namely, a world view presented with such brevity and eloquence, such depth and understanding, in the Populist motto: "Equal Rights to All, Special Privileges to None."

APPENDIX

TABLE I
Pearsonian Coefficents of Correlation between Pairs of Selected Variables

	Virginia		North Carolina		South Carolina		Georgia		Florida		Alabama	
	% For Harrison	% For Weaver	% For Harrison	% For Weaver	% For Harrison	% For Weaver	% For Harrison	% For Weaver	% For Harrison	% For Weaver	% For Harrison	% For Weaver
A. % for Harrison (GOP)—1888 Presidential Election	*	.10	*	—48	*	.10	*	—41	*	.29	*	.13
B. % for Weaver (GOP)—1892 Presidential Election	—18	*	—36	*	—18	*	—37	*	—25	*	.07	*
C. % of Population Negro	42	—66	20	—37	—42	—66	.07	—08	.34	—31	—29	.13
D. % of Population in Towns of 2,500 or More	.00	—27	20	—09	.00	—27	.14	—28	.50	—35	.02	.13
E. % of Farms Operated by Owners	.66	.01	—13	—29	66	.01	.18	—22	.06	.30	.25	—26
F. Value of Farmland Per Acre	—31	.17	10	—19	—31	.17	—03	.06	—02	—17	.09	.20

TABLE I (*continued*)

	Mississippi		Louisiana		Arkansas		Texas		Tennessee	
	% For Harrison	% For Weaver	% For Harrison	% For Weaver	% For Harrison	% For Weaver	% For Harrison	% For Weaver	% For Harrison	% For Weaver
A. % for Harrison (GOP)—1888 Presidential Election	*	−20	*		*	−34	*	−34	*	−61
B. % for Weaver (Pop.)—1892 Presidential Election	−32	*			−41	*	38	*	−58	*
C. % of Population Negro	.39	−47	.09		.73	−23	.59	−06	−32	.30
D. % of Population in Towns of 2,500 or More	.09	−31	.08		.22	−01	.14	−20	−01	−10
E. % of Farms Operated by Owners	−33	.27	.19		−64	.25	−10	−13	.24	−23
F. Value of Farmland Per Acre	.50	−40	.39		.56	−25	.08	.03	−13	.06

ªNot on ballot.

TABLE II

*Pearsonian Coefficients of Correlation (by county) between Selected
Variables and Populist Gubernatorial Elections*

| | Virginia | | North Carolina | | South Carolina[a] |
	% For Cocke (Pop.)—1893 Gubernatorial Election	% For Cocke (Pop.)—1897 Lieutenant Gubernatorial Election	% For Exum (Pop.)—1892 Gubernatorial Election	% For Guthrie (Pop.)—1896 Gubernatorial Election	
A. % of Harrison (GOP)—1888 Presidential Election	.42	—03	—30	—54	
B. % for Weaver (Pop.)—1892 Presidential Election	.46	.29	.93	.81	
C. % of Population Negro	—26	—32	.59	.56	
D. % of Population in Towns of 2,500 or More	—35	—23	—02	—02	
E. % of Farms Operated by Owners	.47	.02	—07	—09	
F. Value of Farmland Per Acre	.25	—39	—33	—29	

[a]Not on ballot.

TABLE II (*continued*)

	Louisiana		Arkansas	
	% For Tannehill (Pop.)—1892 Gubernatorial Election	% For Pharr (Pop.)—1896 Gubernatorial Election	% For Baker (Pop.)—1894 Gubernatorial Election	% For Morgan (Pop.)—1898 Gubernatorial Election
A. % for Harrison (GOP)—1888 Presidential Election	—30	.06	—55	—47
B. % for Weaver (Pop.)—1892 Presidential Election	a	a	.78	.73
C. % of Population Negro	—21	—08	—04	.02
D. % of Population Towns of 2,500 or More	—32	—28	—04	—10
E. % of Farms Operated by Owners	.29	—09	.10	.14
F. Value of Farmland Per Acre	—33	—34	—11	—19

aNot on ballot.

TABLE II (*continued*)

	Georgia	Florida	Alabama		Mississippi
	For Hines (Pop.)—1894 Gubernatorial Election	% For Weeks (Pop.)—1896 Gubernatorial Election	% For Kolb (Pop.)—1894 Gubernatorial Election	% For Goodwin (Pop.)—1896 Gubernatorial Election	% For Burkitt (Pop.)—1895 Gubernatorial Election
A. % for Harrison (GOP)—1888 Presidential Election	—03	—33	—11	.06	—42
B. % for Weaver (Pop.)—1892 Presidential Election	—70	.70	.19	.02	—16
C. % of Population Negro	.11	—06	.20	—23	—39
D. % of Population in Towns of 2,500 or More	.22	—28	.02	—23	—43
E. % of Farms Operated by Owners	—40	.59	—13	.08	.02
F. Value of Farmland Per Acre	—01	—48	.05	—14	.02

TABLE II (*continued*)

	Texas	Tennessee	
	% For Nugent (Pop.)—1892 Gubernatorial Election	% For Buchanan (Pop.)—1892 Gubernatorial Election	% For Mims (Pop.)—1894 Gubernatorial Election
A. % for Harrison (GOP)—1888 Presidential Election	—42	—68	—63
B. % for Weaver (Pop.)—1892 Presidential Election	.94	.94	.89
C. % Population Negro	.13	.44	.47
D. % of Population in Towns of 2,500 or More	—21	—04	.04
E. % of Farms Operated by Owners	—22	—21	—16
F. Value of Farmland Per Acre	.07	.17	.25

TABLE III

Pearsonian Coefficients of Correlation between Pairs of Selected Variables (by county) for Virginia

	A	B	C	D	E	F	G	H
A. % for Weaver (GOP)—1888 Presidential Election	*	.05	.39	.06	—14	—05	.22	—20
B. % for Weaver (Pop.)—1892 Presidential Election	.07	*	.31	.30	—38	—35	.24	—33
C. % for Cocke (Pop.)—1893 Gubernatorial Election	.42	.46	*	.35	—26	35	.47	.25
D. % for Cocke (Pop.)—1897 Lieutenant Gubernatorial Election	—03	.29	.32	*	—32	—23	.02	—39
E. % of Population Negro	.47	.12	.29	—02	*	.37	—42	.17
F. % of Population in Towns of 2,500 or More	—18	—38	—43	—25	—09	*	—50	.07
G. % of Farms Operated by Owners	.05	—06	.25	.04	—30	—35	*	.07
H. Value of Farmland Per Acre	—06	—41	—46	—26	—21	.23	.20	o

N=118 counties in the state, 62 with less than 40 percent Negro population.

TABLE IV

Pearsonian Coefficients of Correlation between Pairs of Selected Variables (by county) for North Carolina

	A	B	C	D	E	F	G	H
A. % for Harrison (GOP)—1888 Presidential Election	*	—41	—46	—58	—19	—01	.03	.12
B. % for Weaver (Pop.)—1892 Presidential Election	—36	*	.98	.88	.60	.01	—13	—29
C. % for Exum (Pop.)—1892 Gubernatorial Election	—30	.93	*	.88	.59	—02	—07	—33
D. % for Guthrie (Pop.)—1896 Gubernatorial Election	—54	.81	.78	*	.56	—02	—09	—29
E. % of Population Negro	.20	—37	.40	.28	*	.24	—34	—05
F. % of Population in Towns of 2,500 or More	.20	—09	—10	—11	.25	*	—16	.47
G. % of Farms Operated by Owners	—13	—29	—23	—10	—56	—10	*	.17
H. Value of Farmland Per Acre	.10	—19	—18	—21	—05	.40	—18	*

N=97 counties in the state, 61 with less than 40 percent Negro population.

TABLE V

Pearsonian Coefficients of Correlation between Pairs of Selected Variables (by county) for South Carolina

	A	B	C	D	E	F	G
A. % for Harrison (GOP)—1888 Presidential Election	*	.10	—85	—66	.01	.28	—19
B. % for Weaver (Pop.)—1892	—18	*	.41	—84	—60	—18	—13
C. % for Tillman (Prog.)—1890 Gubernatorial Election	—74	.31	*	.30	.15	—FV	.46
D. % of Population Negro	.42	—66	—49	*	.32	.05	.00
E. % of Population in Towns of 2,500 or More	.00	—27	—18	.09	*	—59	.78
F. % of Farms Operated by Owners	.66	.01	—45	—02	—20	*	—75
G. Value of Farmland Per Acre	—31	.17	.32	—20	.34	—52	*

N=45 counties in the state, 9 with less than 40 percent Negro population.

TABLE VI

Pearsonian Coefficients of Correlation between Pairs of Selected Variables (by county) for Georgia

	A	B	C	D	E	F	G
A. % for Harrison (GOP)—1888 Presidential Election	*	—41	—06	—21	—26	.19	—04
B. % for Weaver (Pop.)—1892 Presidential Election	—37	*	.74	.10	.22	—51	.14
C. % for Hines (Pop.)—1894 Gubernatorial Election	—03	.70	*	—11	—22	—40	—01
D. % of Population Negro	.07	—08	—15	*	.32	—18	.11
E. % of Population in Towns of 2,500 or More	.14	—28	—32	.12	*	—06	.24
F. % of Farms Operated by Owners	.18	—22	—17	.53	—02	*	—36
G. Value of Farmland Per Acre	—03	.06	—04	—06	.25	—20	*

N=137 counties in the state, 55 with less than 40 percent Negro population.

TABLE VII

Pearsonian Coefficients of Correlation between Pairs of Selected Variables (by county) for Florida

	A	B	C	D	E	F	G
A. % for Harrison (GOP)—1888 Presidential Election	*	.29	.34	.55	.36	—19	.10
B. % for Weaver (Pop.)—1892 Presidential Election	—25	*	.76	—07	—30	.27	—39
C. % for Weeks (Pop.)—1896 Gubernatorial Election	—33	.70	*	—06	—28	.59	—48
D. % of Population Negro	.34	—31	—30	*	.23	—01	—36
E. % of Population in Towns of 2,500 or More	.50	—35	—29	.19	*	—28	.03
F. % of Farms Operated by Owners	.06	.30	.38	—57	.02	*	—25
G. Value of Farmland Per Acre	—02	.17	—29	—43	—00	.10	*

N=45 counties in the state, 26 with less than 40 percent Negro population.

TABLE VIII

Pearsonian Coefficients of Correlation between Pairs of Selected Variables (by county) for Alabama

	A	B	C	D	E	F	G	H	I
A. % for Harrison (GOP)—1888 Presidential Election	*	.13	.22	—29	—19	—18	—19	—03	.22
B. % for Weaver (Pop.)—1892 Presidential Election	.07	*	.10	.19	.09	.18	—06	—21	.03
C. % for Kolb (Pop.)—1892 Presidential Election	.30	—01	*	.10	.14	.16	—36	—24	.10
D. % for Kolb (Pop.)—1894 Gubernatorial Election	—11	—19	—07	*	.08	.20	.02	—13	.05
E. % for Goodwyn (Pop.)—1896 Gubernatorial Election	.06	.02	.20	—00	*	—23	—23	.08	—14
F. % of Population Negro	—29	.13	—59	—00	—33	*	.25	—34	.52
G. % of Population in Towns of 2,500 or More	.02	.13	—35	.30	—15	.12	*	—35	.52
H. % of Farms Operated by Owners	.25	—26	.42	—04	.22	—75	—02	*	.70
I. Value of Farmland Per Acre	.09	.20	—34	—03	—15	.30	.62	—45	*

N=66 counties in the state, 34 counties with less than 40 percent Negro population.

TABLE IX

Pearsonian Coefficients of Correlation between Pairs of Selected Variables (by county) for Mississippi

	A	B	C	D	E	F	G
A. % for Harrison (GOP)—1888 Presidential Election	*	—20	—49	.09	.23	.03	.14
B. % for Weaver (Pop.)—1892 Presidential Election	—23	*	.76	.01	—46	—61	.33
C. % for Burkitt (Pop.)—1895 Gubernatorial Election	—42	.85	*	—16	—39	—43	.02
D. % of Population Negro	.39	—47	—62	*	.11	.07	.36
E. % of Population in Towns of 2,500 or More	.09	—31	—21	.11	*	.34	—00
F. % of Farms Operated by Owners	—33	.27	.48	—86	—04	*	—69
G. Value of Farmland Per Acre	.50	—40	—55	.73	.03	—73	*

N=75 counties in the state, 25 with less than 40 percent Negro population.

TABLE X

Pearsonian Coefficients of Correlation between Pairs of Selected Variables (by county) for Louisiana

	A	B	C	D	E	F	G	H
A. % for Harrison (GOP)—1888 Presidential Election	*		—50	—27	.14	.52	.03	.58
B. % for Weaver (Pop.)—1892 Presidential Election	a	*	a	a	a	a	a	a
C. % for Tannehill (Pop.)—1892 Gubernatorial Election	—30	a	*	.56	—21	—32	.29	—33
D. % for Pharr (Pop.)—1896 Gubernatorial Election	.06	a	.39	*	—08	—28	—09	—34
E. % of Population Negro	.09	a	—47	—53	*	.10	—32	.14
F. % of Population in Towns of 2,500 or More	.08	a	—17	.00	—12	*	—15	.97
G. % of Farms Operated by Owners	.19	a	.33	.49	—82	.07	*	—19
H. Value of Farmland Per Acre	.39	a	—31	—05	—01	.73	.07	*

N=59 parishes in the state, 15 with less than 40 percent Negro population.

TABLE XI
Pearsonian Coefficients of Correlation between Pairs of Selected Variables (by county) for Arkansas

	A	B	C	D	E	F	G	H	I	J
A. % for Harrison (GOP)—1888 Presidential Election	*	—34	.33	.43	—45	—39	.28	.18	—04	.12
B. % for Weaver (Pop.)—1892 Presidential Election	—41	*	.15	.12	.79	.73	.08	—02	.94	—11
C. % for Norwood (Union Labor)—1888 Gubernatorial Election	.64	—06	*	.88	.23	.20	.03	—03	.01	—14
D. % for Fizer (Union Labor)—Union Labor)Gubernatorial Election	.73	—12	.88	*	.18	.12	.03	.10	—01	.01
E. % for Barker (Pop.)—1894 Gubernatorial Election	—55	.78	—11	—17	*	.87	.04	—04	.10	—11
F. % for Morgan (Pop.)—1898 Gubernatorial Election	—47	.73	—06	—14	.87	*	.02	.10	.14	—19
G. % of Population Negro	.73	—23	.46	.56	.40	—34	*	—02	—13	—15
H. % of Population in Towns of 2,500 or More	.22	—01	.14	.06	—04	—10	.06	*	—02	.36
I. % of Farms Operated by Owners	—64	.25	—42	—55	.39	.37	—73	—07	*	—57
J. Value of Farmland Per Acre	.56	—25	.27	.40	—34	—31	.48	.27	—76	*

N=95 counties in the state, 52 with less than 40 percent Negro population.

TABLE XII

Pearsonian Coefficients of Correlation between Pairs of Selected Variables (by county) for Texas

	A	B	C	D	E	F	G	H	I
A. % for Harrison (GOP)—1888 Presidential Election	*	—34	—63	—30	—38	.36	.18	.08	.04
B. % for Weaver (Pop.)—1892 Presidential Election	—38	*	.27	.29	.94	.09	—20	—20	.07
C. % for Hogg (Prog.)—1890 Gubernatorial Election	—75	.CB	*	.41	.35	—41	—41	.07	—06
D. % for Railroad Commission 1890	—35	.41·	.43	*	.32	—22	—26	.09	—04
E. % for Nugent (Pop.)—1892 Gubernatorial Election	—42	.94	.37	.33	*	.13	—21	—22	.07
F. % of Population Negro	.59	—06	.59	—28	—03	*	.23	—41	.40
G. % of Population in Towns of 2,500 or More	.14	—20	—11	—23	—21	.18	*	—22	.40
H. % of Farms Operated by Owners	—10	—13	.09	.15	—15	—47	—22	*	—62
I. Value of Farmland Per Acre	.08	.03	.09	—06	—03	.32	.38	—62	*

N=227 counties in state, 202 with less than 40 percent Negro population.

TABLE XIII

Pearsonian Coefficients of Correlation between Pairs of Selected Variables (by county) for Tennessee

	A	B	C	D	E	F	G	H	I
A. % for Harrison (GOP)—1888 Presidential Election	*	—61	—1.00	—71	—67	—35	.03	.20	—15
B. % for Weaver (Pop.)—1892	—58	*	.60	.94	.89	.36	—11	—22	.08
C. % for Taylor (Prog.)—1888 Gubernatorial Election	—99	.57	*	.70	.65	.33	—03	—09	.12
D. % for Buchanan (Prog.)—1892 Gubernatorial Election	—68	.94	.67	*	.92	.44	—04	—21	.17
E. % for Mims (Pop.)—1894 Gubernatorial Election	—63	.89	.62	.92	*	.47	.04	—16	.25
F. % of Population Negro	—32	.30	.34	.35	.41	*	.36	—36	.65
G. % of Population Negro of 2,500 or More	—01	—10	.01	—01	.04	.41	*	.03	.59
H. % of Farms Operated by Owners	.24	—23	—27	—22	—22	—66	—18	*	—16
I. Value of Farmland Per Acre	—13	.06	.10	.16	.23	.44	.56	—14	*

N=96 counties in the state, 87 with less than 40 percent Negro population.

TABLE XIV

Voting and Negro Population Characteristics for the North
Carolina Congressional Election of 1896*

	Total Vote	Populist Vote	Percentage Populist in Total Vote	Negro Population	Percentage Negro in Total Population
FIRST DISTRICT					
Beaufort	4,636	2,647	57.09	9,203	43.7
Camden	1,141	646	56.61	2,320	40.9
Carteret	2,231	1,094	49.03	2,297	21.2
Chowan	1,934	1,211	62.61	5,156	56.2
Currituck	1,387	620	44.70	2,016	29.9
Dare	877	473	53.93	406	10.8
Gates	1,904	1,046	54.93	4,713	46.0
Hertford	2,677	1,827	68.24	7,944	57.4
Hyde	1,864	993	53.27	3,941	44.3
Martin	3,034	1,608	52.99	7,383	48.5
Pamlico	1,491	990	66.39	2,379	33.3
Pasquotank	2,548	1,688	66.24	5,546	53.2
Perquimans	1,676	1,007	60.08	4,574	49.2
Pitt	5,593	3,133	56.01	12,327	48.3
Tyrrell	788	480	60.91	1,225	20.0
Washington	1,792	1,261	70.36	5,238	51.4
	35,573	20,724	58.25	76,668	41.4**
SECOND DISTRICT					
Bertie	3,855	216	5.60	11,291	58.9
Edgecomb	4,886	370	7.57	15,599	64.7
Greene	2,217	202	9.11	4,758	47.4
Halifax	6,216	205	3.29	19,293	66.7
Lenoir	3,348	291	8.69	6,362	42.8
Northampton	4,203	144	3.42	12,018	56.6
Warren	3,336	61	1.82	13,480	69.6
Wayne	5,408	438	8.09	10,984	42.1
Wilson	3,979	811	20.38	7,760	41.6
	37,448	2,738	7.31	101,454	41.2**

TABLE XIV (*continued*)

	Total Vote	Populist Vote	Percentage Populist in Total Vote	Negro Population	Percentage Negro in Total Population
THIRD DISTRICT					
Bladen	2,878	1,522	52.88	8,117	48.4
Craven	4,800	3,078	64.12	13,358	65.1
Cumberland	4,717	2,834	60.08	12,341	45.2
Duplin	3,581	2,043	57.05	7,087	37.9
Harnett	2,738	1,480	54.05	4,220	30.8
Jones	1,512	849	56.15	3,518	47.5
Moore	4,159	2,454	59.00	6,479	31.6
Onslow	2,178	1,011	46.41	2,911	28.3
Sampson	3,962	2,718	68.60	9,316	36.4
	30,255	17,989	59.45	67,577	41.2**
FOURTH DISTRICT					
Chatham	4,221	2,525	59.81	8,199	32.3
Franklin	5,002	2,750	54.97	10,335	49.0
Johnston	5,284	2,172	41.10	7,322	26.9
Nash	4,505	2,938	65.21	8,521	41.2
Randolph	5,215	2,939	56.35	3,347	13.3
Vance	3,079	2,033	66.02	11,143	63.4
Wake	10,076	5,620	55.77	23,109	47.0
	37,382	20,977	56.11	71,976	33.8**
FIFTH DISTRICT					
Alamance	4,647	119	2.56	5,583	30.6
Caswell	3,065	6	.19	9,389	58.6
Durham	4,349	36	.82	7,329	40.6
Granville	4,447	155	3.48	12,360	50.5
Guilford	6,989	75	1.07	8,223	29.3
Orange	2,979	67	2.24	5,242	35.1
Rockingham	5,115	40	.78	10,164	40.1
Stokes	3,522	10	.28	2,813	16.4
	35,113	508	1.44	61,103	37.6**
SIXTH DISTRICT					
Anson	3,204	1,547	48.28	9,789	48.9
Brunswick	2,141	1,323	61.79	4,761	43.7
Columbus	3,169	1,752	55.28	6,052	33.9

TABLE XIV (*continued*)

	Total Vote	Populist Vote	Percentage Populist in Total Vote	Negro Population	Percentage Negro in Total Population
SIXTH DISTRICT					
(continued)					
Mecklenburg	8,700	4,378	50.32	19,526	45.8
New Hanover	5,427	3,217	59.27	13,935	58.0
Pender	2,436	1,363	55.95	6,546	52.3
Richmond	4,674	2,859	61.16	12,959	54.1
Robeson	5,777	3,622	62.69	14,672	46.6
Union	3,758	1,990	52.95	5,547	26.1
	39,286	22,051	56.12	93,777	45.4**
SEVENTH DISTRICT					
Cabarrus	3,240	1,867	57.62	5,459	30.1
Catawba	3,647	1,949	53.44	2,616	14.0
Davidson	4,432	2,611	58.91	3,528	16.3
Davie	2,090	1,491	71.33	2,852	24.5
Iredell	4,889	2,430	49.70	5,939	23.3
Lincoln	2,398	1,292	53.87	2,558	20.3
Montgomery	2,311	1,453	62.87	2,257	20.1
Rowan	4,519	2,089	46.22	6,980	28.9
Stanly	1,842	855	46.41	1,507	12.4
Yadkin	2,590	1,632	63.01	1,368	9.9
	31,958	17,669	55.28	35,064	19.9**

*United States Department of Commerce, *Bureau of Census, Negro Population, 1790–1915,* 784–785; North Carolina Department of Archives and History, ''North Carolina Congressional Election Returns, 1896.'' These figures were tabulated from a number of sources including the official returns, as a part of the University of Michigan's Political Consortium project to gather and tabulate state election returns.

**All district totals of Negro population are expressed as arithmetic means.

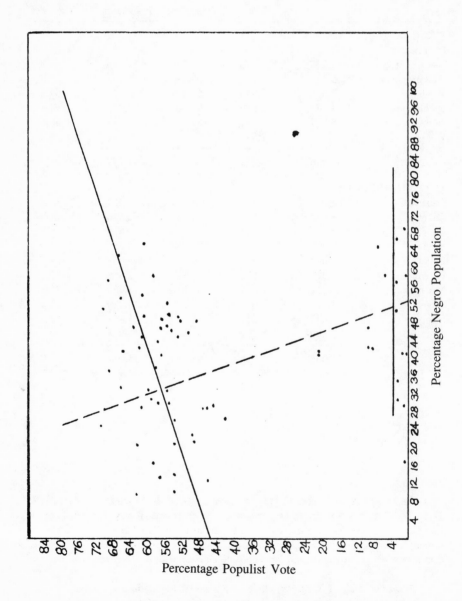

Figure 1. Relationship Between Negro Density and Populism in the
North Carolina Congressional Election of 1896.

TABLE XV

Voting and Negro Population Characteristics for the
Alabama Congressional Election of 1896*

	Total Vote	Populist Vote	Percentage Populist in Total Vote	Negro Population	Percentage Negro in Total Population
THIRD DISTRICT					
Barbour	4,518	463	10.24	21,442	61.4
Bullock	2,681	16	.59	21,005	77.6
Coffee	1,619	872	53.86	1,933	15.9
Dale	2,532	1,157	45.69	3,358	19.5
Geneva	1,321	802	60.71	1,026	9.6
Henry	3,801	995	26.17	8,809	35.5
Lee	3,268	422	12.91·	16,497	57.5
Russell	2,444	32	1.30	18,279	75.9
	22,184	4,759	21.45	92,369	44.1**
FIFTH DISTRICT					
Autauga	1,648	399**	24.21	8,418	63.2
Chambers	3,119	1,050	33.66	13,858	52.7
Clay	1,894	895	47.25	1,704	10.8
Coosa	1,954	1,192	61.00	5,354	33.7
Elmore	3,250	1,965	60.46	10,288	47.3
Lowndes	3,679	272	7.39	26,985	85.5
Macon	1,337	268	20.04	14,188	76.9
Randolph	2,075	870	41.92	3,305	19.2
Tallapoosa	3,373	1,831	54.28	8,508	33.4
	22,329	8,742	39.15	92,608	49.1***
SEVENTH DISTRICT					
Cherokee	2,431	1,345	55.32	2,803	13.7
Cullman	1,738	710	40.85	38	0.3
Dekalb	2,949	305	10.34	1,204	5.7
Etowah	2,691	863	32.06	3,755	17.1
Franklin	1,591	531	33.37	1,160	10.9
Marshall	2,476	1,128	45.55	1,279	6.8
St. Clair	2,283	1,228	53.78	3,050	17.6
Winston	1,074	58	5.40	36	0.5
	17,233	6,168	35.79	13,325	9.0***

*Department of Commerce, *Bureau of Census, Negro Population, 1790–1915,* 776;
Secretary of State, *Official Returns,* 55th Congress, 1896 Congressional Election.

**Democrat affiliated with Populist.

***All district totals of Negro population are expressed as arithmetic means.

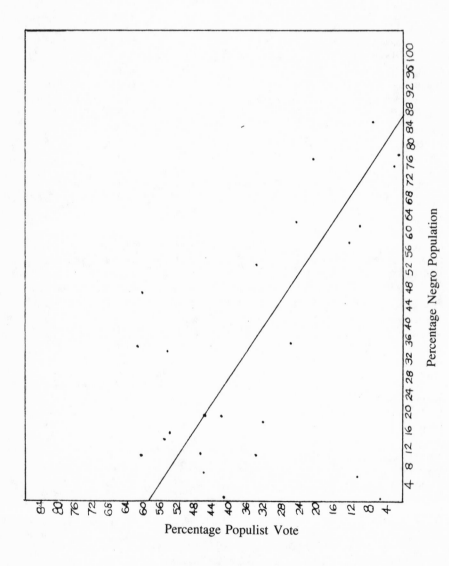

Figure 2. Relationship Between Negro Density and Populism in the
Alabama Congressional Election of 1896.

TABLE XVI

Voting and Negro Population Characteristics for the
Tennessee Congressional Election of 1896*

	Total Vote	Populist Vote	Percentage Populist in Total Vote	Negro Population	Percentage Negro in Total Population
THIRD DISTRICT					
Monroe	3,248	3	.09	1,247	8.1
Hamilton	8,109	43	.53	17,717	33.1
Warren	2,979	3	.10	2,011	14.0
Franklin	3,382	82	2.42	3,570	18.9
Meigs	1,371	2	.14	698	10.1
	19,089	133	.69	25,243	12.8**
FIFTH DISTRICT					
Cannon	2,053	2	.09	952	9.4**
SIXTH DISTRICT					
Davidson	13,023	95	.72	41,315	38.2**
SEVENTH DISTRICT					
Williamson	4,465	411	9.20	10,084	38.3
Maury	6,580	385	5.85	15,910	41.7
Giles	6,327	372	5.87	12,320	35.2
Lawrence	2,517	7	.27	779	6.3
Wayne	2,243	42	1.87	884	7.7
Lewis	522	26	4.98	252	6.3
Hickman	2,523	219	8.68	2,744	18.9
Dickson	2,790	334	11.97	2,101	15.4
	27,967	1,796	6.42	45,074	21.2**
EIGHTH DISTRICT					
Henry	4,563	125	2.73	5,853	27.8
Benton	2,235	123	5.50	617	5.5
Perry	1,568	123	7.84	670	8.6
Decatur	1,881	12	.63	1,304	14.5
Hardin	3,506	5	.23	2,401	13.6
McNairy	2,975	69	2.31	1,881	12.1
Henderson	3,346	6	.08	2,365	14.5
Madison	4,716	323	6.84	14,669	48.1
Carroll	4,523	289	6.38	5,664	24.0
Chester	1,690	167	9.88	1,776	19.6
	31,003	1,239	3.99	37,200	18.8**

TABLE XVI (*continued*)

	Total Vote	Populist Vote	Percentage Populist in Total Vote	Negro Population	Percentage Negro in Total Population
NINTH DISTRICT					
Weakley	5,895	2,199	37.30	4,520	15.6
Gibson	6,181	2,711	43.86	9,337	26.0
Crockett	2,561	933	36.43	4,186	27.6
Haywood	3,024	743	24.57	15,569	66.1
Lauderdale	3,012	1,094	36.32	7,810	41.6
Dyer	3,369	1,174	34.84	4,690	23.6
Obion	4,863	1,733	35.63	4,333	15.9
Lake	947	127	13.41	1,075	20.3
	29,852	10,714	35.89	51,520	29.5**
TENTH DISTRICT					
Hardeman	3,700	156	4.21	8,787	41.8
Fayette	3,725	54	1.44	20,492	71.0
Shelby	10,430	225	2.15	61,613	54.7
Tipton	4,551	491	10.78	11,770	48.5
	22,406	926	4.13	102,662	54.0**

*United States Department of Commerce, *Bureau of Census, Negro Population, 1790–1915,* 787–788; *Tennessee Election Returns,* November 3, 1896.

**All district totals of Negro populations are expressed as arithmetic means.

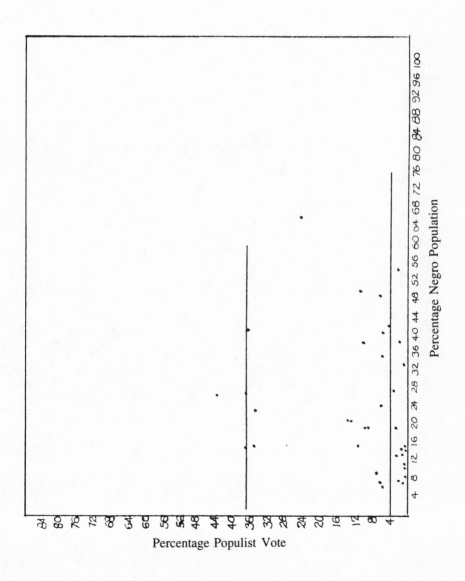

Figure 3. Relationship Between Negro Density and Populism in the
Tennessee Congressional Election of 1896.

TABLE XVII

*Voting and Negro Population Characteristics for the
Mississippi Congressional Election of 1896**

	Total Vote	Populist Vote	Percentage Populist in Total Vote	Negro Population	Percentage Negro in Total Population
FIRST DISTRICT					
Alcorn					26.8
Itawamba					8.4
Lee					37.6
Lowndes					77.8
Monroe					63.0
Oktibbeha					67.4
Prentiss					20.8
Tishomingo					10.7
	8,398	742	8.83	67,450	39.6**
SECOND DISTRICT					
Benton					46.5
DeSota					71.2
LaFayette					43.1
Marshall					62.6
Panola					54.7
Tallahatchie					64.1
Tate					55.9
Tippah					22.6
Union					25.6
	9,884	1,472	14.89	91,917	50.8**
FOURTH DISTRICT					
Calhoun					23.2
Carroll					56.5
Chickasaw					57.3
Choctaw					24.3
Clay					69.8
Grenada					74.0
Kemper					56.0
Montgomery					48.5
Noxubee					82.8
Pontotoc					29.1
Webster					24.7
Yalobusha					53.8
	11,737	3,086	26.29	108,095	50.0**

TABLE XVII (*continued*)

	Total Vote	Populist Vote	Percentage Populist in Total Vote	Negro Population	Percentage Negro in Total Population
FIFTH DISTRICT					
Attala					42.5
Clarke					51.2
Holmes					77.1
Jasper					49.3
Lauderdale					49.3
Leake					33.9
Neshoba					19.5
Newton					37.0
Scott					39.3
Smith					16.1
Wayne					40.9
Yazoo					76.1
	13,051	2,218	16.99	115,026	44.3**
SIXTH DISTRICT					
Adams					76.4
Amite					58.2
Covington					35.8
Greene					23.9
Hancock					30.2
Harrison					27.2
Jckson					30.5
Jones					15.0
Lawrence					49.3
Marion					31.5
Pearl-River					22.2
Perry					28.9
Pike					50.1
	10,477	2,683	25.60	80,757	36.8**
SEVENTH DISTRICT					
Claiborne					75.6
Copiah					51.6
Franklin					47.3
Hinds					72.2
Jefferson					81.0
Lincoln					42.4
Madison					77.9

TABLE XVII (continued)

	Total Vote	Populist Vote	Percentage Populist in Total Vote	Negro Population	Percentage Negro in Total Population
SEVENTH DISTRICT (continued)					
Rankin					58.1
Simpson					38.6
	8,647	898	10.37	116,437	60.0**

*United States Department of Commerce, *Bureau of Census, Negro Population, 1790–1915,* 783–784; Office of the Mississippi Secretary of State, *Vote of Mississippi.* November 16, 1896. The vote of Mississippi during this period was expressed as a condensed statement of district totals.

**All district totals of Negro population are expressed as arithmetic means.

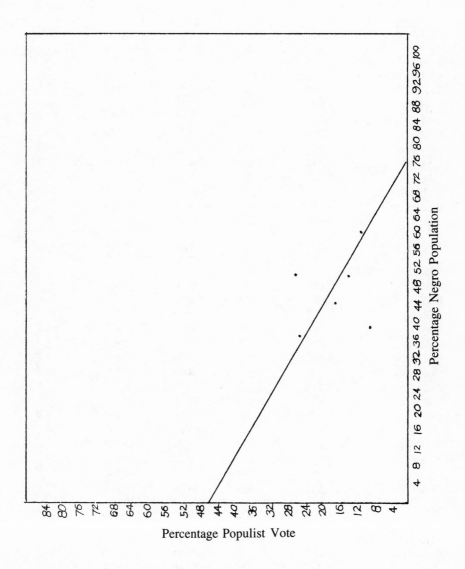

Figure 4. Relationship Between Negro Density and Populism in the Mississippi Congressional Election of 1896.

TABLE XVIII

Voting and Negro Population Characteristics for the
Georgia Congressional Election of 1896*

	Total Vote	Populist Vote	Percentage Populist in Total Vote	Negro Population	Percentage Negro in Total Population
FIRST DISTRICT					
Bryan	454	16	3.52	2,687	48.7
Bulloch	1,869	465	24.87	4,689	34.2
Burke	1,772	125	7.05	22,680	79.6
Chatham	4,859	253	5.20	34,757	60.2
Effingham	689	111	16.11	2,210	39.5
Emanuel	1,498	485	32.37	5,306	36.1
Liberty	1,204	219	18.18	8,673	67.3
McIntosh	789	2	.25	5,212	80.6
Screven	1,510	614	40.66	7,507	52.0
Tattnall	1,530	378	24.70	3,115	30.4
	16,174	2,672	16.52	96,836	52.9**
SECOND DISTRICT					
Baker	607	65	10.70	4,549	76.2
Berrien	955	196	20.52	2,417	22.6
Calhoun	772	51	6.60	6,199	73.5
Clay	907	179	19.73	4,815	61.6
Colquitt	667	259	38.83	477	9.9
Decatur	1,890	392	20.74	10,811	54.2
Dougherty	521	24	4.60	10,231	83.8
Early	1,174	372	31.68	6,122	62.5
Miller	484	159	32.85	1,574	36.8
Mitchell	848	234	27.59	6,106	56.0
Quitman	499	74	14.82	3,050	68.2
Randolph	1,157	177	15.29	9,473	62.0
Terrell	1,387	171	12.32	9,169	63.2
Thomas	1,453	284	19.54	17,450	57.5
Worth	1,181	398	33.70	8,412	31.0
	14,502	3,035	20.92	100,855	54.6**
THIRD DISTRICT					
Crawford	455	94	20.65	5,156	55.3
Dooly	1,402	458	32.66	8,914	49.1
Houston	1,067	186	17.43	16,341	75.6
Lee	451	161	35.69	7,642	83.5
Macon	871	283	32.49	9,181	63.3

TABLE XVIII (*continued*)

	Total Vote	Populist Vote	Percentage Populist in Total Vote	Negro Population	Percentage Negro in Total Population
THIRD DISTRICT					
(continued)					
Pulaski	927	172	18.55	10,001	60.4
Schley	630	223	35.39	3,205	58.9
Stewart	852	212	24.88	11,484	73.2
Sumter	1,503	390	25.94	15,098	68.3
Taylor	594	354	59.59	4,068	46.9
Twiggs	527	108	20.49	5,447	66.5
Webster	433	201	46.42	3,272	57.5
Wilcox	884	254	28.73	3,155	39.5
	10,596	3,096	29.21	102,964	61.3**
SIXTH DISTRICT					
Baldwin	977	424	43.39	9,343	64.0
Bibb	2,626	665	25.32	23,336	55.1
Butts	1,002	412	41.11	5,398	51.1
Fayette	980	386	39.38	3,074	35.2
Henry	1,259	503	39.95	7,591	46.8
Jones	890	314	35.28	8,778	69.1
Monroe	1,342	546	39.22	12,516	65.4
Pike	1,766	755	42.75	8,077	49.6
Spalding	881	166	18.84	7,281	55.5
Upson	1,209	525	43.42	6,123	50.2
	12,932	4,696	36.31	91,517	54.2**
SEVENTH DISTRICT					
Bartow	1,868	287	15.36	6,041	29.3
Catoosa	747	194	25.97	636	11.7
Chattooga	1,483	348	23.46	1,998	17.8
Cobb	2,285	412	18.03	6,774	30.4
Dade	513	105	20.46	1,093	19.2
Floyd	3,275	212	6.47	10,414	36.7
Gordon	1,426	314	22.01	1,727	13.5
Haralson	1,274	640	50.23	1,117	9.9
Murray	931	212	22.77	484	5.7
Paulding	1,654	800	48.36	1,505	12.6
Polk	1,477	477	23.49	4,654	31.1
Walker	1,689	168	9.94	1,932	14.5
Whitfield	1,440	217	15.06	1,930	14.9
	20,062	4,256	21.21	40,305	19.0**

TABLE XVIII (*continued*)

	Total Vote	Populist Vote	Percentage Populist in Total Vote	Negro Population	Percentage Negro in Total Population
EIGHTH DISTRICT					
Clarke	1,194	81	6.78	8,111	9.8
Elbert	1,659	181	10.91	7,884	51.3
Franklin	1,516	696	45.91	3,298	22.5
Greene	1,665	545	32.73	11,719	68.7
Hart	1,352	509	37.64	2,957	27.2
Jasper	785	55	7.00	8,487	61.1
Madison	884	118	13.34	3,662	33.2
Morgan	1,518	87	5.73	10,997	68.6
Oconee	917	316	34.46	3,832	49.7
Oglethorpe	1,426	104	7.29	11,264	66.5
Putnam	459	17	3.70	10,903	73.5
Welkes	1,384	253	18.28	12,464	48.4
	14,759	2,962	20.06	95,578	48.4**
NINTH DISTRICT					
Banks	1,147	303	26.41	1,563	18.3
Cherokee	1,597	463	28.99	1,508	9.8
Dawson	634	58	9.14	259	4.6
Fannin	1,418	8	.56	112	1.3
Forsyth	840	231	27.50	1,288	11.5
Gilmer	1,214	17	1.40	69	0.8
Gwinnett	2,424	996	41.08	2,996	15.1
Habersham	1,093	76	6.95	1,589	13.7
Hall	1,886	331	17.55	2,767	15.3
Jackson	2,669	899	33.68	5,396	28.1
Lumpkin	904	41	4.53	414	6.0
Milton	735	246	33.46	672	10.8
Pickens	1,140	26	2.28	349	4.3
Rabun	509	7	1.37	166	3.0
Towns	642	5	.77	74	1.8
Union	1,010	72	7.12	165	2.1
White	523	147	28.10	662	10.8
	20,385	3,926	19.25	20,049	9.3**
TENTH DISTRICT					
Columbia	884	619	70.02	8,038	71.3
Glascock	483	320	66.25	1,168	31.4
Hancock	1,153	203	17.60	12,410	72.4

TABLE XVIII (*continued*)

	Total Vote	Populist Vote	Percentage Populist in Total Vote	Negro Population	Percentage Negro in Total Population
TENTH DISTRICT					
(continued)					
Jefferson	1,733	1,008	58.16	10,763	62.5
Lincoln	853	634	74.32	3,673	59.8
McDuffie	822	667	81.14	5,522	62.8
Richmond	5,849	702	12.00	22,818	50.5
Taliaferro	685	472	68.90	4,827	66.2
Warren	1,009	747	74.03	6,756	61.7
Washington	2,565	1,202	46.86	14,925	59.1
Wilkinson	1,188	531	44.69	5,214	48.4
	17,224	7,105	41.25	97,114	58.7**
ELEVENTH DISTRICT					
Appling	1,106	593	53.61	2,462	28.4
Brooks	846	125	14.77	7,637	54.6
Camden	412	123	32.52	4,137	67.0
Charlton	No returns listed for any party				
Clinch	523	146	27.91	2,360	35.5
Coffee	1,333	810	60.76	3,858	36.8
Dodge	939	395	42.06	5,309	46.4
Echols	228	108	47.36	1,020	33.1
Glynn	1,008	162	16.07	7,741	57.7
Irwin	1,044	380	36.39	2,075	32.9
Johnson	592	287	48.47	1,456	23.8
Laurens	1,299	645	49.65	6,093	44.3
Lowndes	1,344	598	44.49	7,974	52.8
Montgomery	1,051	488	46.43	3,658	39.6
Pierce	672	250	37.20	1,983	31.1
Telfair	945	125	13.22	2,335	42.6
Wayne	946	511	54.01	2,195	29.3
Ware	900	262	29.11	3,619	41.1
	15,188	6,019	39.62	65,912	41.0**

*United States Department of Commerce, *Bureau of Census, Negro Population, 1790–1915,* 778-780; *Atlanta Constitution,* November 4, 1896; *Georgia Consolidated Election Returns,* 55th Congress, 1896.

**All district totals of Negro population are expressed as arithmetic means.

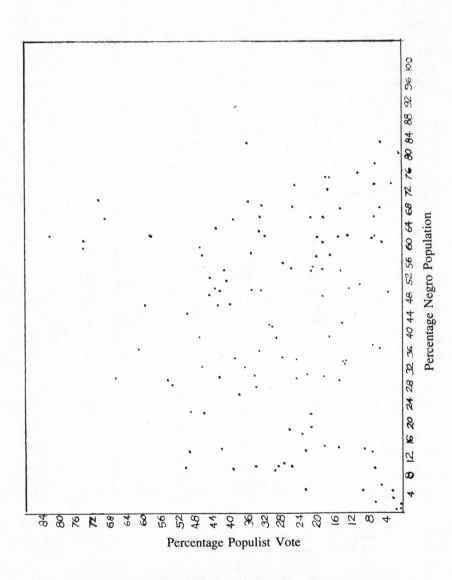

Figure 5. Relationship Between Negro Density and Populism in the
Georgia Congressional Election of 1896.

TABLE XIX

*Voting and Negro Population Characteristics for the
Texas Congressional Election of 1896**

	Total Vote	Populist Vote	Percentage Populist in Total Vote	Negro Population	Percentage Negro in Total Population
FIRST DISTRICT					
Chambers	521	92	17.85	757	33.8
Freestone	3,246	1,313	40.44	6,675	41.8
Grimes	4,587	2,392	52.14	11,664	54.7
Harris	11,850	5,033	42.47	13,522	36.3
Leon	3,067	1,508	49.16	5,377	38.8
Madison	1,716	847	49.35	2,070	24.3
Montgomery	2,779	1,209	43.50	5,488	46.6
Trinity	1,615	639	39.56	1,903	24.9
Walker	2,490	1,050	42.16	7,232	56.2
Waller	2,638	1,105	41.88	6,703	61.6
	34,509	15,189	44.01	61,391	41.9+
SECOND DISTRICT					
Anderson	4,769	796	16.69	9,502	45.4
Angelina	2,190	823	37.57	601	9.5
Cherokee	4,063	1,522	37.46	7,705	33.4
Hardin	908	122	13.43	967	24.4
Harrison	3,807	411	10.79	18,191	68.1
Houston	4,500	1,828	40.62	8,467	43.7
Jasper	1,133	428	37.77	2,378	42.5
Jefferson	2,035	184	9.04	2,218	37.9
Nacogdoches	3,829	1,943	50.74	4,257	26.6
Newton	946	204	21.56	1,558	33.5
Orange	1,263	62	4.90	829	17.4
Panola	2,840	598	21.05	9,204	44.3
Polk	2,453	841	34.28	3,837	37.1
Sabine	960	520	54.16	1,084	21.8
San Augustine	1,523	800	52.52	2,131	31.9
San Jacinto	1,670	167	10.00	4,328	58.8
Shelby	3,223	1,125	34.90	2,954	22.6
Tyler	2,062	448	21.72	2,392	22.0
	43,214	12,822	29.67	82,603	34.5+

TABLE XIX (*continued*)

	Total Vote	Populist Vote	Percentage Populist in Total Vote	Negro Population	Percentage Negro in Total Population
THIRD DISTRICT					
Gregg	1,865	540	28.95	5,349	56.9
Henderson	3,197	1,510	47.23	2,988	24.3
Hunt	8,344	3,074	36.84	2,953	9.3
Rains	1,058	604	47.08	415	10.6
Rockwall	1,517	380	25.04	216	3.6
Rusk	4,334	2,110	48.68	7,624	41.1
Smith	6,569	3,117	47.45	12,690	44.8
Upshur	2,737	1,245	45.48	3,929	30.9
Van Zandt	4,522	2,216	49.00	1,098	6.8
Wood	3,418	1,555	45.49	3,249	23.3
	37,561	16,351	43.53	40,511	25.2+
FOURTH DISTRICT					
Bowie	4,496	1,477	32.85	7,591	37.5
Camp	1,426	666	46.70	3,296	49.8
Cass	4,226	2,018	47.75	8,512	37.7
Delta	2,225	1,271	57.12	728	8.0
Franklin	1,421	508	35.74	819	12.6
Hopkins	4,496	2,183	48.55	2,838	13.8
Lamar	8,015	2,259	28.18	9,378	25.1
Marion	1,991	594	29.83	6,989	64.4
Morris	1,499	567	37.82	2,610	39.7
Red River	5,112	1,151	22.51	6,628	30.9
Titus	2,204	1,009	45.78	1,760	21.5
	37,361	13,703	36.67	51,149	31.0+
FIFTH DISTRICT					
Collin	9,610	2,353	24.48	2,525	6.9
Cooke	5,207	1,097	21.06	1,351	5.5
Denton	5,431	1,008	18.56	1,707	8.0
Grayson	11,517	2,839	24.65	6,712	12.6
Montague	4,959	1,753	35.34	87	0.5
	36,724	9,050	24.64	12,382	6.7+

TABLE XIX (*continued*)

	Total Vote	Populist Vote	Percentage Populist in Total Vote	Negro Population	Percentage Negro in Total Population
SIXTH DISTRICT					
Bosque	3,347	1,668	49.83	641	4.5
Dallas	15,780	7,151	45.31	11,177	16.7
Ellis	10,390	4,152	39.96	3,376	10.6
Hill	8,544	3,521	41.21	2,096	7.6
Johnson	6,316	2,816	44.58	852	3.8
Kaufman	5,776	2,160	37.39	3,176	14.7
Navarro	8,222	3,762	45.75	6,266	23.8
	58,375	25,230	43.22	27,584	11.7+
SEVENTH DISTRICT					
Bell	8,715	2,661	30.53	2,650	7.9
Brazos	3,855	351	9.10	8,433	50.6
Falls	6,672	798	11.96	7,961	38.4
Limestone	6,180	2,047	33.12	4,459	20.6
McLennan	12,014	1,780	14.81	10,381	26.5
Milan	7,040	1,997	28.36	6,220	25.1
	44,476	9,634	21.66	40,104	28.2+
EIGHTH DISTRICT					
Brown	2,816	1,371	48.68	73	0.6
Coleman	1,572	679	43.19	69	1.1
Comanche	2,782	1,493	53.66	8	0.1
Coryell	4,026	1,775	44.08	459	2.7
Erath	5,242	2,960	56.46	723	3.3
Hamilton	2,308	1,253	54.28	13	0.1
Hood	1,728	763	44.15	274	3.6
Lampasas	1,421	846	59.53	262	3.5
Mills	1,328	714	53.76	57	1.0
Parker	5,094	2,091	41.04	671	3.1
Runnels	723	327	45.22	31	1.0
Somervell	744	372	50.00	6	0.2
Tarrant	9,413	2,866	30.44	4,316	10.5
	39,197	17,510	44.67	6,962	2.3+

TABLE XIX (*continued*)

	Total Vote	Populist Vote	Percentage Populist in Total Vote	Negro Population	Percentage Negro in Total Population
NINTH DISTRICT					
Bastrop	4,677	1,300	27.79	8,898	42.9
Burleson	3,261	358	10.97	5,727	44.1
Burnet	2,033	834	41.02	307	2.9
Caldwell	3,406	1,009	29.62	4,878	30.9
Hays	2,534	392	15.46	2,171	19.1
Lee	2,561	472	18.43	3,102	26.0
Travis	8,207	676	8.23	10,090	27.8
Washington	5,931	96	1.61	15,200	52.1
Williamson	7,009	1,650	23.54	2,755	10.6
	39,618	6,787	17.13	53,128	28.5+
TENTH DISTRICT					
Austin	3,789	239	6.30	5,185	29.0
Brazoria	2,891	237	8.19	8,523	74.1
Colorado	3,985	395	9.91	8,845	45.3
Fayette	6,695	593	8.85	8,446	26.8
Fort Bend	3,126	221	7.06	8,981	84.8
Galveston	8,613	643	7.46	7,009	22.3
Gonzales	4,413	1,874	42.46	5,869	32.6
Lavaca	4,704	1,262	26.82	4,253	19.4
Matagorda	1,009	12	1.18	2,621	65.8
ιV̄z̄z̄z̄z̄ +					
ELEVENTH DISTRICT					
Aransas	471	65	13.80	137	7.5
Atascosa	1,369	426	31.11	285	4.4
Bee	1,485	196	13.19	317	8.5
Calhoun	374	74	19.78	168	20.6
DeWitt	6,582	249	3.78	3,995	27.9
Dimmit	211	65	30.80	37	3.5
Duval	1,195	1	0.08	7	0.1
Frio	832	151	18.14	102	3.3
Goliad	1,421	298	20.97	1,644	27.8
Guadalupe	3,378	206	6.09	4,415	29.0
Jackson	1,061	210	19.79	1,822	55.5
Karnes	1,700	637	3.74	544	15.0
Live Oak	545	162	29.72	49	2.4

TABLE XIX (*continued*)

	Total Vote	Populist Vote	Percentage Populist in Total Vote	Negro Population	Percentage Negro in Total Population
ELEVENTH DISTRICT					
(continued)					
Nueces	2,048	26	1.26	707	8.7
Refugio	324	17	5.24	324	26.2
San Patricio	619	117	18.90	25	1.9
Victoria	2,210	34	1.53	3,519	40.3
Wharton	2,010	112	5.57	6,119	80.7
Wilson	2,426	1,003	41.34	1,053	9.9
Zavala	153	21	13.72	3	0.3
	30,414	4,254	14.87	25,272	18.7+
TWELFTH DISTRICT					
Bandera	789	161	20.40	126	3.3
Bexar	10,793	382	3.53	5,504	11.2
Blanco	922	300	32.53	210	4.5
Coke	450	173	38.44	none listed**	**
Comal	1,365	14	1.02	180	2.8
Concho	64	1	1.58	14	1.3
Edwards	496	36	7.25	6	0.3
Gillespie	1,542	108	7.00	108	1.5
Kendall	793	41	5.17	216	5.6
Kerr	979	125	12.76	92	2.4
Kimble	418	77	18.42	5	0.2
Llano	1,319	426	32.29	52	0.8
Mason	1,007	278	27.60	31	0.6
McCullock	689	214	31.05	12	1.4
Medina	1,458	125	8.57	283	4.9
Menard	457	103	22.53	23	1.9
Midland	327	9	2.75	3	0.3
Pecos	256	1	.39	8	0.6
Presidio	1,454	520	35.76	26	1.5
San Saba	1,301	520	39.96	53	0.8
Sterling	213	84	39.43	none listed**	**
Sutton	363	2	0.55	1	0.2
Tom Green	1,258	30	2.38	202	3.9
	28,712	3,210	11.17	7,155	1.9+

TABLE XIX (*continued*)

	Total Vote	Populist Vote	Percentage Populist in Total Vote	Negro Population	Percentage Negro in Total Population
THIRTEENTH DISTRICT					
Archer	540	79	14.62	12	0.6
Armstrong	199	74	37.18	285	4.4
Baylor	487	142	29.15	6	0.2
Borden	103	42	40.77	5	2.3
Briscoe	175	85	48.57	**	**
Callahan	1,449	595	41.06	31	0.6
Carson	108	3	2.77	1	0.3
Childress	382	74	19.37	2	0.2
Clay	1,734	442	25.49	102	1.4
Collingsworth	189	53	28.04	**	**
Cottle	123	18	14.63	**	**
Crosby	115	22	19.13	1	0.3
Dallam	44	7	15.90	**	**
Deaf Smith	108	19	17.59	**	**
Dickens	112	35	31.25	**	**
Donely	336	116	34.52	40	3.8
Eastland	2,794	1,346	48.17	25	0.2
El Paso	3,685	1,428	38.75	377	2.4
Fisher	500	227	45.40	15	6.5
Floyd	279	110	39.42	**	**
Foard	300	175	58.33	**	**
Hale	275	84	30.54	3	0.4
Hall	300	67	22.33	1	0.1
Hansford	28	10	35.71	**	**
Hardeman	570	131	22.98	21	0.5
Hartley	113	13	11.50	1	0.4
Haskell	332	81	24.39	6	0.4
Hemphill	143	25	17.48	9	1.7
Howard	378	161	42.59	34	2.8
Jack	1,987	915	46.04	97	1.0
Jones	947	490	51.74	7	0.2
Kent	121	70	57.85	**	**
King	91	1	1.09	2	1.2
Knox	306	94	30.71	**	**
Lipscomb	131	31	23.66	**	**
Lubbock	101	9	8.91	2	***
Martin	109	14	12.84	**	**
Mitchell	509	193	37.91	99	4.8

TABLE XIX (*continued*)

	Total Vote	Populist Vote	Percentage Populist in Total Vote	Negro Population	Percentage Negro in Total Population
THIRTEENTH DISTRICT (continued)					
Moore	37	21	56.75	**	**
Motley	162	33	20.37	3	2.2
Nolan	384	138	35.93	32	2.0
Ochiltree	38	13	34.21	**	**
Oldham	79	9	11.39	3	1.1
Palo Pinto	2,088	981	46.98	67	0.8
Potter	347	118	34.00	14	1.6
Randall	132	39	29.54	**	**
Reeves	597	70	11.72	7	0.6
Roberts	141	22	15.60	2	0.6
Scurry	373	197	52.81	2	0.1
Shackelford	515	230	44.66	167	8.3
Stephens	1,224	564	46.07	5	0.1
Swisher	204	89	43.62	**	**
Taylor	1,666	834	50.06	174	2.5
Throckmorton	325	144	44.30	11	1.2
Ward	157	51	32.48	3	***
Wheeler	100	17	17.00	16	2.1
Wichita	974	221	22.68	128	2.6
Wilbarger	1,026	287	27.97	26	0.4
Wise	5,584	2,218	39.72	161	0.7
Young	1,205	448	37.17	15	0.3
	37,561	14,219	38.85	2,020	1.2+

*United States Bureau of Commerce, *Bureau of Census, Negro Population, 1790–1915*, 789–792; *Report of Secretary of State*, November 3, 1896, 61–64; *Southern Mercury*, October 29, 1896.

**The census did not report any Negro population in these counties.

***Percent not shown since the base is less than 100.

+All district totals of Negro Population are expressed as arithmetic means.

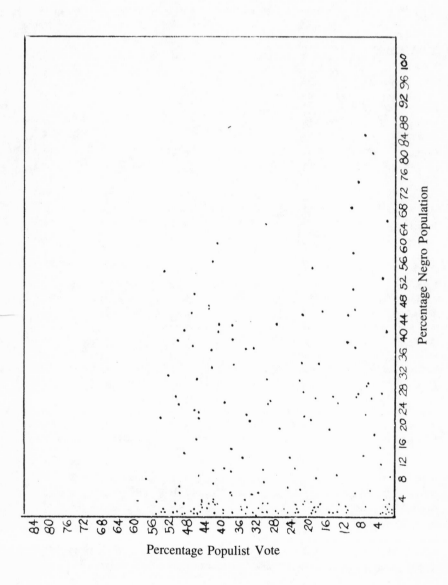

Figure 6. Relationship Between Negro Density and Populism in the
Texas Congressional Election of 1896.

TABLE XX

Voting and Negro Population Characteristics for the
*Florida Congressional Election of 1894**

	Total Vote	Populist Vote	Percentage Populist in Total Vote	Negro Population	Percentage Negro in Total Population
FIRST DISTRICT					
Calhoun	183	104	56.83	549	32.7
Citrus	247	39	15.78	304	12.7
DeSoto	706	250	35.41	139	2.8
Escambia	2,013	20	.99	8,706	43.1
Franklin	236	49	20.76	1,358	41.1
Hernando	189	66	34.92	892	36.0
Hillsborough	3,133	216	6.89	2,917	19.5
Holmes	277	156	56.31	184	4.2
Jackson	793	220	27.74	11,211	63.9
Lee	112	1	.89	80	5.7
Leon	937	23	2.45	14,631	82.4
Levy	307	29	9.44	2,129	32.3
Liberty	141	74	52.48	634	43.7
Manatee	333	103	30.93	181	6.3
Monroe	942	16	1.69	5,935	31.6
Pasco	367	78	21.25	376	8.8
Polk	736	280	38.04	784	9.9
Santa Rosa	181	4	2.20	2,192	27.5
Taylor	73	23	31.50	151	7.4
Walton	408	196	48.03	743	15.4
Washington	432	188	43.51	1,339	20.8
	12,746	2,135	16.75	55,435	26.1**
SECOND DISTRICT					
Alachua	652	63	9.66	13,260	57.8
Baker	317	181	57.09	745	22.4
Bradford	435	83	19.08	1,555	20.7
Brevard	352	20	5.68	541	15.9
Clay	243	66	27.16	1,521	29.5
Columbia	581	120	20.65	6,484	50.4
Duval	1,886	366	19.40	14,802	55.2
Hamilton	355	31	8.73	3,170	37.3
Lake	1,020	150	14.70	1,844	23.0
Marion	1,177	482	40.95	11,485	55.2
Nassau	577	109	18.89	4,338	52.3

TABLE XX (*continued*)

	Total Vote	Populist Vote	Percentage Populist in Total Vote	Negro Population	Percentage Negro in Total Population
SECOND DISTRICT (continued)					
Orange	726	33	4.54	3,536	28.1
Osceola	219	52	23.74	476	15.2
Putman	463	78	16.84	4,778	42.7
St. Johns	351	17	4.84	3,195	36.7
Sumter	662	305	46.07	1,498	27.9
Suwannee	431	13	3.01	4,943	47.0
Volusia	564	165	29.25	2,462	29.1
	11,011	2,334	21.19	80,633	35.9**

*United States Bureau of Commerce, *Bureau of Census, Negro Population, 1790–1915*, 778; *Congressional Directory*, 54th Congress, 1st Session, 27; Florida *National Elections*, November 6, 1894, 6–7; *Appletons* Annual Cyclopaedia, *1894, 283*.

**All district totals of Negro population are expressed as arithmetic means.*

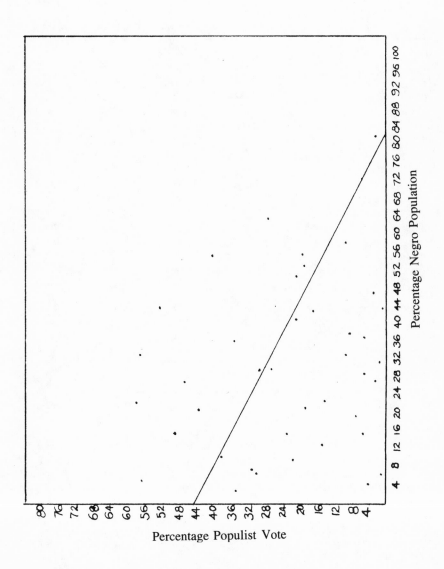

Figure 7. Relationship Between Negro Density and Populism in the
Florida Congressional Election of 1894.

TABLE XXI

Voting and Negro Population Characteristics for the
Arkansas Congressional Election of 1894*

	Total Vote	Populist Vote	Percentage Populist in Total Vote	Negro Population	Percentage Negro in Total Population
FIRST DISTRICT					
Randolph	700	45	6.42	595	4.1
Clay	452	134	29.64	43	0.4
Greene	777	362	46.58	161	1.2
Lawrence	614	135	21.98	833	6.4
Sharp	637	160	25.11	177	1.7
Jackson	494	57	11.53	4,329	28.5
Craighead	503	121	24.05	519	4.3
Poinsett	201	18	8.95	546	12.8
Cross	286	34	11.88	2,890	37.6
St. Francis	531	207	38.98	8,000	59.1
Lee	676	16	2.36	14,187	75.1
Phillips	668	2	.29	19,640	77.5
Woodruff	566	8	1.41	7,556	53.9
	7,105	1,299	18.28	59,476	27.9**
SECOND DISTRICT					
Lincoln	258	1	.38	8,451	63.1
Drew	544	52	9.55	9,865	56.9
Dallas	343	7	2.04	3,265	35.1
Hot Spring	362	7	1.93	1.249	10.8
Polk	152	3	1.97	46	0.5
Scott	456	18	3.94	31	0.2
	2,115	88	4.16	22,907	27.8**
FOURTH DISTRICT					
Franklin	1,253	204	16.28	677	3.4
Johnson	992	246	24.79	631	3.8
Logan	1,433	190	13.25	1,124	5.4
Pulaski	2,123	216	10.17	21,935	46.3
Conway	1,143	99	8.66	7,671	39.4
Pope	1,537	279	18.15	1,621	8.3
Yell	1,138	166	14.58	1,362	7.6
Perry	502	157	31.27	941	17.0
	10,121	1,557	15.38	35,962	16.4**

TABLE XXI (*continued*)

	Total Vote	Populist Vote	Percentage Populist in Total Vote	Negro Population	Percentage Negro in Total Population
FIFTH DISTRICT					
Benton	2,032	25	1.23	92	0.3
Washington	2,089	36	1.72	1,010	3.2
Carroll	1,384	101	7.29	82	0.5
Boone	927	2	.21	91	0.6
Newton	717	16	2.23	6	0.1
Crawford	1,464	14	.95	2,296	10.6
Van Buren	602	135	22.42	162	1.9
Faulkner	1,736	421	24.25	3,348	18.3
Searcy	701	9	1.28	28	0.3
	11,652	759	6.51	7,115	4.0**

*United States Bureau of Commerce, *Bureau of Census, Negro Population, 1790–1915,* 777; *Biennial Report of the Secretary of State of Arkansas,* November, 1894, 65–67; *Congressional Directory,* 1st Session, 54th Congress, 18–20.

**All district totals of Negro population are expressed as arithmetic means.

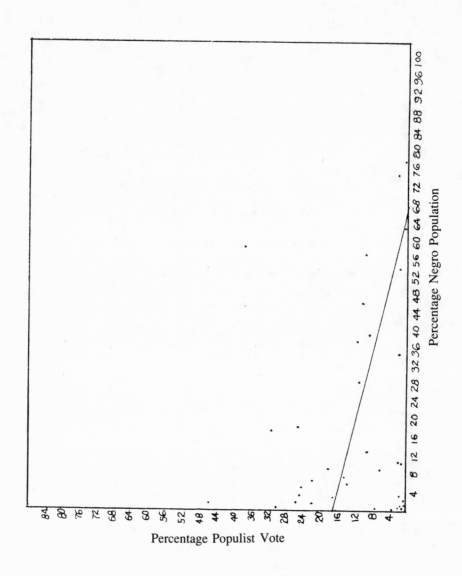

Figure 8. Relationship Between Negro Density and Populism in the
Arkansas Congressional Election of 1894.

TABLE XXII

*Voting and Negro Population Characteristics for the
Louisiana Congressional Election of 1892* *

	Total Vote	Populist Vote	Percentage Populist in Total Vote	Negro Population	Percentage Negro in Total Population
FIRST DISTRICT					
Orleans	12,859	40	3.11	64,491	26.6
St. Bernard	733	12	1.63	1,977	45.7
	13,592	52	0.38	66,468	36.2**
THIRD DISTRICT					
Iberville	2,241	595	26.55	15,142	69.3
Assumption	2,003	696	34.76	8,890	45.3
Lafourche	3,160	93	2.94	7,819	35.4
Terrebonne	1,577	346	21.94	9,699	48.1
St. Mary	1,580	249	15.75	14,395	64.2
Iberia	616	28	4.54	10,477	49.9
St. Martin	485	2	.41	7,821	52.5
Lafayette	665	1	.15	6,884	43.1
Vermilion	560	237	42.32	2,899	20.4
Cameron	188	6	3.19	426	15.1
Calcasieu	1,756	692	39.40	3,194	15.8
Ascension	2,319	178	7.67	11,270	57.7
	17,157	3,123***	18.20	98,916	43.1**
FOURTH DISTRICT					
Rapides	3,672	457	12.44	15,800	57.2
Sabine	1,270	760	59.84	2,067	22.0
DeSoto	1,921	346	18.01	13,220	66.6
Natchitoches	1,679	594	35.37	15,551	60.2
Red River	1,241	288	23.20	7,760	68.6
Caddo	2,483	251	10.10	23,541	74.6
Bossier	3,015	72	2.38	16,225	79.8
Winn	992	791	79.73	1,010	14.3
Grant	838	500	59.66	3,416	41.3
Bienville	2,074	443	21.35	6,268	44.4
Vernon	694	369	53.17	540	9.1
Webster	1,720	296	17.20	7,289	58.5
	21,609	5,167+	23.91	12,687	49.7**

TABLE XXII (*continued*)

	Total Vote	Populist Vote	Percentage Populist in Total Vote	Negro Population	Percentage Negro in Total Population
FIFTH DISTRICT					
Caldwell	909	224	24.64	3,106	53.4
Franklin	830	25	3.01	4,040	58.6
Tensas	2,564	11	0.42	15,492	93.1
Madison	3,206	3	0.09	13,204	93.4
Ouachita	2,964	151	5.09	12,344	68.6
Jackson	866	466	53.81	2,608	35.0
Lincoln	1,753	1,084	61.83	6,269	42.5
Union	2,012	647	32.15	7,403	42.8
Morehouse	1,231	96	7.79	13,267	79.0
East Carroll	1,392	22	1.58	11,360	91.9
West Carroll	416	9	2.16	2,310	61.6
Claiborne	2,574	1,121	43.55	13,512	58.0
Catahoula	1,570	442	28.15	4,976	41.5
	22,287	4,301***	19.29	109,891	63.0**
SIXTH DISTRICT					
Acadia	369	96	26.01	1,629	12.3
St. Landry	2,034	899	44.19	22,274	55.3
Avoyelles	1,609	3	0.18	12,161	48.4
East Feliciana	1,427	102	7.14	12,707	71.0
E.Baton Rouge	1,533	287	18.72	16,420	63.3
W.Baton Rouge	1,601	30	1.87	5,964	71.3
St. Helena	382	78	20.41	4,589	56.9
Livingston	567	245	43.20	871	15.1
Tangipahoa	892	114	12.78	4,698	37.1
Washington	541	127	23.47	2,062	30.8
St. Tammany	124	62	50.00	3,702	36.4
	11,079	2,043	18.44	87,072	45.3**

*United States Bureau of Commerce, *Bureau of Census, Negro Population, 1790–1915,* 782–783; State of Louisiana, *Report of the Secretary of State,* "Official Vote of 1892 Congressional Election," 98–100; *Congressional Directory,* 3rd Session, 53rd Congress, 47–48.

**All district totals of Negro population are expressed as arithmetic means.

***These candidates represented both the Republican and the Populist Party in their districts. Only Ross Carlin in the first district ran expressly as a Populist candidate. See Charles W. Dabney, Jr., *Congressional Directory,* 3rd Session, 53rd Congress, 47–48.

+T. J. Guice appears to have been a Farmers' Alliance candidate running against a Democrat, N. C. Blanchard. As such, Guice probably received the Populist, Republican, and Farmers' Alliance vote in the Fourth District since these were the only two candidates. He is, therefore, included *as a Populist candidate* for this reason. See "Fourth district," *Congressional Record,* 2nd Session, 52nd Congress, 45; Melvin J. White, "Populism in Louisiana During the Nineties," *Mississippi Valley Historical Review,* V (June, 1918), 5–6.

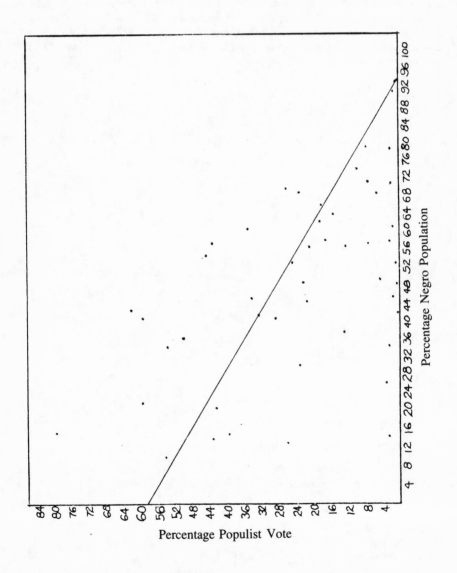

Figure 9. Relationship Between Negro Density and Populism in the
Louisiana Congressional Election of 1892.

TABLE XXIII

Voting and Negro Population Characteristics for the
Virginia Congressional Election of 1892*

	Total Vote	Populist Vote	Percentage Populist in Total Vote	Negro Population	Percentage Negro in Total Population
FIRST DISTRICT					
Accomack	5,352	1,630	30.45	9,730	35.7
Caroline	2,742	1,475	53.79	9,322	55.9
Essex	1,839	933	50.73	6,462	64.3
City of Fredericksburg	944	176	18.64	1,682	37.1
Gloucester	2,356	1,440	61.12	6,216	53.3
King & Queen	1,616	55	52.90	5,430	56.2
Lancaster	1,891	874	46.21	4,020	55.9
Mathews	1,565	619	39.55	2,137	28.2
Middlesex	536	255	47.57	4,317	57.9
Northampton	1,622	387	23.85	5,479	53.1
Northum- berland	1,791	812	45.33	3,090	39.2
Richmond County	1,328	609	45.85	3,148	44.1
Spotsylvania	1,560	673	43.14	4,395	46.3
Westmoreland	1,561	807	51.69	4,737	56.4
	26,703	11,545	43.23	70,165	48.9**
SECOND DISTRICT					
Charles City	883	4	0.45	3,717	73.4
Elizabeth City	2,124	114	5.36	7,774	48.1
Isle of Wight	2,202	80	3.63	5,144	45.5
Nansemond	3,392	226	6.66	10,765	54.7
Norfolk	5,094	62	1.21	19,216	66.5
City of Norfolk	6,050	8	0.13	16,244	46.6
Portsmouth	2,751	3	0.10	4,018	30.3
Princess Anne	1,077	66	6.12	4,130	43.4
Surry	1,297	139	10.71	5,017	60.8
Southampton	2,571	245	9.52	11,782	58.7
Warwick	1,644	12	.72	1,320	60.0
York	1,355	17	1.25	4,395	57.9
	30,440+	976	3.20	93,522	53.8**

TABLE XXIII (*continued*)

	Total Vote	Populist Vote	Percentage Populist in Total Vote	Negro Population	Percentage Negro in Total Population
THIRD DISTRICT					
Chesterfield	2,982	1,241	41.61	10,811	41.2
Goochland	1,466	811	55.32	5,874	59.0
Hanover	2,833	1,336	47.15	8,211	47.2
Henrico	4,318	1,966	45.53	11,265	51.2
King William	1,346	656	48.73	5,685	59.2
New Kent	838	445	53.10	3,545	64.3
Manchester	1,821	574	31.52	***	***
City of Richmond	13,480	3,459	25.66	32,330	39.7
	29,084+	10,488	36.06	77,721	51.7**
FOURTH DISTRICT					
Amelia	1,116	588	52.68	6,045	66.7
Brunswick	2,206	1,122	50.86	10,584	61.4
Dinwiddie	1,649	842	51.06	8,394	62.1
Greensville	802	436	54.36	5,311	64.5
Lunenburg	1,278	457	35.75	6,736	59.2
Mecklenburg	3,179	1,816	57.12	16,030	28.2
Nottoway	1,511	442	29.25	7,623	65.8
Petersburg	3,599	1,023	28.42	12,221	53.9
Powhatan	1,210	816	67.43	4,433	65.3
Prince Edward	1,541	764	49.57	9,924	67.5
Prince George	842	569	67.57	5,132	65.2
Sussex	879	587	66.78	7,576	68.3
	19,812	9,462	47.75	100,009	6.07**
SIXTH DISTRICT					
Bedford	4,986	1,731	34.71	11,149	35.7
Campbell	3,467	1,694	48.86	9,998	46.8
Charlotte	2,405	967	40.20	9,361	62.1
Halifax	5,660	2,384	42.12	19,416	56.4
Lynchburg	3,789	1,362	35.94	9,802	49.7
Montgomery	2,643	1,341	50.73	3,515	19.8
Radford	783	185	23.62	***	***
Roanoke City	4,605	1,879	40.80	4,929	30.4
Roanoke County	2,936	1,306	44.48	4,076	29.2
	31,274+	12,849	41.08	72,246	41.3**

TABLE XXIII (*continued*)

	Total Vote	Populist Vote	Percentage Populist in Total Vote	Negro Population	Percentage Negro in Total Population
EIGHTH DISTRICT					
City of					
Alexandria	3,154	1,153	36.55	5,113	35.7
Alexandria	839	470	56.01	2,123	49.9
Culpeper	2,502	904	36.13	6,085	46.0
Fairfax	3,389	1,187	35.02	5,069	30.4
Fauquier	4,166	1,383	33.19	7,904	35.0
King George	1,027	474	46.15	3,208	48.3
Loudoun	4,186	1,448	34.59	6,578	28.3
Louisa	2,662	1,373	51.57	9,805	57.7
Orange	2,221	883	39.75	6,241	48.7
Prince William	1,791	275	15.35	2,595	26.5
Stafford	1,267	516	40.72	1,469	20.0
	27,204 +	10,066	37.00	56,190	38.8**
NINTH DISTRICT					
Bland	945	262	27.72	241	4.7
Buchanan	910	71	7.80	24	0.4
Craig	778	73	9.38	149	3.9
Dickenson	779	47	6.03	26	0.5
Lee	2,773	23	0.82	1,213	6.7
Russell	2,749	386	14.04	1,203	7.5
Scott	3,540	309	8.72	968	4.5
Smyth	2,314	126	5.44	1,224	9.2
Tazewell	3,432	72	2.09	3,504	17.6
Washington	4,730	138	2.91	2,965	11.4
Wise	1,879	26	1.38	582	6.2
Wythe	3,413	176	5.15	3,170	17.6
	28,242	1,709	6.05	15,269	7.5**
TENTH DISTRICT					
Alleghany	1,193	855	71.66	2,328	25.1
Amherst	1,670	1,161	69.52	7,628	43.5
Appomattox	1,687	905	53.64	4,336	45.2
Augusta	3,645	2,211	60.65	6,112	20.4
Bath	490	374	76.32	761	16.6
Botetourt	1,692	1,188	70.21	3,732	25.1
Buckingham	1,286	1,043	81.10	7,597	52.8
Cumberland	554	980	63.88	6,622	69.8
Flwanna	925	546	59.02	4,457	46.9

TABLE XXIII (*continued*)

	Total Vote	Populist Vote	Percentage Populist in Total Vote	Negro Population	Percentage Negro in Total Population
TENTH DISTRICT					
(continued)					
Highland	607	401	66.66	422	7.9
Nelson	1,431	1,097	76.65	6,303	41.1
Rockbridge	2,209	1,631	73.83	5,131	22.2
Buena Vista	342	83	24.26	***	***
	16,826+	12,475	74.14	55,428	34.7**

*United States Bureau of Commerce, *Bureau of Census, Negro Population, 1790–1915*, 792–793, 797; *Congressional Directory*, 3rd Session, 53rd Congress, 115–118; Commonwealth of Virginia, *Election Record*, No. 92, 22–31.

**All district totals of Negro population are expressed as arithmetic means.

***Figures not available for these areas.

+The population of the independent cities is not included in the population given for counties.

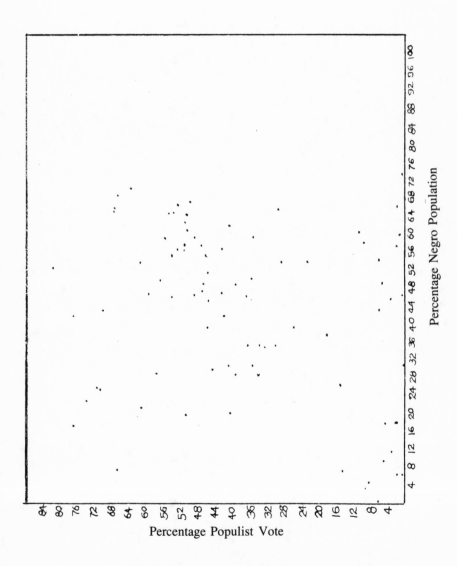

Figure 10. Relationship Between Negro Density and Populism in the
Virginia Congressional Election of 1892.

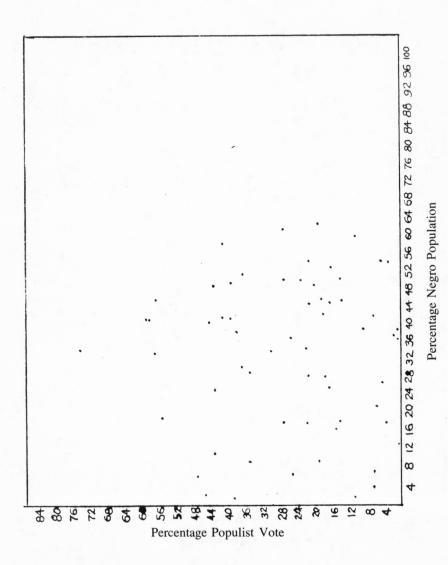

Figure 11. Relationship Between Negro Density and Populism by
Congressional District in the South.

NOTES

Notes to Introduction

1. Carl N. Degler, "Racism in the United States: An Essay Review," *Journal of Southern History,* XXXVIII (February, 1972), 101.
2. Richard Reeves, "The New Populism and the Old: A Matter of Words," *Saturday Review,* April 8, 1972, pp. 46–47.
3. Degler, "Racism in the United States," 102.
4. Robert Sherrill, *Gothic Politics in the Deep South: Stars of the New Confederacy* (New York, 1968), 122.
5. Pat Watters, *The South and the Nation* (New York, 1969), 59.

Notes to Chapter 1

1. *People's Party Paper* (Atlanta), August 28, 1896.
2. According to Professor Hicks, "Perhaps half of the members of the [Southern] Alliance gave the new party their support. The rest were unwilling to risk the reality of white supremacy in what might prove to be a vain struggle for a new order." However, under pressure to conform to private principles, ultimately "it was no longer possible to be a good Allianceman unless one also was a good Populist." The initial formation of the Populist Party was probably a catalyst to attract the less aggressive members. John D. Hicks, *The Populist Revolt: A History of the Farmers' Alliance and the People's Party* (Lincoln, 1931; 1961), 243, 270–73. For a study of the germination and growth of such movements, see C. Wendell King, *Social Movements in the United States* (New York, 1967), 40–48.
3. Theodore Saloutos, *Farmer Movements in the South: 1865–1933* (Lincoln, 1960), 70–1; Hicks, *Populist Revolt,* 104–05. A good discussion of the Texas Alliance can be found in Ralph Smith, "The Farmers' Alliance in Texas, 1875–1900," *Southwestern Historical Quarterly,* XLVIII (October, 1948), 346–69.
4. For a discussion of the background and plans of C. W. Macune, see Fred A. Shannon, "C. W. Macune and the Farmers' Alliance," *Current History,* XXVIII (June, 1955), 330–35; Ralph Smith, " 'Macuneism' or the Farmers of Texas in Business," *Journal of Southern History,* XIII (May, 1947), 220–44; Annie L. Diggs, "The Farmers' Alliance and Some of its Leaders," *Arena,* V (1891–1892), 598–99.
5. *Progressive Farmer* (Raleigh), September 9, 1887; C. Vann Woodward, *Tom Watson: Agrarian Rebel* (New York, 1938; 1963), 136.
6. Saloutos, *Farmer Movements,* 69; C. Vann Woodward, *Origins of the New South, 1877–1913* (New York, 1951; 1966), 190–91; Ina W. Van Noppen, ed., *The South: A Documentary History* (Princeton, 1958), 404–05. See also Clifton Paisley, "The Political Wheelers," *Arkansas Historical Quarterly,* XXV (Spring, 1966), 3–21; *Appleton's Annual Cyclopedia, 1886,* XI (New York, 1887), 42; *ibid., 1890,* XV, 299.
7. James W. Vander Zanden, "The Ideology of White Supremacy," *Journal of the History of Ideas, XX* (June-September, 1959), 385–402; Guion Griffis Johnson, "The Ideology of White Supremacy, 1876–1910," in Fletcher Green, ed., *Essays in Southern History* (Chapel Hill, 1949), 125–56; Rhett Jones, "Proving Blacks Inferior, 1870–1930," *Black World,* XX (February, 1971), 4–19.
8. Saloutos, *Farmer Movements,* 72.
9. Fred A. Shannon, *The Farmers' Last Frontier: Agriculture, 1860–1897* (New York, 1968), 77–100, 314, 418; Hicks, *Populist Revolt,* 114; Woodward, *New South,* 205–06.
10. *National Economist,* July 4, 1891. This paper served as the official organ of the

Southern Alliance from its beginning. The first copy of the paper was issued on March 14, 1889, from Washington, D.C. See also William D. Sheldon, *Populism in the Old Dominion* (Princeton, 1935), 3–4; Paul Lewinson, *Race, Class, and Party: A History of Negro Suffrage and White Politics in the South* (New York, 1932; 1965), 71. A similar "resolution" was adopted in 1889 by the "committee on co-operation" of the National Alliance concerning the "detrimental" effects "to both white and colored to allow conditions to exist that force our colored farmers and laborers to sell their products for less and pay more for supplies than the market justifies." *Weekly Toiler* (Nashville), January 23, 1889.

11. Saloutos, *Farmer Movements*, 69–70, 74, 77, 79; August Meier, *Negro Thought in America 1880–1915* (Ann Arbor, 1966), 44; Hicks, *Populist Revolt*, 108.

12. *Ibid.*, 98; Saloutos, *Farmer Movements*, 69–70, 79.

13. R. M. Humphrey, "History of the Colored Farmers National Alliance and Cooperative Union," in *The Farmers' Alliance and Agriculture Digest*, N. A. Dunning, ed. (Washington, 1891), 288. Milton George ostensibly had helped establish the first Negro Alliance in Prairie County, Arkansas, in 1882. Humphrey, however, failed to recognize this early effort in his official account. Roy V. Scott, "Milton George and the Farmers' Alliance Movement," *Mississippi Valley Historical Review*, XLV (June, 1958), 107.

14. Humphrey, "The Colored Alliance," 288.

15. *Ibid.; Weekly Toiler*, March 27, 1889. Van Noppen, *Documentary*, 405. *The Progressive Farmer in Documentary* has interwoven details of the 1886 convention with the national convention of 1888.

16. Meier, *Negro Thought in America*, 42–58, 121–38; Edwin S. Redkey, *Black Exodus: Black Nationalist and Back-to-Africa Movements, 1890–1910* (New Haven, 1969), 1–23; Purvis M. Carter, "Robert Lloyd Smith and the Farmers' Improvement Society, A Self-Help Movement in Texas," *Negro History Bulletin, XXIX* (Fall, 1966), 175–76, 190–91.

17. Van Noppen, *Documentary*, 405.

18. Humphrey, "The Colored Alliance," 289; *National Economist*, June 7, 1890; Atlanta *Constitution*, December 4, 1890; William J. Northen Scrapbook I, 83, in Northen Collection, State of Georgia Archives, Atlanta.

19. *Ibid.*

20. Humphrey, "The Colored Alliance," 289; Colored Farmers' Alliance Charter, Office of Recorder of Deeds, Corporation Division, Instrument #1606, Incorporation Liber #4, Folio 354, Washington, D.C.

21. Woodward, *New South*, 192. For further evidence, see *Weekly Toiler*, July 4, 1888.

22. *Ibid.*, August 21, 1889.

23. William W. Rogers, "The Negro Alliance in Alabama," *Journal of Negro History, XXXXV* (January, 1960), 40.

24. *Ibid.*, 39–40. *Weekly Toiler*, January 30, 1889; William W. Rogers, *The One-Gallused Rebellion: Agrarianism in Alabama, 1865–1896* (Baton Rouge, 1970), 141–44.

25. Rogers, "The Negro Alliance," 39–44. See also *Appleton's Annual Cyclopedia, 1890*, 301.

26. Union Springs *Bullock County Reporter*, October 18, 1889, quoted in Rogers, *One-Gallused Rebellion*, 143–44.

27. Rogers, "The Negro Alliance," 43–44; Rogers, *One-Gallused Rebellion*, 144–45. For further information on the agrarian movement in Alabama, see William Warren Rogers, "Agrarianism in Alabama, 1865–1896" (Unpublished Doctoral dissertation, University of North Carolina at Chapel Hill, 1959).

28. *Weekly Toiler,* July 18, 1888. The *Toiler* served as the official state organ of the Tennessee white and Colored Alliance. J. H. McDowell purchased the paper on August 28, 1888, and thereafter turned it into a major Alliance organ. "The policy of the *Toiler* in the future," said the new editor, "will be conservative. . . ." *Ibid.,* September 12, 1888. Nevertheless, the Negro Alliance received extensive coverage under McDowell and L. K. Taylor, who later replaced McDowell, while the major state papers ignored its very existence.

29. *Ibid.,* July 4, 1888. Vaughan served as the Tennessee General Superintendent of the Colored Alliance in the early years, but was later replaced by J. W. Brown of Prospect, Tennessee. As with so many of the Colored Alliance officers, nothing is known of his financial posture or race.

30. *Ibid.,* October 7, 1888.

31. *Ibid.,* July 1, 1888.

32. *Ibid.,* July 31, 1889. For evidence of financial shortages in the white Tennessee Alliance, see Nashville *Banner,* October 4, 1891.

33. Plans were made, however, to establish a local co-op at Fayetteville, Tennessee. See *Weekly Toiler,* July 31, 1889.

34. *National Economist,* August 23, 1890.

35. Saloutos, *Farmer Movements,* 113–14; *National Economist,* quoted in *Toiler,* December 2, 1891.

36. Nashville *Banner,* August 9, 1892; *National Economist* in *Toiler,* December 2, 1i91; Corinne Westphal, "The Farmers' Alliance in Tennessee" (Unpublished Master's thesis, Vanderbilt University, 1929), 79–81; *Appleton's Annual Cyclopedia, 1890,* 299–301; Daniel H. Robison, "Tennessee Politics and the Agrarian Movement, 1886–1896," *Mississippi Valley Historical Review,* XX (December, 1933), 365; Roger L. Hart, *Redeemers, Bourbons, and Populists: Tennessee, 1870–1896* (Baton Rouge, 1975). For statements of the Alliance Democrat, Rice Pierce, in the Tennessee House of Representatives concerning the race issue, see *National Economist,* February 28, 1891.

37. George B. Tindall, *South Carolina Negroes, 1877–1900* (Columbia, 1952), 114–15; Saloutos, *Farmer Movements,* 80.

38. *Ibid.;* Tindall, *South Carolina Negroes,* 115–17.

39. *Ibid.,* 117–18. The year 1890 appears to have been one of continued growth for the South Carolina Colored Alliance.

40. *Ibid.,* 117.

41. *Ibid.,* 118–19; Francis Butler Simkins, *The Tillman Movement in South Carolina* (Durham, 1926), 128–29, 132–33. A contemporary agrarian sympathizer believes the Colored Alliance did support Tillman. Joseph C. Manning, *The Fade out of Populism* (New York, 1928), 17.

42. Tindall, *South Carolina Negroes,* 118–19.

43. John D. Hicks and John D. Barnhart, "The Farmers' Alliance," *North Carolina Historical Review,* VI (July, 1929), 268.

44. *Ottawa, Kansas Journal,* quoted in *National Economist,* August 15, 1891.

45. *National Economist,* February 28, 1891.

46. *Ibid.,* June 13, 1891.

47. *Ibid.,* August 16, 1890.

48. *Ibid.,* July 12, 1890. See also J. H. Turner, "The Race Problem," in *Farmers' Alliance Digest,* 272–79. Turner was the Secretary-Treasurer of the Southern Alliance.

49. *National Alliance* (Houston, Texas), quoted in *National Economist,* April 4, 1891.

Based at Houston, Texas, under the editorship of R. M. Humphrey, the *National Alliance* as the official organ of the Colored Alliance. An extensive correspondence has failed to uncover a single issue of the paper. See Jack Abramowitz, "Negro in the Agrarian Revolt," *Agricultural History,* XXIV–XXV (1950–51), 91–92.

50. *Ottawa, Kansas Journal,* quoted in *National Economist,* August 15, 1891.

51. *National Economist,* June 20, 1891.

52. Humphrey, "The Colored Alliance," 290.

53. *Congressional Record,* 51 Cong., 2 Sess., 158. J. J. Shuffer was the first elected president as of December, 1886.

54. *Progressive Farmer,* December 23, 1890.

55. Nonpayment of dues for six months automatically suspended a member; he was then, in theory, forced to wear his badge backwards until he paid his delinquent dues.

56. Abramowitz, "Accommodation and Militancy," 50.

57. *Ibid.*

58. Sheldon, *Populism in the Old Dominion,* 35; Saloutos, *Farmer Movements,* 80; Hicks, *Populist Revolt,* 115; Van Noppen, *Documentary,* 404–05; Woodward, *New South,* 192; Abramowitz, "Negro in the Agrarian Revolt," 91; *Appleton's Annual Cyclopedia, 1890,* 301.

59. Saloutos, *Farmer Movements,* 81; *Progressive Farmer,* December 23, 1890.

60. Saloutos, *Farmer Movements,* 80.

61. *Ibid.*

62. Tindall, *South Carolina Negroes,* 118.

63. An example of this was the National Headquarters' establishment of trading posts and exchanges in the cities of Houston, New Orleans, Mobile, Charleston, and Norfolk. A $2 fee was charged each member for trading privileges. Humphrey, "Colored Alliance," 289–90; Rogers, "Negro Alliance," 42; Rogers, *One-Gallused Rebellion,* 143.

64. *National Alliance,* quoted in *National Economist,* June 21, 1890.

65. Dr. James Sparkman, "The Negro" (1889?), in Joel Williamson, ed., *The Origins of Segregation* (New York, 1968) 67.

66. *National Economist,* June 7, 1890.

67. *Cleveland Gazette,* September 26, 1891, in Herbert Aptheker, *A Documentary History of the Negro People in the United States* (2 vols., New York, 1932), II, 810.

68. "Our muscle is our stock in trade," Humphrey reported, "and . . . labor is the basis of all [our] wealth. . . ." *National Economist,* June 7, 1890; United States Bureau of the Census, *Negro Population in the United States, 1790–1915* (Washington, 1918), 459–61, 503–06.

69. The Negro, a debtor, reportedly paid interest rates as high as 100 percent, which prevented him from realizing any yearly profit from his labor. Humphrey, "Colored Alliance," 290. See also Woodward, *New South,* 180–81.

70. Gerald Grob, "Terence V. Powderly and the Knights of Labor," *Mid-America,* XXXIX (January, 1957), 51–53; Roger Wallace Shugg, "The New Orleans General Strike of 1892," *Louisiana Historical Quarterly,* XI (April, 1938), 550; Sidney H. Kessler, "The Organization of Negroes in the Knights of Labor," *Journal of Negro History,* XXVII (July, 1952), 248–76; William W. Rogers, "Negro Knights of Labor in Arkansas: A Case Study of the 'Miscellaneous' Strike," *Labor History,* X (Summer, 1969), 498–505; William I. Hair, *Bourbonism and Agrarian Protest: Louisiana Politics, 1877–1900* (Baton Rouge, 1969), 171–85, 227; Woodward, *New South,* 229–31. These actions would seem to suggest a reinterpretation of the stereotyped docile Southern black laborer. Also, these studies cast

doubt on the traditional view that the Knights were not fomenters of strikes. While the overt stages of these strikes were black efforts, the role of the Knights as promoters of these actions is implicit in several of these studies.

71. William F. Holmes, *The White Chief: James Kimble Vardaman* (Baton Rouge, 1970), 35. William Holmes, "The Lefore County Massacre and the Demise of the Colored Farmers' Alliance," *Phylon, XXXIV* (September, 1973), 267–74. See also *Leavenworth Advocate,* September 28, 1889; Washington, D.C. *Bee,* September 27, 1889 for further indications of such black Alliance efforts in Mississippi during this same period.

72. Aptheker, *Documentary,* II, 810. A copy of one such circular was reprinted in the *American Citizen* (Topeka), September 11, 1891, a black newspaper.

73. Tindall, *South Carolina Negroes,* 117–18.

74. *Ibid;* Abramowitz, "Accommodation and Militancy," 43; William Holmes, "The Arkansas Cotton Pickers Strike of 1891 and the Demise of the Colored Farmers' Alliance," *Arkansas Historical Society,* XXXII (Summer, 1973), 107–19.

75. *National Economist,* September 26, 1891. Emphasis added. The text of the column indicates that the strike remained minor, receiving little publicity—favorable or unfavorable—from the major newspapers of the region.

76. Quoted in Abramowitz, "Accommodation and Militancy," 43.

77. *National Economist,* September 26, 1891.

78. *Weekly Toiler,* October 14, 1891; John Hope Franklin, *From Slavery to Freedom* (3rd ed., New York, 1967), 36; Woodward, *Tom Watson,* 219; Atlanta *Constitution,* September 23, 1891; William J. Northen Scrapbook, No. I, 213, Northen Papers; a good discussion of the strike is found in Abramowitz, "Accommodation and Militancy," 42–49.

Notes to Chapter 2

1. *National Economist,* May 24, 1890.

2. *Toiler,* January 8, 1890.

3. Hicks, *Populist Revolt,* 119.

4. *National Economist,* September 6, 1890; Hicks, *Populist Revolt,* 108, 119–27. See also *Toiler,* December 11, 18, 1889; January 15, 1890.

5. Hicks, *Populist Revolt,* 112; Frank M. Drew, "The Present Farmers' Movement," *Political Science Quarterly,* VI (June, 1891), 285, citing *Proceedings of Farmers' and Laborers' Union, 1889,* 57.

6. Woodward, *New South,* 201.

7. Lord Bryce, *American Commonwealth,* quoted in Clement Eaton, *The Waning of the Old South Civilization, 1860–1880* (Athens, 1968), 137.

8. Woodward, *New South,* 201.

9. Humphrey, "Colored Alliance," 291; *Toiler,* December 18, 1889.

10. Humphrey, "Colored Alliance," 291; *Toiler,* January 23, 1889.

11. *National Economist,* May 31, 1890.

12. *Toiler,* January 23, 1889; *Appleton's Annual Cyclopedia, 1890,* 301.

13. *National Economist,* April 12, 1890.

14. In North Carolina, for example, blacks were specifically excluded from the Farmers' Alliance. Alliance membership was open to "white persons only, with the exception of Cherokee Indians in Clay, Graham, Haywood, Jackson, Macon and Swain Counties if they are of pure Indian blood and not less than half white." Croatan Indians located on the

eastern shore were also included in the same category. Helen G. Edmonds, *The Negro and Fusion Politics in North Carolina, 1894–1901* (Chapel Hill, 1951), 24.

15. Gerald Grob, *Workers and Utopia* (New York, 1969), 54; *Toiler,* December 25, 1889.

16. Jamie Lawson Reddick, "The Negro in the Populist Movement in Georgia" (Unpublished Master's thesis, Atlanta University, 1937), 28; Saloutos, *Farmer Movements,* 18; Abramowitz, "Populist Movement," 258. See also James O. Knauss, "Farmers' Alliance in Florida," *South Atlantic Quarterly,* XXV (July, 1926), 300–16; Samuel Proctor, "National Farmers' Alliance Convention of 1890 and its Ocala Demands," *Florida Historical Quarterly,* XVIIII (January, 1950), 167–69.

17. Humphrey, "Colored Alliance," 291–92; Dunning, *Farmers' Agricultural Digest,* 153.

18. Humphrey, "Colored Alliance," 292.

19. *National Economist,* January 10, 1891.

20. Dunning, *Farmers' Agricultural Digest,* 153–54; *Progressive Farmer,* December 9, 1890.

21. Philadelphia *Times,* December 5, 1890, in *Public Opinion,* X, No. 10 (New York, 1890), 220; Atlanta *Constitution,* December 4, 1890; Augusta *Chronicle,* December 4, 1890; Dunning, *Farmers' Agricultural Digest,* 153–54.

22. *Boston Journal,* December 8, 1890, in *Public Opinion,* X, 220.

23. *National Economist,* March 7, 1891, in Aptheker, *Documentary,* II, 807–09.

24. *Cong. Record,* 51 Cong., 2 Sess., 158. The full text of a telegram to the Senate Committee on Agriculture is included in the record.

25. Atlanta *Constitution,* December 7, 1890; Northen Scrapbook, No. I, 83–84, in Northen Collection.

26. Woodward, *New South,* 220.

27. Drew, "Present Farmers' Movement," 285.

28. Saloutos, *Farmer Movements,* 119.

29. Woodward, *New South,* 212.

30. Atlanta *Constitution,* December 4, 1890; Northen Scrapbook, No. I, 83.

31. Dunning, *Farmers' Agricultural Digest,* 95, 142; Hicks, *Populist Revolt,* 217; Hair, *Bourbonism and Agrarian Protest,* 211.

32. *National Economist,* April 11, 1891, in Aptheker, *Documentary, II,* 809–10.

33. Atlanta *Constitution,* January 13, 1890, quoted in Woodward, *Tom Watson,* 144.

34. Hicks, *Populist Revolt,* 178, 208.

35. *National Economist,* March 7, 1891, in Aptheker, *Documentary,* II, 805,890.

36. Woodward, *New South,* 193. See also Woodward, *The Burden of Southern History* (New York, 1960), 153.

37. Barnhart, "The Farmers' Alliance," 271; Drew, "Present Farmers' Movement," 286; Hicks, *Populist Revolt,* 115.

38. Meier, *Negro Thought,* 60; August Meier and Elliot Rudwick, *From Plantation to Ghetto* (New York, 1960), 158–59. For other reports of such open conflicts of interest between black and white Alliance men, see *Atlanta Constitution,* September 11, 1889; *New York Age,* January 4, 1890.

39. Charles Crowe, "Tom Watson, Populists and Blacks Reconsidered," *Journal of Negro History,* LV (April 1970), 108–09; Jack Abramowitz, "The Negro in the Populist Movement," *Journal of Negro History,* XXXVIII (July, 1953), 258–60; *Progressive Farmer,* December 9, 1890; *Philadelphia Times,* December 5, 1890, in *Public Opinion,* X, 220; *National Economist,* January 10, 17, 1891.

Notes to Chapter 3

1. Rogers, *One-Gallused Rebellion*, 142.

2. Norman Pollack, ed., *The Populist Mind* (Indianapolis, 1967), xxx–xxxiii. The history of these movements has been adequately chronicled elsewhere and need not be repeated here in abbreviated form. A list of the more significant studies can be found in *ibid*, lx. See also Saloutos, *Farmer Movements*, 1–68.

3. *People's Party Paper*, August 28, 1896.

4. *Ibid.*, June 28, 1895.

5. Greensboro *Daily Record*, March 7, August 19, 1892, quoted in Hicks, *Populist Revolt*, 239.

6. Atlanta *Constitution*, January 13, 1890, quoted in Woodward, *Tom Watson*, 144.

7. Woodward, *New South*, 80. For similar descriptions of attitudes in two southern states, see John B. Clark, *Populism in Alabama, 1874–1896* (Auburn, 1927), 80; Albert D. Kirwan, *Revolt of the Rednecks: Mississippi Politics, 1876–1925* (New York, 1965), 95.

8. Quoted in David Alan Harris, "The Political Career of Milford W. Howard, Populist Congressman from Alabama" (Unpublished Master's thesis, Auburn University, 1957), 57–58.

9. *Ibid*.

10. Woodward, *Tom Watson*, 223. In Alabama a comparable situation occurred with Joseph Manning, whose brother edited a newspaper which opposed him. Likewise, his father and brother remained staunch Democrats. The salient fact here is that politics, like "the late war," literally turned brother against brother. Jerrell H. Shoftner and William Warren Rogers, "Joseph C. Manning: Militant Agrarian, Enduring Populist," *Alabama Historical Quarterly*, XXIX (Spring-Summer, 1967), 36.

11. Quoted in *ibid.*, 239. For a description of one such event, see Ralph McGill, *The South and the Southerner* (Boston, 1963), 126–27.

12. Thomas K. Hearn, "The Populist Movement in Marshall County [Alabama]" (Unpublished Master's thesis, University of Alabama, 1935), 66.

13. For a summary of such treatment in one Southern state, see Frederick A. Bode, "Religion and Class Hegemony: A Populist Critique in North Carolina," *Journal of Southern History*, XXXVII (August, 1971), 417–38.

14. Quoted in Helen M. Blackburn, "The Populist Party in the South" (Unpublished Master's thesis, Howard University, 1941), 51.

15. *Biblical Recorder* (Raleigh), January 3, 1894, quoted in Bode, "Religion and Class Hegemony," 425.

16. Quoted in *ibid.*, 427.

17. Raleigh *Caucasian*, July 25, 1895, quoted in *ibid*, 433.

18. *People's Party Paper*, September 29, 1893.

19. William H. Skaggs, *The Southern Oligarchy: An Appeal in Behalf of the Silent Masses of Our County Against the Despotic Rule of the Few* (New York, 1924), 126, 424; Logan, *Negro in American Life and Thought*, 61–64, 67–73.

20. For discussions of the Lodge Bill, see *Cong. Record*, 51 Cong., 1 Sess., 5789–93, 6538–45, 6851, 6869.

21. Reddick, "Negro in the Populist Movement in Georgia," 25.

22. Frenise A. Logan, *The Negro in North Carolina, 1876–1894* (Chapel Hill, 1964), 61.

23. For the case against the bill's being logically tagged as a "Force Bill," see Richard E. Welch, "The Federal Elections Bill of 1890: Postscripts and Preludes," *Journal of*

American History, LII (December, 1965), 511–26.

24. For a discussion of the role the Republican "silverites" played in the defeat of the Lodge Bill, see Fred Wellborn, "The Influence of the Silver-Republican Senators, 1889–1891," *Mississippi Valley Historical Review,* XIV (March, 1928), 402–80.

25. *People's Weekly Tribune* (Birmingham), May 28, 1896.

26. Wilbur J. Cash, *The Mind of the South* (New York, 1941), 174. See also Kirwan, *Revolt of the Rednecks,* 95.

27. *People's Party Paper,* August 28, 1896.

28. The use of the "Force Bill" as a measure to create political conformity in the South can be very aptly traced in the newspapers and periodicals of that day. To follow this issue, see *Public Opinion,* 1889–90, VIII, 551–53; 1890–91, C, 330–31; 1893, XIII, 420–21; 1892–93, XIV, 103–04, 223; 1893, XV, 377–78, 614–15; 1893–94, XVI, 43–04, 71.

29. *National Economist,* July 26, 1890.

30. *Ibid.,* April 18, 1891.

31. *Progressive Farmer,* December 9, 1890; *National Economist,* July 26, 1890.

32. *Ibid.,* January 10, 1891. For further information on the Lodge Bill, see Ruth E. Byrd, "The History of the Force Bill of 1890 and its Effect upon State Constitutions" (Unpublished Master's thesis, University of North Carolina at Chapel Hill, 1939); Hoke Smith, "Disastrous Effects of the Force Bill," *Forum,* XIII, August, 1892), 686–92; Henry Cabot Lodge and Terrence V. Powderly, "The Federal Election Bill," *North American Review,* CLI (September, 1890), 257–73; A. W. Shaffer, "A Southern Republican on the Lodge Bill," *ibid.,* CLI (November, 1890), 601–09; Thomas B. Reed, "The Federal Control of Elections," *ibid.,* CLI (June, 1890), 671–80; *Progressive Farmer,* January 27, 1891; H. D. Hutchison to L. L. Polk, April 15, 1892, Leonidas L. Polk Papers, Southern Historical Collection, University of North Carolina at Chapel Hill.

33. On this philosophy, see Meier, *Negro Thought,* 42–46, 62–63, 74–76, 80–99, 105–06, 119–57, 208–47; Robert L. Factor, *The Black Response to America: Men, Ideals, and Organization from Frederick Douglass to the NAACP* (Reading, 1970), 109–16.

34. "An Open Letter from Charles A. Roxborough Resigning from the Republican Committee, with his Reasons Therefore, July 31, 1891." Charles A. Roxborough Letter, Louisiana State University Archives, Louisiana State University, Baton Rouge. Roxborough was a black leader of the Republican party in Louisiana during the 1880s. In the above letter, he hints for the Negro to support the Democrats rather than the Republicans.

35. Rayford W. Logan, *The Betrayal of the Negro: From Rutherford B. Hayes to Woodrow Wilson* (New York, 1965), 80; Louis Harlan, *Booker T. Washington: The Making of a Black Leader. 1865–1901* (New York, 1972), 164.

36. Meier, *Negro Thought in America,* 77. Interviewed by the Atlanta *Constitution,* a white Democratic paper, Professor Meier believes that the blacks made such statements "for white ears. . . ." However, I am of the opinion that the views of middle-class prosperous blacks differed little from whites of the same level on the Lodge Bill.

37. Quoted in *ibid.,* 192.

38. *Ibid.,* 80–82; W. E. Burghardt DuBois, *The Souls of Black Folk: Essays and Sketches* (Greenwich, 1961), 47; *Progressive Farmer,* January 27, 1891.

39. Meier, *Negro Thought in America,* 38.

40. Earl E. Thorpe, *The Mind of the Negro: An Intellectual History of Afro-Americans* (Westport, 1970), 275.

41. *National Economist,* August 15, 1891.

42. Hicks, *Populist Revolt,* 207–12.

43. *Ibid.*, 212–13; Blackburn, "Populist Party in the South," 15–16; Sheldon, *Populism in the Old Dominion,* 66. Out of the estimated 1,400 delegates, the two states of Kansas and Ohio had over 700 representatives. It also appears that Negroes were not viewed as "Southern delegates" by the press.

44. Quoted in Hicks, *Populist Revolt,* 212.

45. Clipping in Tom Watson Scrapbook #22, 24, Tom Watson Papers, Southern Historical Collection, University of North Carolina at Chapel Hill. See also Henry D. Lloyd, "The Populists at St. Louis," *Review of Reviews,* XIV (September, 1896), 299–300.

46. Reddick, "Negro in the Populist Movement in Georgia," 30.

47. Blackburn, "Populist Party in the South," 16–17.

48. Sheldon, *Populism in the Old Dominion,* 66. See also *National Economist,* November 28, 1891.

49. New York *Times,* May 21, 1891.

50. Reddick, "Negro in the Populist Movement in Georgia," 92; Blackburn, "Populist Party in the South," 16.

51. Quoted in Hicks, *Populist Revolt,* 215.

52. Quoted in Stuart Noblin, *Leonidas Lafayette Polk* (Chapel Hill, 1949), 269–70.

53. The Cincinnati platform can be found in Hicks, *Populist Revolt,* 433–35.

54. Various newspaper opinions on the third party question as well as the region's attitude toward its chance of success are discussed in *Public Opinion,* 1891, XI, 167–71.

55. *National Economist,* April 11, 1891.

56. *Ibid.,* June 13, 1891. Emphasis added. ". . . the first distinctive political body known as the People's party" was not formed until nearly six months later at Indianapolis. *People's Party Paper,* December 17, 1891.

57. *Alliance Vindicator,* quoted in *National Economist,* June 27, 1891.

58. Saloutos, *Farmer Movements in the South,* 123.

59. *People's Party Paper,* March 17, 1892.

60. *Ibid.*

61. Blackburn, "Populist Party in the South," 22.

62. A list of the number of seats allotted to each individual order can be found in Hicks, *Populist Revolt,* 226.

63. Reddick, "Negro in the Populist Movement in Georgia, 34–35; Blackburn, "Populist Party in the South," 22–23.

64. *People's Party Paper,* March 17, 1892.

65. *National Economist,* March 5, 1892.

66. The events of the St. Louis Convention can be found in *People's Party Paper,* February 25, 1892; *National Economist,* February 27, March 5, 1892.

67. Saloutos, *Farmer Movements in the South,* 124.

68. *National Economist,* March 5, 1892.

69. *Ibid.,* February 27, 1892; *People's Party Paper,* February 25, 1892.

70. Tom Watson Scrapbook, #27, 1; *National Economist,* March 5, 1892. These two accounts, both newspapers, differ little in their reporting of the actions that occurred. However, the difference involved a portrayal of attitudes and motivations that surrounded this event, one indicating self-interest, the other humane intentions. Probably the event was a mixture of the two.

71. Robert M. Saunders, "The Southern Populists and the Negro in 1892," *Essays in History,* XII (1966–67), University of Virginia, 10.

72. Saloutos, *Farmer Movements in the South,* 139. See also Sheldon, *Populism in the Old Dominion,* 1–21; *Southern Mercury,* January 28, 1897; Logan, *Negro in North Carolina,* 76–78.

73. Nashville *Banner,* October 4, 1891; *Philadelphia Press,* October 24, 1891, quoted in *Public Opinion,* 1891–92, XII, 99.

74. Hicks, *Populist Revolt,* 229.

75. *Ibid.,* 230. One author agrees that eight representatives were elected at large, but states that eight, rather than four, additional delegates were selected from each congressional district. Anna Rochester, *The Populist Movement in the United States* (New York, 1943), 66.

76. James H. "Cyclone" Davis, for example, when speaking to an audience would keep several volumes of Jefferson's works near him to use in buttressing the principles of Populism. See Woodward, *New South,* 245. See also, "Jefferson on the Race Question," *Progressive Farmer,* October 21, 1890; Thomas E. Watson, "The Creed of Jefferson, the Founder of Democracy" in *The Life and Speeches of Thomas E. Watson* (Nashville, 1908), 127–33; R. M. Goodman to Robert Felton, September 18, 1892, in Rebecca Latimer Felton Collection, University of Georgia Library, Athens, Georgia.

77. Hicks, *Populist Revolt,* 230–31.

78. Blackburn, "Populist Party in the South," 27.

79. See Simkins, *Tillman Movement in South Carolina,* 111–13, 180–81.

80. Blackburn, "Populist Party in the South," 27; Saunders, "The Southern Populists," 10.

81. Columbus *Advocate,* quoted in Abramowitz, "Negro in the Populist Movement," 278.

82. Kansas City *American Citizen,* October 2, 1891, quoted in Chafe, "The Negro and Populism," 410.

83. Omaha *Daily Bee,* quoted in Abramowitz, "Accommodation and Militancy," 34.

84. *People's Party Paper,* January 21, 1892.

85. *National Economist,* July 9, 1892. The rest of the platform can be found in Hicks, *Populist Revolt,* 439–44.

86. C. Vann Woodward, *The Strange Career of Jim Crow* (New York, 1957), 13–48.

87. See Noblin, *L. L. Polk,* 284–88; Hicks, *Populist Revolt,* 232–33; C. Vann Woodward, *Tom Watson: Agrarian Rebel* (New York, 1963), 30. Polk died on June 11, 1892.

88. Undated newspaper clipping in Tom Watson Scrapbook, #27, 1.

89. Noblin, *L. L. Polk,* 28, 199.

90. *People's Party Paper,* September 30, 1892. While this plan was described by Tom Watson to a Negro audience during his 1892 campaign, it seems unlikely, in view of his great admiration for the man, that he would have invented such a scheme which would discredit the memory of Polk. See Noblin, *L. L. Polk,* 155, 285, 291, 297.

91. The Alabama Populist Party advocated a similar plan in their 1894 platform. While calling for a separate state, the declaration favored relocating only those Negroes who voluntarily agreed to leave. The wording of the measure indicates that this was a humanitarian and paternalistic move designed to protect the Negro from recent white violence, rather than any expression of hostility toward the black man. The text of the declaration can be found in *Appleton's Annual Cyclopedia, 1894,* 4. See also Quarles, *Negro in the Making of America,* 157, concerning Negro sentiment in Texas for a separate state.

92. The relevant literature on this subject has been collected in Bracey *et al., Black Nationalism,* lxi–lxx.

93. Meier, *Negro Thought,* 63.

94. James T. Haley, ed. and compiler, *Afro-American Encyclopedia* (Nashville, 1895), 9. A copy of this rare volume is available in the Negro Collection, Fisk University, Nashville, Tennessee.

95. The Reverend Garland H. White to Governor W. J. Northen, March 29, 1894, in "The Negro at the South: Letters by Governor W. J. Northen," Northen Papers, State of Georgia Archives, Atlanta, folder marked "Speeches 1889–1891," 9–10. The best narrative of Bishop Turner's role can be found in Redkey, *Black Nationalism.*

96. Haley, *Afro-American Encyclopedia,* 9.

97. *Louisiana Populist* (Natchitoches), November 29, 1805.

98. Meier, *Negro Thought,* 62.

99. Hicks, *Populist Revolt,* 235. Judge Gresham declined the nomination, threw his support to Cleveland, and later became his secretary of state. Sheldon, *Populism in the Old Dominion,* 83.

100. For newspaper opinion of Weaver's chance to break the solid South in 1892, as well as his presidential campaign, see *Public Opinion,* 1892, XIII, 319–25, 1892–1893, XIV, 78–79.

101. Sheldon, *Populism in the Old Dominion,* 83–85; Arnett, *Populist Movement in Georgia,* 141–42; *National Economist,* July 9, 1892; *People's Party Paper,* July 8, 22, 1892. "General" James Field never attained any rank above major. His title was purely honorary.

102. Montgomery *Advertiser,* September 16, 1892; *The Daily News* (Birmingham), September 16, 1892, quoted in M. A. Booras, "A Case Study of . . . the Birmingham . . . Populist Party Convention" (Unpublished Master's thesis, University of Alabama, 1952), 113.

103. *Louisiana Populist,* January 24, 1896.

104. The circumstances distinguishing the growth and motivations of such movements can be found in King, *Social Movements,* 39–64.

105. *National Economist,* September 17, 1892.

106. The myth of the liberating proletariat has been soundly disproven by one modern political sociologist who views this type of individual as prone to express ethnic prejudice, political authoritarianism, and fundamentalist religious beliefs. Seymour Lipset, "Workingclass Authoritarianism," in *Political Man* (New York, 1963), 86–126. This essay is also found in *American Sociological Review,* XXIV (August, 1959), 482–501. For other modern evidence which further disputes this myth, see Morris Janowitz and Dwaine Marvick, "Authoritarianism and Political Behavior," *Public Opinion Quarterly,* XLVII (Summer, 1953), 185–201; Louis Wirth, "Race and Public Policy," *Scientific Monthly,* LXVIII (April, 1944), 304; William MacKinnon and Richard Centers, "Authoritarianism and Urban Stratification," *American Journal of Sociology,* LXI (May, 1966), 616.

107. Sheldon, *Populism in the Old Dominion,* 83.

Notes to Chapter 4

1. Woodward, *New South,* 245, 249–50. For additional use of the Jacksonian-Jeffersonian doctrine, see the statements of Davis and Milford W. Howard, the Populist congressman from Alabama, in Pollack, *The Populist Mind,* 203–30.

2. Copy of an untitled speech, 1896, Box 3, folder 19, Marion Butler Papers, Southern

Historical Collection. For a similar assertion by "Stump" Ashby, see Pollack, *Populist Mind,* 226.

3. Historians are divided over the question of whether or not Populism's utopia was in the future or the past. The present writer accepts the thesis of Richard Hofstadter: "The utopia of the Populists was in the past, not the future." Hofstadter, *Age of Reform,* 62.

4. Woodward, *Jim Crow,* 43. A similar comment can be found in Ignatius Donnelly's *Doctor Huquet* (1891), a novel of the post-Civil War South. Pollack, *Populist Mind,* 491. See also Hair, *Bourbonism and Agrarian Protest,* 193–94.

5. Thomas E. Watson, "The Negro Question in the South," *Arena,* VI (October, 1892), 540–50.

6. Woodward, *New South,* 252. See also Hofstadter, *Age of Reform,* 64–65.

7. Marion Butler to J. A. Simms, February 17, 1896, Box 2, Butler Papers.

8. B. S. Heath, *Labor and Finance Revolution* (1892) quoted in Hofstadter, *Age of Reform,* 63.

9. *Louisiana Populist,* October 18, 1895.

10. "National People's Party Platform," *The World Almanac, 1893* (New York, 1893), 83–84.

11. Wayne Alvord, "T. L. Nugent, Texas Populist," *Southwestern Historical Quarterly,* LVII (July, 1953), 65–81.

12. Shofner and Rogers, "Joseph C. Manning," 7–37; Summersell, "The Alabama Governor's Race of 1892," 22.

13. The roots and subsequent development of the Social Gospel have been traditionally assumed to be of a non-Southern, urban, clergy focus. Although the movement was "not unknown" in the South, according to Professor Woodward it had but "few spokesmen" in the region. Woodward, *New South,* 452. The present writer's examination of the literature of Populism has convinced him that the principles of the Social Gospel were incorporated into the movement and had wide circulation in the South. The studies of individuals by Professors Alvord, Bode, Shofner, and Rogers, cited above, reveal that individual Southern Populists, however rustic and ineffective, sympathetically presented the Social Gospel. Another individual who must be included in the group of Southern Social Gospelers is Milford Howard. Elmer F. Suderman, "The Social Gospel Novelists' Criticisms of American Society," *Midcontinent American Studies Journal,* VII (Spring, 1966), 60. Such a movement deserves more treatment in depth than I have been able to accord it here. For traditional surveys of the Social Gospel movement which exclude the South's role, see Charles Howard Hopkins, *The Rise of the Social Gospel in American Protestantism, 1866–1915* (New Haven, 1940); Sidney Fine, *Laissez Faire and the General-Welfare State* (Ann Arbor, 1950; 1966), 169–97.

14. Alvord, "T. L. Nugent," 72, 78.

15. Bode, "Religion and Class Hegemony," 421–23.

16. *Louisiana Populist,* December 6, 1895.

17. *Ibid.,* February 7, 1896. For a similar comment by W. Scott Morgan, see *ibid.,* July 12, 1895.

18. Booras, "Birmingham's Populist Party Convention," 85, 110.

19. Dallas *Morning News,* June 25, 1892, quoted in Woodward, *New South,* 247.

20. Montgomery *Advertiser,* September 16, 1892; *The Daily News* (Birmingham), September 16, 1892, in Booras "Birmingham Populist Party Convention," 85, 110.

21. *People's Weekly Tribune,* May 14, 21, 1896.

22. Shofner and Rogers, "Joseph C. Manning," 9.

23. Woodward, *New South,* 245–46.

24. Letter from W. R. Elmore, July 6, 1894, printed in *West Alabama Breeze,* July 12, 1894, quoted in Charles G. Summersell, "A Life of Reuben Kolb" (Unpublished Master's thesis, University of Alabama, 1930), 108–09.

25. J. H. Buchanan to Marion Butler, August 27, 1896, Box 3, folder 33, Butler Papers.

26. Summersell, "Reuben Kolb," 111.

27. W. J. Pearson to Marion Butler, May 18, 1896, Box 2, folder 27, Butler Papers. For an example of "an Alliance lay sermon" which further shows the religious tinge and moral attitude of the Southern agrarian revolt, see the letter of Linn Tanner of the Cheyneyville, Louisiana, in *National Economist,* June 13, 1891.

28. Hofstadter, *Age of Reform,* 62.

29. *Facts and Figures,* quoted in *Louisiana Populist,* December 14, 1894.

30. Quoted in Hofstadter, *Age of Reform,* 64.

31. *Ibid.*

33. *Town Talk,* quoted in *ibid.,* January 17, 1896.

34. Hofstadter, *Age of Reform,* 23–59; Paul Gaston, *New South Creed: A Study of Southern Mythmaking* (New York, 1970), 7–13; Edwin C. Rozwenc and John C. Matlon, eds., "The Agrarian Myth in American History," in *Myth and Reality in the Populist Revolt* (Boston, 1967), 1–6.

35. *Oneonta Star,* quoted in *People's Weekly Tribune,* December 3, 1896.

36. *Louisiana Populist,* August 24, 1894.

37. John Sparkman, "The Kolb-Oates Campaign of 1894" (Unpublished Master's thesis, University of Alabama, 1924), 2.

38. *People's Weekly Tribune,* May 21, 1896.

39. The "opulent theme," exalted in the New South, can be traced in Gaston's, "The Opulent South," in *The New South Creed,* 43–80.

40. Dorothy Scarborough, *In the Land of Cotton* (New York, 1923), 162.

41. The most complete study of these ideas can be found in Irvin G. Wyllie, *The Self-Made Man in America* (New Brunswick, 1954).

42. Quoted in Hofstadter, *Age of Reform,* 74.

43. *Louisiana Populist,* January 10, 1896.

44. Joel A. Tarr, "Goldfinger, the Gold Conspiracy and the Populists," *Mid-continent American Studies Journal,* VII (Fall, 1966), 49–52. For other contemporary examples of such thought patterns, see Daniel Bell, ed., *The Radical Right* (New York, 1964).

45. Hofstadter, *Age of Reform,* 71.

46. *Congressional Record,* quoted in William Loren Katz., ed., *Eyewitness: The Negro in American History* (New York, 1967), 339.

47. E. Franklin Frazier, *The Negro in the United States* (New York, 1949), 160. An enclosed chart illustrates the rising pattern of lynchings.

48. Compiled from data in Benjamin Brawley, *A Short History of the American Negro* (New York, 1950), 154, and Woodward, *New South,* 351. See also Logan, *Negro in American Life and Thought,* 76.

49. Clarence A. Bacote, "Negro Proscriptions, Protests and Proposed Solutions in Georgia, 1880–1908," in Dwight Hoover, ed., *Understanding Negro History* (Chicago, 1968), 205.

50. V. O. Key, Jr., *Politics, Parties, and Pressure Groups* (Cambridge, 1942; 1964), 14, n. 11; Cash, *Mind of the South,* 173–74.

51. Quoted in Redkey, *Black Exodus,* 9–10.

52. Quoted in Tindall, *Negro in South Carolina*, 251–52.

53. John B. Brownlow to Oliver P. Temple, January 1, 1894, Box 12, folder 4, Temple papers, Special Collections, University of Tennessee, Knoxville.

54. M. A. M'Cardy, "Duty of the State to the Negro," in *Afro-American Encyclopedia*, 143–44.

55. Tindall, *South Carolina Negroes*, 248.

56. *Ibid.*, 247. For various opinions, black and white, on "federal interference," see Open Letter Club Correspondence, folder 5, State of Tennessee Archives, Nashville.

57. See particularly George Wilson to Marion Butler, May 30, 1896, Box 2, folder 27, Butler papers; John B. Brownlow to Oliver P. Temple, December 19, 1897, Box 14, folder 2; Brownlow to Temple, July 29, 1894, Box 12, folder 5, Temple papers. For two perceptive interpretations of southern Republicanism and northern attitudes on the race question during the period, see Vincent P. DeSantis, *Republicans Face the Southern Question–The New Departure Years, 1877–1897* (New York, 1959) and Stanley P. Hirshson, *Farewell to the Bloody Shirt: Northern Republicans and the Southern Negro, 1877–1893* (New York, 1962).

58. Reverend A. L. Phillips, "God's Problem for the South," in *Afro-American Encyclopedia*, 23.

59. "Choice Thoughts and Utterances of Wise Colored People," in *ibid.*, 527; Charles W. Chestnutt, Letter No. 2, Open Letter Club Correspondence.

60. "Choice Thoughts and Utterances," 527.

61. Meier, *Negro Thought*, 35, 40; Bracey *et al.*, *Black Nationalism*, 223.

62. Bacote, "Negro Proscriptions in Georgia," 202.

63. Charles E. Wynes, *Race Relations in Virginia, 1870–1902* (Charlottesville, 1961), 117. See also Logan, *Negro in North Carolina*, 175.

64. Richmond *Planet*, April 6, 1895, in Wynes, *Race Relations in Virginia*, 118.

65. *Voice of Missions*, December 1, 1900, in Bracey *et al.*, *Black Nationalism*, 227. This comment was made by William Hooper Councill, president of the State Normal School at Huntsville, Alabama, who was "an even more extreme accommodator" than Booker T. Washington. *Ibid.*, 223. For additional information on Councill, see Meier, *Negro Thought*.

66. Quoted in Aptheker, *Documentary*, II, 757.

67. Ridgley Torrence, *The Story of John Hope* (New York, 1948), 114–15.

68. Gaston, *New South Creed*, 129–35.

69. Meier, *Negro Thought*, 101. For a discussion of "the contrast between a natural legend of moral innocence, in which Southerners always claimed to share, and the reality of Southern determination to maintain a master class," see Gaston, "The Innocent South," *New South Creed*, 119–50.

70. *Toiler*, April 17, 1889. See also, Summersell, "Alabama Governor's Race," 34, n. 59.

71. Quoted in Wynes, *Race Relations in Virginia*, 45.

72. *Ibid.*, 45–46.

73. Quoted in Woodward, *New South*, 219. The story of the Texas Lily-White Republican movement can be found in Paul Douglas Casdorph, "Norris Wright Cuney and Texas Republican Politics, 1883–1896," *Southern Historical Quarterly*, LXVIII (January, 1965), 455–64; Maud Cuney Hare, "The Lily Whites," in *Norris Wright Cuney* (Austin, 1913; 1968), 92–104.

74. Quoted in Woodward, *New South*, 220. See also, Joseph F. Steelman, "Vicis-

situdes of Republican Party Politics: The Campaign of 1892 in North Carolina," *North Carolina Historical Review*, XXXXIII (Autumn, 1966), 430–42.

75. John Roy Lynch, *Reminiscences of an Active Life: The Autobiography of John Roy Lynch* (Chicago, 1970), 334, ed. by John Hope Franklin. Lynch's comments on the motivations behind the Lily-White movement seem sound. However, his attempt to downplay their role and scope would appear to this writer, to be open to question. As a black Mississippi Republican, perhaps his intentions were honorable. The author of the standard biography of L. Q. C. Lamar, Wirt Armstead Cate, has challenged the accuracy of Lynch's case: "Generally speaking, little or no dependence can be placed on the writings of the Mississippi Negro ex-Congressman, John R. Lynch. . . . [He] perverted the facts . . . in all cases that suited his purpose and in some where falsifying apparently brought him no advantage." *Ibid.*, 318.

76. Quoted in Woodward, *New South*, 220.

Notes to Chapter 5

1. Woodward, *Strange Career of Jim Crow*, 46. Professor Woodward has repeated the essence of this statement in his earlier and later works on Populism. See Woodward, *Tom Watson*, 222; "The Populist Heritage and the Intellectual," in *Burden of Southern History*, 157; "Tom Watson and the Negro in Agrarian Politics," *Journal of Southern History*, IV (February, 1938), 21. This stimulating statement, which was largely responsible for the initiation of this study, has received wide acceptance by many other historians studying the period. For example, see Hair, *Bourbon Protest*, 241. See Joel Williamson, *Origins of Segregation*, v–ix, for a discussion of the Woodward thesis. Woodward has moderated his stance considerably in more recent years. See particularly Woodward, *American Counterpoint*.

2. See particularly Woodward, "Tom Watson and the Negro."

3. Abramowitz, "Negro in the Populist Movement," 288. See also McGill, *The South and the Southerner*, 128.

4. National Economist, September 10, 1892; People's Party Paper, August 12, 1892.

5. *National Economist*, November 26, 1892. This was a part of Loucks' presidential address to the Supreme Council of the Southern Alliance at Memphis on November 16, 1892.

6. Meier and Rudwick, "Introductory Note" to Herbert Schapiro, "The Populists and the Negro: A Reconsideration," *Making of Black America*, II, 27. Professor Schapiro's essay also examines this viewpoint, reaching a similar conclusion.

7. Gaither, "Negro in the Ideology of Southern Populism," 172–215, examines the inverse linear relationship between the black population and the Populist congressional vote in the various Southern states. See also Kirwan, *Revolt of the Rednecks*, 96.

8. Roscoe C. Martin, *The People's Party in Texas, A Study in Third Party Politics*, University of Texas Bulletin No. 3308 (Austin, 1933), 93–94; Lawrence D. Rice, *The Negro in Texas, 1874–1900* (Baton Rouge, 1971), 86–87; Abramowitz, "Negro in the Populist Revolt," 267–68.

9. Edmonds, *Fusion Politics*, 17, 225–27.

10. For statistical evidence on this phenomenon, see Gaither, "Negro in the Ideology of Southern Populism," 172–215.

11. Richmond *State* [n.d.], quoted in *Public Opinion*, XIII, 320.

12. For example, see statements in the *National Economist,* March 26, 1892; H. S. Scomp to W. H. Felton, September 11, 1894, Felton Collection. See also Woodward, "Populist Heritage," 150–51.

13. Psychologists, ostensibly unlike many historians, have long been aware of the inconsistency between verbal attitudes and inner commitment. For further information on this subject, see Richard T. La Piere, "Attitudes vs. Actions," *Social Forces,* XIII (December, 1934), 230–37; Bernard Kutner, Carol Wilkins and Penny Yarrow, "Verbal Attitudes, and Overt Behavior Involving Racial Prejudice," *Journal of Abnormal and Social Psychology,* XLVII (July, 1952), 649–52; Lawrence S. Linn, "Verbal Attitudes and Overt Behavior: A Study of Racial Discrimination," *Social Forces,* XLV (March, 1965), 353–64; Milton Malof and Albert Lott, "Ethnocentrism and the Acceptance of Negro Support in a Group Situation," *Journal of Abnormal and Social Psychology,* LXV (October, 1962), 254–58.

14. Woodward, *Origins of the New South,* 254. See also T. Harry Williams, *Romance and Realism in Southern Politics* (Baton Rouge, 1966), 53.

15. Carl Carmer, *Stars Fell on Alabama* (New York, 1934), 67.

16. Mrs. William H. Felton, *My Memoirs of Georgia Politics* (1911), quoted in Francis M. Wilhoit, "An Interpretation of Populism's Impact on the Georgia Negro," *Journal of Negro History,* LII (April, 1967), 123. William H. Felton was a candidate of the earlier Independents and later unsuccessful Populist movement in north Georgia. For the careers of W. H. Felton and his wife, see William P. Roberts, "The Public Career of Dr. William Harrell Felton" (Unpublished Doctoral dissertation, University of North Carolina, 1952); John E. Talmadge, *Rebecca Latimer Felton: Nine Stormy Decades* (Athens, 1960).

17. Richmond *Virginia Sun,* December 20, 1894, quoted in Woodward, *Origins of the New South,* 258.

18. *Louisiana Populist,* August 31, 1894. See also *Capitol Item* quoted in *ibid.,* August 31, 1894; and *ibid.,* September 21, 1894, for similar comments.

19. *Ibid.,* August 24, 1894.

20. *Progressive Farmer,* May 3, 1892, quoted in Florence E. Smith, "Populist Party in North Carolina" (Unpublished Doctoral dissertation, University of Chicago, 1929), 77–78.

21. Quoted in Thomas K. Hearn, "The Populist Movement in Marshall County [Alabama]" (Unpublished Master's thesis, University of Alabama, 1935), 56.

22. Alwyn Barr, *Reconstruction to Reform: Texas Politics, 1876–1901* (Austin, 1971), 152.

23. *Greensboro Watchman,* quoted in *People's Weekly Tribune,* May 28, 1896.

24. Atlanta *Constitution,* August 19, October 3, 1896, quoted in Olive Hall Shadgett, *The Republican Party in Georgia: From Reconstruction through 1900* (Athens, 1964), 117.

25. Quoted in Logan, *Negro in North Carolina,* 19.

26. Welsh *Crescent,* quoted in Hair, *Bourbonism and Agrarian Protest,* 187.

27. *People's Party Paper,* August 26, 1892.

28. See Alvord, "T. L. Nugent, Texas Populist," for a discussion of Nugent as a Social Gospeler.

29. Catherine Nugent, ed., *Life Work of Thomas L. Nugent* (1890), quoted in Saunders, "Southern Populists and the Negro in 1892," p. 17, n. 59.

30. *Ibid.*

31. Dallas *Morning News,* July 31, 1892, quoted in *ibid.*

32. Hackney, *Populism to Progressivism in Alabama,* 45–47.

33. Robert L. Saunders, "The Transformation of Tom Watson, 1894–1895," *Georgia Historical Quarterly,* LIV (Fall, 1970), 350.

34. Crowe, "Tom Watson, Populists, and Blacks Reconsidered," 102. See also Lawrence J. Friedman, *The White Savage: Racial Fantasies in the Postbellum South* (Englewood Cliffs, 1970), 80, for additional primary evidence to support this viewpoint.

35. See particularly Woodward, *Tom Watson,* 408–86.

36. Wilhoit, "Populism's Impact on the Georgia Negro," 117.

37. *People's Party Paper,* September 28, 1894; Bacote, "Negro Proscriptions in Georgia," 202–03; E. Merton Coulter, *Georgia: A Short History* (Chapel Hill, 1960), 392.

38. Crowe, "Tom Watson, Populists, and Blacks Reconsidered," 107–108.

39. *People's Party Paper,* September 28, 1894; Saunders, "Southern Populists and the Negroes, 1893–1895," 252.

40. For black and white opinion on the bill, see Bacote, "Negro Proscriptions in Georgia," 202–04.

41. Savannah *Tribune,* October 17, 1891, quoted in *ibid.,* 203.

42. Hair, *Bourbonism and Agrarian Protest,* 196–97. See also Henry C. Dethloff and Robert R. Jones, "Race Relations in Louisiana, 1877–1898," *Louisiana History,* IX (Fall, 1968), 314–16.

43. Wynes, *Race Relations in Virginia,* 47.

44. *Virginia Sun,* October 26, 1892, quoted in Saunders, "Southern Populists and the Negro in 1892," 7–8, n 2.

45. Wynes, *Race Relations in Virginia,* 47–50. Cf. Saunders, "Southern Populists and the Negro in 1892," 12–13 for a contrasting interpretation of Virginia Populism and blacks on the local level.

46. Woodward, *New South,* 257. See also Woodward, *Jim Crow,* 46.

47. Woodward, *New South,* 257. For a critical examination of Woodward's evidence, see Saunder's "Southern Populists and the Negro, 1893–1895," 246–47.

48. Rice, *Negro in Texas,* 256.

49. Dethloff and Jones, "Race Relations in Louisiana," 304, 310.

50. Perhaps the best known and most often cited incident alluded to by Professor Woodward concerns H. S. Doyle, a black preacher, who campaigned in Watson's behalf during the 1892 Georgia congressional election. Threatened with lynching, he was protected for two nights by "fully two thousand" white Populists. Woodward, *Tom Watson,* 239–40.

51. John William Graves, "Negro Disfranchisement in Arkansas," *Arkansas Historical Quarterly,* XXVI (August, 1967), 207.

52. Saunders, "Southern Populists and the Negro, 1893–1895," 247–248.

52. *Ibid.* Saunders, "Transformation of Tom Watson," 250. Friedman, *White Savage,* 81.

54. Woodward, *Jim Crow,* 45–46.

55. Quoted in Abramowitz, "Negro in the Populist Movement," 267–68.

56. Cf. Saunders, "Southern Populists and the Negro in 1892," 11; Wynes, *Race Relations in Virginia,* 48.

57. Graves, "Negro Disfranchisement in Arkansas," 203.

58. Quoted in Saunders, "Southern Populists and the Negro in 1892," 11.

59. *Ibid.;* Saunders, "Southern Populists and the Negro, 1893–1895," 241.

60. Lucia E. Daniel, "The Louisiana People's Party," *Louisiana Historical Quarterly,* XXVI (October, 1943), 1080.

61. Saunders, "Southern Populists and the Negro, 1893–1895," 243. Minority participation was clearly not one of the distinguishing features of Populist conventions. Amid a heady cynicism it would be easy at this point to wax eloquent about how a self-professed reform movement failed to achieve proportional representation for oppressed minorities. However, on examination, our contemporary standard does not appear to be significantly better than the Populist model. Alluding to a prevailing myth in American folklore, the Democratic party has been the political vehicle for minorities since the depression period of the 1930s; and yet, as recent as the 1968 Democratic convention in Chicago, blacks made up only 5.5 percent of the delegates although they were 20 percent of the total that eventually voted for Hubert Humphrey, the party's presidential candidate. Although they eventually provided 52 percent of the Democratic vote in 1968, women made up only 13 percent of the delegates. On examination, the convention delegates were predominantly middle-aged middle-class, white, and male. The persistence through time of this pattern reveals one the problems of using the American party system as an instrument of reform by individuals seeking surcease from their discontents. "Democrats: Trying for Party Reform," *Time,* December 6, 1971, 17.

62. Saunders, "Southern Populists and the Negro, 1893–1895," 243.

63. New York *Times,* March 23, 1965, 28; Willie Morris, *North Toward Home* (New York, 1970), 398–99. Twenty history professors, including Woodward, were involved in the march on Montgomery. At one point, Woodward and several fellow historians gathered in a circle and gave three cheers for Martin Luther King.

64. Woodward, *Strange Career of Jim Crow,* 46.

65. Augusta *Chronicle,* August 12, 1886, in Watson papers, Box 1, folder 2; Philip S. Foner, *Frederick Douglass: A Biography* (New York, 1964), 341–42, 431, n. 20. There is the same telling force of directness and fervor in Populist press coverage of the Douglass episode that is found in later Southern press coverage of the famous "dinner at the White House" episode in 1901. See Dewey W. Grantham, Jr., "Dinner at the White House: Theodore Roosevelt, Booker T. Washington, and the South," *Tennessee Historical Quarterly,* XVII (June, 1958), 112–30. Transposing the two names across time, there is illustrated in the language of the press an attitude so similar as to approach something akin to plagiarism. This further illustrates the homogeneity in racial attitudes of Southern whites, be they Populist or Democrat.

66. *National Economist,* September 17, 1892. See also *Caucasian,* March 21, 1895; *People's Party Paper,* April 12, 1895; Abramowitz, "Negro in the Agrarian Revolt," 95.

67. *Progressive Farmer,* September 18, 1894; *People's Party Paper,* October 28, 1892, August 24, 31, 1894; *weekly Toiler,* November 2, 1892. Many Populists advocated and openly supported education for blacks on a segregated basis. See *Progressive Farmer,* August 7, 1894; *Southern Mercury,* July 26, 1894; Kirwan, *Revolt of the Rednecks,* 98; Edmonds, *Fusion Politics,* 35; William D. McCain, "Populist Party in Mississippi" (Unpublished Master's thesis, University of Mississippi, 1931), 46–48; *Appleton's Annual Cyclopedia, 1892,* 740.

68. Saunders, "Transformation of Tom Watson," 350; Saunders, "Southern Populists and the Negro, 1893–1895," 245. For Frederick Douglass's viewpoint on "mixed schools," see Philip S. Foner, ed., *The Life and Writings of Frederick Douglass* (4 vols., New, 1955), IV, 288–90.

69. *People's Party Paper,* May 25, 1894, quoted in Friedman, *White Savage,* 79. See also *People's Party Paper,* July 22, 1892, for a similar statement issued by the Georgia People's Party.

70. *Caucasian,* April 4, 1895.

71. *People's Party Paper,* March 13, 1896, quoted in Friedman, *White Savage,* 79–80.

72. *People's Party Paper,* September 22, 29, October 13, 1893, quoted in *ibid.,* 81.

73. *Progressive Age* quoted in *Louisiana Populist,* September 14, 1894. Taylor was found guilty later of soliciting election funds from black government employees. The penalty was three years in prison, $5,000, or both. It does not appear that the sentence was carried out. *Ibid.;* Bacote, "Negro Proscription in Georgia," 223, n. 71.

74. Meier, *Negro Thought in America,* 32, 36, 50; Redkey, *Black Exodus,* 54–55, 80, 188; Bacote, "Negro Proscription in Georgia," 214, 223, n. 71.

75. Quoted in Meier, *Negro Thought in America,* 32.

76. *Southern Mercury,* August 9, 1894; *People's Party Paper,* April 5, 1895; Meier, *Negro Thought in America,* 32, 36, 50.

77. *People's Weekly Tribune,* June 18, 1896.

78. Friedman, *White Savage,* 81.

79. *People's Weekly Tribune,* June 4, 1896.

80. *Ibid., People's Party Paper,* March 22, 1895, quoted in Saunders, "Transformation of Tom Watson," 352.

81. Saunders, "Southern Populists and the Negro, 1893–1895," 252, 260, n. 49.

82. *People's Party Paper,* May 22, 1895, quoted in Friedman, *White Savage,* 81.

83. *Ibid.,* March 22, 1895, quoted in Saunders, "Transformation of Tom Watson," 352. Emphasis added.

84. For other such volatile incidents, See Edmonds, *Fusion Politics in North Carolina,* 42–43; *Louisiana Populist,* March 15, November 1, 1895; *Alliance Farmer,* quoted in *Louisiana Populist,* March 22, 1895; *Progress,* quoted in *ibid.,* March 22, 1895; and *People's Weekly Tribune,* June 11, 25, July 2, 1896, Birmingham *State Herald,* June 5, 1896. The first set of citations relates to an 1895 incident in North Carolina over legislative adjournment in honor of Frederick Douglass; the second concerns a contested congressional election case (Murray vs. Elliot, 1896) in South Carolina. Murray, a black, was seated over Elliot, a Caucasian, who had resorted to fraud in order to win his seat.

85. Kansas City *American Citizen,* December 23, 1892, quoted in Chafe, "Negro and Populism," 415.

86. *Ibid.*

Notes to Chapter 6

1. The formation and general characteristics of such movements are traced in King, *Social Movements,* 25–38.

2. The following discussion is based primarily on Watson, "The Negro Question," 541–49. This same article also appeared in Watson's personal newspaper, *The People's Party Paper,* September 16, 1892, and C. H. Pierson's *Virginia Sun,* October 19, 1892, just prior to the elections in Georgia and Virginia. It further illustrates the white Populist efforts to acquaint the black voter with their basic philosophy of "self interest."

3. *People's Party Paper,* September 16, 1892. The Louisiana People's Party, which met on February 17, 1892, adopted, almost verbatim, this same proposal into their platform. *Ibid.,* March 10, 1892.

4. Watson, "The Negro Question," 546. Author's emphasis added.

5. Hofstadter, *Age of Reform,* 83.

6. Watson, "The Negro Question," 550. For similar statements by Watson, see Watson, *Life and Speeches*, 127–65; *People's Party Paper*, September 16, March 17, 1892. The Georgia People's Party Convention also endorsed the viewpoint that "there is no southern man who will advocate social equality." *Ibid.*, July 22, 1892. For a summary of this same philosophy in Alabama, see *People's Weekly Tribune*, May 28, 1896.

7. *Caucasian*, April 4, 1895. See also Robert Wayne Smith, "A Rhetorical Analysis of the Populist Movement in North Carolina, 1892–1896" (Unpublished Doctoral dissertation, University of Wisconsin, 1957), 85. Microfilm copy in the North Carolina Collection, University of North Carolina at Chapel Hill.

8. *Southern Mercury*, January 14, 1897.

9. *People's Party Paper*, July 29, 1892. A similar proposal had been adopted into the platform of the Louisiana Populist Party. *Ibid.*, March 10, 1892.

10. *Ibid.*, July 15, 1892. See also C. Vann Woodward, "Tom Watson and the Negro in Agrarian Politics," *Journal of Southern History*, IV (February, 1938), 14–20.

11. Quoted in Gerald T. Bryant, "J. B. Rayner, A Negro Populist," *Negro History Bulletin*, III (May, 1940), 125.

12. See, for example, Leslie H. Fishel, Jr., "The Negro in Northern Politics, 1877–1900," *Mississippi Valley Historical Review*, XLII (December, 1955), 466–89; Vincent P. De Santis, "Negro Dissatisfaction with Republican Policy," *Journal of Negro History*, XXXVI (April, 1951), 148–59.

13. Blackburn, "Populist Party in the South," 45. This appears to be true of the Virginia Colored Alliance as well. Sheldon, *Populism in the Old Dominion*, 222. Cf. Saunders, "Southern Populists and the Negro in 1892," 10, for a different viewpoint.

14. Quoted in Sheldon, *Populism in the Old Dominion*, 222. Serving as president of the Virginia Alliance for three years, Page was subsequently elected president of the National Alliance. In addition, he was a major leader in the Virginia Populist Party.

15. *Virginia Sun*, July 20, 1892, quoted in Saunders, "Southern Populists and the Negro in 1892," 12.

16. *Ibid.*, 12–13.

17. Quoted in Sheldon, *Populism in the Old Dominion*, 86.

18. Allen W. Moger, *Virginia: Bourbonism to Byrd, 1870–1925* (Charlottesville, 1968), 95–98.

19. Richard L. Morton, *The Negro in Virginia Politics, 1885–1902* (Charlottesville, 1919), 98–132; Moger, *Virginia*, 47–75.

20. Quoted in Sheldon, *Populism in the Old Dominion*, 87–88. In the Southern ideological system, whites sharply distinguished themselves from blacks, conceiving the latter in terms of a marked physical contrast. Under this mythical system, "blue" cuticles were traits ascribed to Negro physical characteristics, or were regarded as a measure of Negro blood in one's heritage. Conversely, white cuticles were properties of the white man and stood as the antithesis of the character and properties of the black man. In substance, white cuticles were pure and desirable; "blue" cuticles were inferior and undesirable.

21. Norfolk *Public Ledger*, December 30, 1893, quoted in Moger, *Virginia*, 115.

22. Richmond, *Planet*, November 11, 25, 1893, quoted in Saunders, "Southern Populists and the Negro, 1893–1895," 240.

23. Sheldon, *Populism in the Old Dominion*, 92.

24. Richmond *Virginia Sun*, November 16, 1892, quoted in Woodward, *Origins of the New South*, 261. In early December, 1896, the *Virginia Sun*, "the populist [sic] organ of this state, gave a loud wail of anguish . . . and 'kicked the bucket.' " *Southern Mercury*,

December 17, 1896.

25. Woodward, *Origins of the New South,* 261; Sheldon, *Populism in the Old Dominion,* 90–92. See also *Southern Mercury,* December 17, 1896.

26. Richmond *Times,* February 6, 1894, quoted in Moger, *Virginia,* 98.

27. *Ibid.,* 108.

28. Quoted in Morton, *Negro in Virginia Politics,* 133.

29. Charles E. Wynes, "Charles T. O'Ferrall and the Virginia Gubernatorial Election of 1893," *Virginia Magazine of History and Biography,* LXIV (October, 1956), 437.

30. Sheldon, *Populism in the Old Dominion,* 102.

31. Edmund Randolph Cocke to H. St. George Tucker, January 25, 1891, quoted in Wynes, *Race Relations in Virginia,* 47. Cocke, grandson of Edmund Randolph, is an excellent example of the many distinguished families involved in the leadership of Virginia Populism.

32. Quoted in Sheldon, *Populism in the Old Dominion,* 101.

33. Wynes, "Charles T. O'Ferrall," 437, 450) Sheldon, *Populism in the Old Dominion,* 102.

34. *Ibid.,* 16; Wynes, *Race Relations in Virginia,* 51; Wynes, "Charles T. O'Ferrall," 450. As usual, the Democrats invoked the all-pervasive race question into the election of 1893. In 1895, the then governor, Charles T. O'Ferrall, a Democrat, invited a Massachusetts delegation to visit him at the Virginia state house; the delegation included, unexpectedly, a Negro. In order to avoid offending the remaining delegates, O'Ferrall, despite his personal feelings, was forced to socialize with the Negro. "The color line is in a kink," Tom Watson loudly proclaimed of this incident. "White supremacy . . . has a wonderful knack of changing color after the election." *People's Party Paper,* March 22, 1895.

35. Morton, *Negro in Virginia Politics,* 137, 144–45.

36. Henry M. Field, *Bright Skies and Dark Shadows,* quoted in Morton, *Negro in Virginia Politics,* 145.

37. Wynes, "Charles T. O'Ferrall," 437, 451. O'Ferrall received 127,940 votes, with Cocke, the Populist candidate, receiving 81,239, giving O'Ferrall a majority of 46,701 votes.

38. Wynes, *Race Relations in Virginia,* 49; Sheldon, *Populism in the Old Dominion,* 103–05; Wynes, "Charles T. O'Ferrall," 451.

39. Morton, *Negro in Virginia Politics,* 131.

40. Lynchburg *Daily Advance,* October 10, 1893, quoted in Wynes, *Race Relations in Virginia,* 49.

41. *Ibid.*

42. *Appleton's Annual Cyclopedia,* 1896, 813; Sheldon, *Populism in the Old Dominion,* 150. Despite the Populists' exaggerated claim that "there are 80,000 populist [sic] in Virginia" as of December 1896, and "the populist party is stronger in Virginia today than ever," the movement was in decline throughout the state. Further evidence of this was the death of the *Virginia Sun,* the major Populist paper in late 1896. *Southern Mercury,* December 17, 1896.

43. Steelman, "Vicissitudes of Republican Party Politics," 438–42; Theron Paul Jones, "The Gubernatorial Election of 1892 in North Carolina" (Unpublished Master's thesis, University of North Carolina at Chapel Hill, 1949), 63–69. Helen Edmonds, however, has concluded that the North Carolina Populists were "in the main, dissatisfied Democrates." Edmonds, *Fusion Politics,* 221.

44. Logan, *Negro in North Carolina Politics,* 22–23.

45. Edmonds, *Fusion Politics,* 221; T. L. Jones to Marion Butler, May 19, 1896, Box 2, folder 27, Butler Papers.

46. Edmonds, *Fusion Politics,* 37–38; *Progressive Farmer,* October 11, 1892; Smith, "Rhetorical Analysis of the Populist Movement," 83–84.

47. Quoted in William Alexander Mabry, "Negro Suffrage and Fusion in North Carolina," *North Carolina Historical Review,* XII (April, 1935), 91.

48. *Progressive Farmer,* March 24, 1896. Ironically, it appears that a large segment of the Colored Alliance probably voted against the Populists in the 1892 election in North Carolina. J. D. Thorne to L. L. Polk, April 20, 1892, Polk Collection; Edmonds, *Fusion Politics,* 26; "Proceedings of the Eleventh Annual Session of the North Carolina Farmers' State Alliance, 1897," in *Proceedings of the North Carolina Farmers' State Alliance, 1888–1906* (n.p., n.d.), 5.

49. B. F. Keith to Marion Butler, October 13, 1896, Box 4, folder 42, Butler Papers.

50. One observer, writing in 1929 of North Carolina politics, noted that not a single political campaign had taken place in the state since the Civil War without the cry of "nigger" by some speakers and newspapers. Smith, "Populist Party in North Carolina," 30. See also Logan, *Negroes in North Carolina,* 22–24; *National Economist,* October 1, 1892; "The South Under the Lash," circular in Marmaduke J. Hawkins Collection, State Archives and Library, Raleigh, North Carolina.

51. *Progressive Farmer,* August 21, 28, 1894; Joseph F. Steelman, "Republican Party Strategists and the Issue of Fusion with Populists in North Carolina, 1893–1894," *North Carolina Historical Review,* XLVII (July, 1970), 251, 264–65; Edmonds, *Fusion Politics,* 37–38.

52. *Progressive Farmer,* December 4, 1894.

53. *Caucasian,* January 4, 1894.

54. Charlotte *News and Observer,* August 18, 1894, quoted in Smith, "Populist Party in North Carolina," 112.

55. Joseph Gregoire De Roulhac Hamilton, *North Carolina Since 1860* (Chicago, 1919), 248–49.

56. *Ibid.,* 249.

57. W. A. Guthrie to Marion Butler, June 7, 1896, Box 2, folder 29; Clipping from *Charlotte Observer* (n.d.) attached to *ibid.,* Butler Papers. Guthrie was a former Republican who had joined the Populist Party and was chosen as gubernatorial candidate in 1896. For an analysis of Guthrie's campaign, see Edmonds, *Fusion Politics,* 56–57.

58. A. J. Nage to Marion Butler, April 30, 1896, Box 2, folder 26(a), Butler Papers.

59. J. H. Wilson to Marion Butler, November 4, 1896, Box 4, folder 46, *ibid.*

60. *Ibid.;* Clipping, *Charlotte Observer,* October 31, 1896, Box 4, folder 45, *ibid.*

61. Walter R. Henry to Marion Butler, October 20, 1896, Box 4, folder 43–44; J. H. Wilson to Butler, October 24, 29, 31, 1896, Box 4, folder 45; Clipping, *Charlotte Observer,* October 31, 1896, Box 4, folder 45, *ibid.*

62. Charles H. Martin to Marion Butler, December 11, 1896, Box 4, folder 50, *ibid.*

63. B. F. White to Marion Butler, June 28, 1896, Box 2, folder 29, *ibid.*

64. T. L. Jones to Marion Butler, May 19, 1896, Box 2, folder 27, *ibid.*

65. B. F. White to Marion Butler, June 28, 1896, Box 2, folder 29, *ibid.* Russell was the successful Republican gubernatorial candidate in 1896.

66. Edmonds, *Fusion Politics,* 37, 321.

67. Steelman, "Republican Party Strategists and the Issue of Fusion," 245.

68. Andrew D. Cowles should not be confused with William H. H. Cowles, a Democrat from the Eighth District. For a sketch of W. H. H. Cowles, see *Congressional Directory,* 1 Sess., 52 Cong., 88.

69. Andrew D. Cowles, "A Card to the Republican Party of Iredell County," Statesville, North Carolina, October 29, 1894, in Marmaduke J. Hawkins Collection, State Archives and Library, Raleigh, North Carolina. Emphasis added. Cowles' letter opposing fusion was widely disseminated. As a former chairman of the Republican Executive Committee from Iredell County, his voice carried considerable weight with the following. Steelman, "Republican Party Strategists and the Issue of Fusion," 268.

70. Hal W. Ayer to Marion Butler, October 6, 1896, Box 4, folder 41, Butler Papers. Ayer was the Populist candidate for auditor in 1896.

71. Campaign pamphlet, "An Appeal to Populists and Defense of Mr. Thos. Watson, Washington, October 20, 1896," Box 4, folder 45, *ibid.*

72. James H. Sherrill to Marion Butler, September 13, 1896, Box 3, folder 36, *ibid.*

73. A. J. Moyr to Marion Butler, September 7, 1896, Box 3, folder 35, *ibid.*

74. H. S. Shufen to Butler, September 8, 1896, Box 3, folder 35, *ibid.*

75. James R. Happs to Butler, September 11, 1896, Box 3, folder 36, *ibid.*

76. W. A. Guthrie to Butler, September 26, 1896, Box 3, folder 39, *ibid.*

77. R. R. Krusey to Butler, May 1, 1896, Box 2, folder 26, *ibid.*

78. Logan, *Negro in North Carolina,* 22.

79. Quoted in *ibid.*

80. Quoted in Meier, *Negro Thought,* 33.

81. Y. C. Morton to Butler, April 30, 1896, Box 2, folder 26(a), Butler Papers.

82. A. H. Paddison to Butler, April 23, 1896, Box 2, folder 26(a), *ibid.*

83. Williard H. Smith, "William Jennings Bryan—A Reappraisal," Indiana Academy of the Social Sciences, *Proceedings, 1965* (New Series, Volume X), 56–69; "William Jennings Bryan and the Social Gospel," *Journal of American History,* LIII (June, 1966), 41–60; "William Jennings Bryan and Racism," *Journal of Negro History,* LIV (April, 1969), 127–49.

84. *The Afro-American Sentinel* (Omaha), August 29, 1896, quoted in Aptheker, *Documentary History,* II, 818–19. This editorial was by Philip H. Brown, an official of the Afro-American Associated Press.

85. Smith, "Bryan and Racism," 137–39.

86. *Ibid.,* 136.

87. A. J. Moyr to Butler, September 7, 1896, Box 3, folder 35, Butler Papers.

88. W. A. Guthrie to Butler, October 6, 1896, Box 4, folder 41, *ibid.*

89. The events of the "Fusionist" victory are detailed in Edmonds, *Fusion Politics.* The 1894 Fusion legislature of North Carolina had been divided in the following manner: in the Senate, eight Democrats, twenty-four Populists, and eighteen Republicans; in the House, forty-six Democrats, thirty-eight Republicans, and thirty-six Populists. *Appleton's Annual Cyclopedia,* 1895, 556. 90. Hugh T. Lefler and Albert Ray Newsome, *North Carolina: The History of a Southern State* (Chapel Hill, 1963), 519.

91. See particularly the handbill, "To the People of North Carolina" (dated July 2, 1896), distributed and endorsed by some of the state's major black leadership. Prominent "anti-Russell" blacks were: R. B. Russell of Maxton; W. H. Quick of Rockingham; R. B. Fitzgerald, A. M. Moore, and J. E. Shepherd of Durham; R. W. H. Leak, L. A. Scruggs, E. A. Johnson, and Bruce Capehart, all of Raleigh. Black leadership generally supported W. A. Guthrie, the former Republican turned Populist. W. A. Guthrie to Butler, June 7, July

11, 1896; Clipping from *Charlotte Observer* (n.d.). Box 2, folders 29–30, Butler Papers.

92. Edmonds, *Fusion Politics,* 222. A similar view can be found in William Alexander Mabry, *The Negro in North Carolina Politics Since Reconstruction* (Durham, 1940), 34–35; Mabry, "Negro Rule and Fusion Politics," 85–86.

93. *Progressive Farmer,* August 23, 1892.

94. *Ibid.,* October 16, 1894.

95. M. C. Birmingham to Butler, December 19, 1896; *Charlotte Observer,* October 29, 31, 1896, Box 4, folder 50, Butler Papers.

96. The Populists supported Tillman, who accepted many of the Alliance and Populist doctrines and incorporated them into the Democratic platform. Like Tennessee, an organized party of considerable strength never existed in South Carolina. In 1892, for example, the South Carolina Populists remained content to nominate presidential electors only. See Simkins, *Tillman Movement,* 172, 180–81; Hicks, *Populist Revolt,* 246; Joseph Church, "The Farmer's Alliance and the Populist Movement in South Carolina, 1887–1896" (Unpublished Master's thesis, University of South Carolina, 1953), 50–52, 75–76.

97. Simkins, *Tillman Movement,* 136–37. See also Francis Butler Simkins, "Ben Tillman's View of the Negro," *Journal of Southern History,* III (May, 1937), 161–74.

98. *National Economist,* October 8, 1892.

99. For a discussion of the Negro and South Carolina Republicanism, see Tindall, *South Carolina Negroes,* 41–68; James W. Patton, "The Republican Party in South Carolina, 1876–1895," in *Essays in Southern History,* 91–111.

100. The "eight ballot box" law passed in 1892, "was in effect, a literacy test for voting," and had, along with trickery and fraud, bitten deeply into the political ranks of the Negro. In the mid-1890s before the 1895 constitutional convention, there were only about 120,000 potential legal Negro voters in the state. Ernest M. Lander, Jr., *A History of South Carolina, 1865–1960* (Chapel Hill, 1960), 28, 40.

101. Tindall, *South Carolina Negroes,* 56–58.

102. See Church, "Farmers' Alliance and Populist Movement in South Carolina," 24–33.

103. *Georgia Baptist,* quoted in *Progressive Farmer,* October 30, 1894.

104. Watson, "The Negro Question," 547; *People's Party Paper,* September 16, 1892. Author's emphasis added.

105. *Georgia Baptist,* quoted in *Progressive Farmer,* October 30, 1894. Emphasis added.

106. *Southern Alliance Farmer* (Atlanta), August 2, 1892, quoted in Pollack, *Populist Mind,* 386–87; Arnett, *Populist Movement in Georgia,* 151–53; Shadgett, *Republican Party in Georgia,* 105–21; Thomas E. Watson to W. H. Felton, September 16, 1894, Felton Collection.

107. For comments on Doyle, see Woodward, *Tom Watson,* 239–40; Woodward, "Tom Watson and the Negro," 48–49; *People's Party Paper,* October 28, 1892; October 27, 1893; October 25, 1895.

108. *People's Party Paper,* March 17, 1892.

109. L. Moody Sims, Jr., "A Note on Sidney Lanier's Attitude Toward the Negro and Toward Populism," *Georgia Historical Quarterly,* LII (September, 1968), 305–37.

110. Additional evidence of this view is found in Saunders, "Southern Populists and the Negro in 1892," 8–9.

111. *People's Party Paper,* July 22, 1892. This issue contains events of Georgia's first People's Party Convention, held in Atlanta on July 20, 1892.

112. *Southern Alliance Farmer,* August 2, 1892, in Pollack, *Populist Mind,* 386–87.

113. Crowe, "Tom Watson, Populists and Blacks," 109.

114. Atlanta *Journal,* December 7–8, 1893, quoted in *ibid.* The Populist record is also examined by Crowe in *ibid.* See also Shadgett, *Republican Party in Georgia,* 117, for the hostile comment of Henry Lincoln Johnson, a black Republican leader in Georgia.

115. Atlanta *Constitution,* October 1, 1892, quoted in *ibid.,* 111.

116. *Ibid.,* 110.

117. Crowe, "Tom Watson, Populists, and Blacks," 109.

118. Shadgett, *Republican Party in Georgia,* 110–11.

119. Atlanta *Constitution,* October 1, 1892, quoted in *ibid.,* 111.

120. *Ibid.*

121. Crowe, "Tom Watson, Populists, and Blacks," 116; Meier, *Negro Thought,* 28. It is germane to the subject to say that the writer received from the Northen papers a picture of a man who sought to protect the black from violence. However, his view on "social equality" between the races was one of considerable resistance. See particularly the folder marked "Mob Violence," Northen Collection.

122. In conjunction with his promise, Northen advocated and the Georgia Legislature subsequently passed an "anti-lynch" bill on December 20, 1893. *Georgia Laws, 1893,* 128. See also Northen, "The Negro at the South," address before the Congregational Club, Boston, Massachusetts, May 22, 1899, in "Speeches, 1889–91," Northen Collection.

123. Meier, *Negro Thought,* 170.

125. Woodward, *New South,* 259.

126. Coulter, *Georgia,* 393–94. Emphasis added. See also Arnett, *Populist Movement in Georgia,* 153–54; Woodward, *Tom Watson,* 241.

127. *People's Party Paper,* January 20, 1893. A similar story is told by a North Carolina black in *Progressive Farmer,* January 24, 1893.

128. Reddick, "Negro in the Populist Movement in Georgia," 58–59; Woodward, *Tom Watson,* 241.

129. *People's Party Paper,* October 14, 1892.

130. *Ibid.,* October 28, 1892.

131. Quoted in Crowe, "Tom Watson, Populists, and Blacks," 109.

132. *National Economist,* October 1, 1892. For an example of the type of "Force Bill" propaganda used against the Georgia Populists, see "The Force Bill, the Farmer and the Tariff" a circular distributed by Charles F. Crisp, a Democrat, "in his usual forcible style." Marmaduke J. Hawkins Collection. For similar tactics, see the full print of a "Rape Circular" issued by W. Y. Atkinson, a prominent Georgia Democrat, in *People's Party Paper,* September 18, 1896.

133. Coulter, *Georgia,* 395.

134. Arnett, *Populist Movement in Georgia,* 183.

135. Bascom Osborne Quillian, Jr., "The Populist Challenge in Georgia in the Year 1894" (Unpublished Master's thesis, University of Georgia, 1948), 60–61.

136. *People's Party Paper,* October 18, 1895.

137. *Ibid.,* June 1, 1894. See also Arnett, *Populist Movement in Georgia,* 183.

138. *People's Party Paper,* March 29, 1895. See also Shadgett, *Republican Party in Georgia,* 117.

139. *People's Guide,* quoted in *People's Party Paper,* October 28, 1895; Woodward, *Tom Watson,* 269–71. If the price is correct, this was a bargain since votes normally sold for $1 each.

140. H. S. Scomp [≥] to W. H. Felton, November 9, 1894, Felton Collection. Felton, a former Democrat and Whig, ran as a Populist Congressional candidate from the seventh District in 1894 against John W. Maddox, an incumbent Democrat.

141. J. D. Cunningham to W. H. Felton, November 8, 1894, *ibid.* Using unfriendly newspaper accounts, one student has concluded that the Negroes voted for the Populists in 1894. Abramowitz, "Negro in the Populist Movement," 275–76.

142. W. H. Hidell to Rebecca Felton, *ibid.,* October 15, 1894; W. H. Hidell to W. H. Welton, November 7, 1894. Rebecca Felton, the wife of W. H. Felton, was a reformer and advocate of temperance and feminine rights.

143. Arnett, *Populist Movement in Georgia,* 184. See also Manning, *Fadeout of Populism,* 22, 25. Despite the fraudulence, 1894, with 44.5% of the total vote, represented the apex of Georgia Populism; Quillan, "Populist Challenge in Georgia," 112.

144. *People's Party Paper,* October 14, 1892.

145. This practice appears to have been widespread. See Arnett, *Populist Movement in Georgia,* 154; Coulter, *Georgia,* 83, Woodward; *Tom Watson,* 241; *Southern Mercury,* October 29, 1896; *People's Party Paper,* September 28, October 5, 1894, July 29, October 14, 1892. Democrats were not alone in having sufficient pressure to force blacks to vote according to their wishes. "It is undoubtedly true" Woodward has written, "that the Populist ideology was dominantly that of the landowning farmer who was, in many cases, the exploiter of landless tenant labor." Woodward, *Tom Watson,* 218.

146. Ralph Wardlaw, *Negro Suffrage in Georgia, 1867–1930,* Phelps-Stokes Fellowship Studies, Number 11, *Bulletin* of the University of Georgia, XXXIII, No. 2a (Athens, 1932), 45–46, 79–80.

147. Murphy [?] to W. H. Felton, December 4, 189. See also H. [?] to Rebecca Felton, December 13, 1894, Felton Collection.

Notes to Chapter 7

1. Clark, *Populism in Alabama,* 182, 26. The governor is not identified by name.

2. William G. Brown, "The South and the Saloon," *Century Magazine,* LXXVI (1908), quoted in Woodward, *New South,* 452.

3. Clark, *Populism in Alabama,* 21, 162–63, 180.

4. Shoftner and Rogers, "Joseph C. Manning," 7–37.

5. *Louisiana Populist,* November 30, 1894.

7. Clark, *Populism in Alabama,* 11–20, 172–74; Manning, *Fadeout of Populism,* 60.

8. Rogers, *One-Gallused Rebellion,* 55; Allen J. Going, *Bourbon Democracy in Alabama, 1874–1890* (University, Alabama, 1951), 47–49, 54–56. Cotton prices in Alabama declined as follows: December 1, 1880, 10 cents; December 1, 1888, 8.5 cents; 1893, 7 cents; 1894, 4.8 cents; 1896, 6.5 cents. Clark, *Populism,* 35, 68.

9. Quoted in *ibid.,* 174.

10. Woodward, *New South,* 244–45.

11. William Warren Rogers, "Reuben F. Kolb: Agricultural Leader of the New South," *Agricultural History,* XXXII (April, 1958), 109–19.

12. Hackney, *From Populism to Progressivism,* 18.

13. Rogers, *One-Gallused Rebellion,* 221.

14. Summersell, "Alabama Governor's Race," 21.

15. Leah R. Atkins, "Populism in Alabama: Reuben F. Kolb and the Appeals to

Minority Groups," *Alabama Historical Quarterly,* XXXII (Fall and Winter, 1970), 169–70, 173–74.

16. *Huntsville Gazette,* January 2, 1892, quoted in Saunders, "Southern Populists and the Negro in 1892," 15.

17. Atkins, "Kolb and the Appeals to Minority Groups," 174.

18. Clark, *Populism in Alabama,* 144; Rogers, *One-Gallused Rebellion,* 233.

19. Atkins, "Kolb and the Appeals to Minority Groups," 174.

20. *Ibid.,* 173.

21. Hackney, *From Populism to Progressivism,* 40; Rogers, *One-Gallused Rebellion,* 238.

22. Saunders, "Southern Populists and the Negro, 1893–95," 240–42, 257.

23. *Choctaw Advocate* (Butler), July 13, 1892, quoted in Atkins, "Kolb and the Appeals to Minority Groups," 173; Rochester, *Populist Movement in the United States,* 59. Emphasis added. As in other states previously examined, the emphasis here was on "political rights" and moral evaluaton, not social rights.

24. Quoted in Rogers, *One-Gallused Rebellion,* 213.

25. Hackney, *From Populism to Progressivism,* 38.

26. Summersell, "Alabama Governor's Race," 19.

27. *Ibid.,* 22.

28. *Ibid.,* 25–26. A listing of blacks who supported Jones is included in *ibid.*

29. Clark, *Populism in Alabama,* 136.

30. For an examination of these charges, see "The Alabama Election," *Public Opinion,* XII (1892), 442–44; Moore, *History of Alabama,* 624; Rogers, *One-Gallused Rebellion,* 221–27.

31. Hackney, *From Populism to Progressivism,* 22–23; Rogers, *One-Gallused Rebellion,* 226.

32. Clark, *Populism in Alabama,* 26–27, 80.

33. Summersell, "Alabama Governor's Race," 27.

34. *Ibid.,* 29–30.

35. Factor, *Black Response to America,* 158.

36. *Ibid.* Additional analyses of the voting in black belt counties can be found in Abramowitz, "Negro in the Populist Movement," 280.

37. Summersell, "Alabama Governor's Race," 5; Clark, *Populism in Alabama,* 175.

38. *Ibid.,* 177–78. Populists in both Alabama and North Carolina generally used the term "co-operation" rather than fusion in their literature. The theme projected was that this effort was a necessary cooperative venture to secure fair elections.

39. Hackney, *From Populism to Progressivism,* 33–34; Clark, *Populism in Alabama,* 142, 152. As an example of how contorted Alabama politics had become, the Lily Whites contained an element of blacks. Hackney, *From Populism to Progressivism,* 33; Rogers, *One-Gallused Rebellion,* 280.

40. Hackney, *From Populism to Progressivism,* 34; Saunders, "Southern Populists and the Negro, 1893–95," 256.

41. Allen J. Going, "Critical Months in Alabama Politics, 1895–1896," *Alabama Review,* V (October, 1952), 276, n. 26.

42. Charles Grayson Summersell, "A Life of Reuben Kolb" (Unpublished Master's thesis, University of Alabama, 1930), 102–03; Sparkman, "Kolb-Oates Election," 33; Clark, *Populism in Alabama,* 153.

43. *Appleton's Annual Cyclopedia,* 1894, 5.

44. Skaggs, *The Southern Oligarchy*, 120. Skaggs played a prominent role in Alabama Populism and his conclusions herein are largely based on his personal observations of the political situation in his state. His conclusions should be balanced against more objective accounts.

45. Atkins, "Kolb and Appeal to Minority Groups," 179–80.

46. Skaggs, *The Southern Oligarchy*, 121; Rogers, *One-Gallused Rebellion*, 280–82.

47. Skaggs, *The Southern Oligarchy*, 121.

48. Rogers, *One-Gallused Rebellion*, 289.

49. Cole, "Populism in Tuscaloosa County," 77–80.

50. Skaggs, *The Southern Oligarchy*, 119; Rogers, *One-Gallused Rebellion*, 281–82.

51. Clark, *Populism in Alabama*, 154.

52. Hicks, *Populist Revolt*, 335; Cole, "Populism in Tuscaloosa County," 77–80.

53. Clark, *Populism in Alabama*, 175.

54. Accounts of Negro disfranchisement can be found in Joseph H. Taylor, "Populism and Disfranchisement in Alabama," *Journal of Negro History*, XXXIV (October, 1949), 410–27; and Hackney, *From Populism to Progressivism*, 147–208. In my estimation, Taylor overemphasizes the Populists' proposal for Negro disfranchisement while Hackney probably minimizes their contribution.

55. Tallapoosa, *New Era*, in *People's Weekly Tribune*, December 3, 1896.

56. *People's Weekly Tribune*, November 26, 1896; January 14, 1897.

57. *Ibid.*

58. I. L. Brock to Oliver D. Street, September 13, 1902, quoted in Hackney, *From Populism to Progressivism*, 203.

59. *Ibid.*, 176. *People's Weekly Tribune*, December 10, 1896. For a contrasting interpretation of Manning, see Shoftner and Rogers, "Joseph Manning," 7–37.

60. Birmingham *News*, February 8, 1894; Redkey, *Black Nationalism*, 193–94; Alfred W. Reynolds, "The Alabama Negro Colony in Mexico, 1894–1896," *Alabama Review*, V (October, 1952), 243–68, and VI (January, 1953), 31–58; *Appleton's Annual Cyclopedia*, 1894, 4. "Plans" to put "all negroes in one place and all whites in another" were absurd, according to Tom Watson. Parting from one's black mammy would be sufficient reason to reject such a proposal. Friedman, *White Savage*, 83.

61. Hackney, *From Populism to Progressivism*, 206.

62. Dethloff and Jones, "Race Relations in Louisiana," 306, 308. A table indicating voter registration by race can be found in Ezell, *South Since 1865*, 176.

63. Hair, *Bourbonism and Agrarian Protest*, 113–14, 234, 237, 241–43, 247, 262–65; Dethloff and Jones, "Race Relations in Louisiana," 305; C. Vann Woodward, *American Counterpoint* (Boston, 1971), 212–13; Ezell, *South Since 1865*, 175–76.

64. Gilbert L. Dupré, *Political Reminiscences*, quoted in Dethloff and Jones, "Race Relations in Louisiana," 308.

65. *Ibid.*, 307–08.

66. Hair, *Bourbonism and Agrarian Protest*, 186–92; Woodward, *Jim Crow*, 29–31. For a description of a pattern of aristocratic paternalism in nearby Arkansas, see Graves, "Negro Disfranchisement in Arkansas," 200–01.

67. Opelousas *Courier*, February 11, 1888, quoted in Dethloff and Jones, "Race Relations in Louisiana," 308.

68. Melvin J. White, "Populism in Louisiana During the 'Nineties," *Mississippi Valley Historical Review*, V (June, 1918), 14–15.

69. *Town Talk in Louisiana Populist*, January 4, 1895. Like any complex movement,

Populism cannot be defined sharply, but suffice it to say that this portrait formed a central theme of the membership's view of its recent past.

70. Hair, *Bourbonism and Agrarian Protest*, 244, 248. See also Hofstadter, *Age of Reform*, 101–02.

71. *Ibid.*, 216–17.

72. *National Economist*, October 17, 1891. Emphasis added.

73. *Ibid.*

74. White, "Populism in Louisiana," 11.

75. Daniel, "Louisiana People's Party," 1080.

76. *National Economist*, December 20, 1890; Abramowitz, "Negro In the Agrarian Revolt," 94–95.

77. Charles A. Roxborough, "An Open Letter."

78. Hair, *Bourbonism and Agrarian Protest*, 223; Daniel, "Louisiana People's Party," 1055.

79. Pollock, *Populist Mind*, 386. This same philosophy was being expressed, almost verbatum, by Tom Watson in Georgia. See particularly *People's Party Paper*, March 17, 1892.

80. Hair, *Bourbonism and Agrarian Protest*, 225. Woodward is clearly wrong in his statement that "Louisiana Populists in combination with Anti-Lottery allies of the Democratic party won an easy victory over the regular Democrats in the state election of 1892." Woodward, *New South*, 261.

81. N. T. N. Robinson (Marshall, U.S. Circuit Court of Appeals, 5th District, La.) to Henry Wise Garrett, Washington, D.C., April 7, 1892, Robinson Letter, Tulane University Library and Archives, Tulane University, New Orleans.

82. Quoted in Ezell, *South Since 1865*, 175.

83. Hair, *Bourbonism and Agrarian Protest*, 235.

84. *Louisiana Populist*, quoted in Woodward, *New South*, 276.

85. Shreveport *Evening Judge*, December 15, 1895, quoted in Hair, *Bourbonism and Agrarian Protest*, 260.

86. *Louisiana Populist*, March 29; May 17, 1895.

87. *Ibid.*, September 7, 1894.

88. *Ibid.*, June 21; July 5, 1895.

89. *Ibid.*, December 6, 1895.

90. *Ibid.*, January 17, 24, 31, 1896.

91. *Ibid.*, May 17, 1895.

92. *Ibid.*, August 31, 1894. See also *ibid.*, August 24, September 21, 1894.

93. *Ibid.*, September 20, 1895.

94. *Ibid.*, September 13, 1895.

95. *Louisiana Populist*, August 31, October 19, 1894; *Shreveport Progress*, in *ibid.*, October 19, 1894.

96. *Ibid.*, May 14, 1894. See also *ibid.*, November 1, 1895.

97. *Ibid.*, October 11, 25, 1895.

98. *Ibid.*, August 16, 1895. White, "Populism in Louisiana," 13–14.

99. *Louisiana Populist*, February 21, 1896.

100. Quoted in Williams, *Romance and Realism in Southern Politics*, 50.

101. Dethloff and Jones, "Race Relations in Louisiana," 307; Hair, *Bourbonism and Agrarian Protest*, 274.

102. Williams, *Romance and Realism in Southern Politics*, 57.

103. Hair, *Bourbonism and Agrarian Protest,* 175.

104. Lewinson, *Race, Class, and Party,* 91; Hair, *Bourbonism and Agrarian Protest,* 276–77; White, "Populism in Louisiana," 18–19.

105. Dethloff and Jones, "Race Relations in Louisiana," 317. A different viewpoint of Populist attitudes can be found in Hair, *Bourbonism and American Protest,* 274.

106. Dethloff and Jones, "Race Relations in Louisiana," 317. These objections sound strangely reminiscent of Northern objections to Southern congressional representation based on slave population prior to the Civil War.

107. *Louisiana Populist,* April 22, 1898, quoted in *ibid.*

108. *Ibid.*

109. *Ibid., 316.*

110. *Ibid.*

111. Lewinson, *Race, Class, and Party,* 81. There is a slight discrepancy between the figures of Lewinson and of Dethloff and Jones. However, on one point all authors agree: a sharp decline in Negro registrants followed the 1898 constitutional convention.

112. Key, *Southern Politics,* 519. An enclosed table indicates voter registration by race and sex.

113. Dethloff and Jones, "Race Relations in Louisiana," 316. See also White, "Populism in Louisiana," 16–19.

114. Barr, *Reconstruction to Reform,* 117–22; Robert C. Cotner, *James Stephen Hogg: A Biography* (Austin, 1959), 250–51.

115. Ernest W. Winkler, ed., *Platforms of Political Parties in Texas* (Austin, 1916), 293. The origin of the Texas Populist party can be traced to the formation of a county ticket in Navarro County, February 1888. E. G. Sessions to Marion Butler, June 11, 1896, Butler Papers, Box 2, folder 29.

116. Winkler, *Political Platforms,* 297–99.

117. Quoted in Abramowitz, "Negro in the Populist Revolt," 267–68.

118. Saunders, "Southern Populists and the Negro in 1892," 11, n. 28; Abramowitz, "Negro in the Populist Revolt," 262–68; *Southern Mercury,* June 30, July 7, 1892.

119. Rice, *Negro in Texas,* 70.

120. Winkler, *Political Platforms,* 316–26; Barr, *Reconstruction to Reform,* 129–37. National Populist platforms supporting free silver can be found in Hicks, *Populist Revolt,* 432–44.

121. Quoted in Barr, *Reconstruction to Reform,* 136.

122. Dallas *Morning News,* June 25, 1892, quoted in Woodward, *New South,* 246.

123. Alvord, "T. L. Nugent, Texas Populist," 65–81.

124. Catherine Nugent, ed., *Life Work of Thomas L. Nugent* (1896), quoted in Saunders, "Populists and the Negro in 1892," 17, n. 59.

125. Dallas *Morning News,* August 9, 1892, quoted in *ibid.*

126. *Ibid., 17.*

127. *Ibid.*

128. *Ibid.*

129. Woodward, *New South,* 261–62; Abramowitz, "Negro in the Populist Revolt," 268.

130. Cotner, *Hogg Biography,* 313.

131. Rice, *Negro in Texas,* 72.

132. Quoted in Cotner, *Hogg Biography,* 312–13.

133. Robert Cotner, ed., *Addresses and State Papers of James Stephen Hogg* (Austin,

1951), 432. See also Harrell Budd, "The Negro in Politics in Texas, 1867–1898" (Unpublished Master's Thesis, University of Texas, 1929), 108; Rice, *Negro in Texas,* 75.

134. *Ibid.,* 76.

135. Cotner, *Hogg Biography,* 313.

136. Rice, *Negro in Texas,* 74. A partial list of other black leaders who supported Hogg is included. A speech by Henry Clay Gray, a black who supported Hogg, can be found in Douglas Geraldyne Perry, "Black Populism: The Negro in the People's Party in Texas" (Unpublished Master's Thesis, Prairie View University, 1945), 58–64.

137. Rice, *Negro in Texas,* 72–77; Barr, *Reconstruction to Reform,* 138–39; Maud Cuney Hare, *Norris Wright Cuney* (Austin, 1913; 1968), 163.

138. Rice, *Negro in Texas,* 80; Martin, *People's Party in Texas,* 73, 76, 78, 90, 96–97. A map illustrating the voting patterns for the various candidates can be found in Cotner, *Hogg Biography,* opposite p. 313.

139. Abramowitz, "John B. Rayner, Grass Roots Leader," 160–93.

140. Abramowitz, "Negro in the Populist Revolt," 270; Bryant, "J. B. Rayner, A Negro Populist," 125.

141. *Ibid.*

142. *Ibid.) Southern Mercury,* October 4, 1894; March 29, 1895; August 18, 1898; June 9, 1898.

143. Rice, *Negro in Texas,* 79.

144. Lewinson, *Race, Class, and Party,* 110.

145. Galveston *Daily News,* quoted in Casdorph, "Norris Wright Cuney," 457.

146. *Ibid.*

147. *Ibid.,* 460; Quarles, *Negro in the Making of America,* 157.

148. Casdorph, "Norris Wright Cuney," 460–64; Hare, *Norris Wright Cuney,* 127–230.

149. *Ibid.,* 204.

150. *Ibid.,* 158.

151. Rice, *Negro in Texas,* 82.

152. *Ibid.,* 83; Casdorph, "Norris Wright Cuney," 460–64.

153. Rice, *Negro in Texas,* 82–84; Perry, "Black Populism," 28–29.

154. Key, *Southern Politics,* 534. An enclosed map traces the rise and decline of Texas Populism.

155. *Ibid.*

156. Rice, *Negro in Texas,* 138.

157. *Ibid.,* 83, 136.

158. Key, *Southern Politics,* 534–35.

159. Rice, *Negro in Texas,* 138–39.

160. Lewinson, *Race, Class, and Party,* 104, 121, 147.

161. Barr, *Reconstruction to Reform,* 141–42, 149–50, 174; Martin, *People's Party in Texas,* 69–87, 105–11, 252–60.

162. Barr, *Reconstruction to Reform,* 173.

163. *Ibid.,* 174.

Notes to Chapter 8

1. Woodward, *New South,* 245–46.

2. Barr, *Reconstruction to Reform,* xii, 149–50.

3. Hackney, *Populism to Progressivism*, 27–31.

4. H. Larry Ingle, "A Southern Democrat at Large: William Hodge Kitchen and the Populist Party," *North Carolina Historical Review*, XXXXV (Spring, 1968), 178–94.

5. Watson, "Negro Question in the South," 541–49. See also *People's Party Paper*, September 16, 1892.

6. Hackney, *Populism to Progressivism*.

7. Hofstadter, *Age of Reform*, 60–93.

8. All election data used herein were secured in data deck form from Dr. Sheldon Hackney, History Department, Princeton, New Jersey. All urban economic and racial statistics were taken from the 1900 census.

9. Incidence of election irregularities in Tennessee and Arkansas increased greatly with the advent of the twentieth century. By mid-century, Professor Key concluded that, of all the Southern states, "Tennessee has the most consistent and widespread habit of fraud, with Arkansas a close second." V. O. Key, Jr., *Southern Politics in State and Nation* (New York, 1949), 443. However, Key believes that election fraud in the American system "has declined over the long term." Key, *Politics, Parties, and Pressure Groups*, 636.

10. W. P. Keller to Marion Butler, September 27, 1896, folder 40, Box 3, Butler Papers.

11. *Arkansas Gazette*, February 3, 1889, quoted in Woodward, *New South*, 56.

12. Vernon Lane Wharton, *The Negro in Mississippi, 1865–1890* (New York, 1965), 204.

13. Albert Burton Moore, *History of Alabama* (Tuscaloosa, 1934), 624; "The Alabama Election," *Public Opinion*, 1892, XIII, 442–44; Rogers, *One-Gallused Rebellion*, 289.

14. Although the Southern election system has an unenviable reputation for fraud, incidents of irregularities can readily be discovered nationwide. In Chicago's ninth ward on April 3, 1883, for example, Abraham Lincoln, James Madison, John Hancock, Thomas Jefferson, and George Washington were "sworn in." Ironically, all of these prominent "voters" were recorded as Democrats. Key, *Politics, Parties, and Pressure Groups*, 629, n. 8.

15. Mingo Scott, Jr., *The Negro in Tennessee Politics and Governmental Affairs, 1865–1965* (Nashville, 1964), 82. See also Joseph Howard Cartwright, "The Negro in Tennessee Politics, 1880–1891" (Unpublished Master's thesis, Vanderbilt University, 1968), 5, 208–58.

16. For additional statistical characteristics which exemplify this pattern at the county level, see the analyses of the 1896 North Carolina congressional elections in Gaither, "Negro in the Ideology of Southern Populism," 172–75.

17. For evidence of this pattern in Louisiana, see J. A. Tetts to Marion Butler, October 3, 1896, Butler Papers, Box 4, folder 41. See also Saunders "Southern Populists and the Negro in 1892," 21–25.

18. Woodward, *New South*, 252.

19. For a discussion of this philosophy, see "The Myths of Coalition," in Carmichael and Hamilton, *Black Power*, 58–84.

Notes to Chapter 9

1. Joseph A. Schlesinger, *Ambition and Politics* (Chicago, 1946), 4–5, 57–58.

2. Quoted in Factor, *Black Response to America*, 59.

3. Quoted in Wharton, *Negro in Mississippi,* 216.

4. Quoted in Francis L. Broderick, *W. E. B. DuBois, Negro Leader in a Time of Crisis* (Stanford, 1966), 86.

5. W. E. B. DuBois, *Dusk of Dawn: An Essay Toward an Autobiography of a Race Concept* (New York, 1940), 29. In later years DuBois "began to believe" that Populism was a party of "deep significance" and its failure was caused by "the established election frauds of the South, of which I knew. . . ." *Ibid.,* 54.

6. Factor, *Black Response to America,* 103.

7. *Tallapoosa, New Era,* quoted in *People's Weekly Tribune,* December 3, 1886. See also Joseph B. Taylor, "Populism and Disfranchisements in Alabama," *Journal of Negro History,* XXXIV (October, 1949), 410–27.

8. Quoted in McGill, *The South and the Southerner,* 123–24.

9. *People's Party Paper,* September 27, 1895, quoted in Saunders, "Southern Populists and the Negro, 1893–1895," 251.

10. *Ibid.,* 260, n. 47.

11. *People's Weekly Tribune,* May 28, 1896.

12. *Ibid.,* December 31, 1896.

Notes to Epilogue

1. For the Wallace philosophy, as distinguished from the Wallace rhetoric, see Jerald R. Burke's *The Political Philosophy of George C. Wallace* (Portals Press, Tuscaloosa, 1976). For the Carter philosophy, see Jimmy Carter, *Why Not the Best?* (Broadman Press, Nashville, 1975).

2. Michael Barone, Grant Ujifusa, and Douglas Matthews, The *Almanac of American Politics, 1976* (E. P. Dutton, New York, 1975), 1–2.

3. George Wallace, *Stand Up for America* (Doubleday, New York, 1976), 115.

4. The information on the Black vote was provided by J. Stanley Alexander, the Voter Education Project, Atlanta, Georgia.

5. The information on the Caucasian vote was developed from Donald S. Strong's *Issue Voting and Party Realignment* (forthcoming from the University of Alabama Press).

BIBLIOGRAPHY

This bibliography is selective rather than exhaustive. Only those materials—primary and secondary—that proved especially valuable and might serve as research aids for future historians of southern Populism and the Negro are listed below. Other materials utilized can be found in the footnotes of the various chapters and appendices.

A. Primary Materials

1. Manuscript Collections

Marion Butler Papers, Southern Historical Collection, University of North Carolina at Chapel Hill.

A huge, invaluable collection, the Butler papers contain much political correspondence from various Populists throughout the South. The major portion consists of letters from little known, local, political leaders who injected comments about the grassroots tactics of the Democrats. Generally erudite and comprehensive in scope, the Butler papers proved to be perhaps the most valuable collection examined during this study.

Rebecca Latimer Felton Collection, University of Georgia Archives, Athens.

Generally composed of memoranda and personal letters, these papers contain major and controversial correspondence about the 1894 political campaign in Georgia. They were immensely useful for a balanced treatment of the state's political history during this period, especially in the Seventh District. Bearing heavy emphasis on the black man's venality, these manuscripts exhibit the characteristic unevenness of various individual accounts and should be approached with caution.

Marmaduke J. Hawkins Papers, North Carolina State Library and Archives, Raleigh, North Carolina.

This small collection contains several prominent examples of the type of political propaganda used during the Populist revolt. Since their circulation was vigorously pushed by Democrats as "inflammatory" material, they were of particular value in assessing the opposition's psychological attack against Populist racial ideology in the South. The two dominating issues of the "Force Bill" and "Negro domination" are animated by several particulars within the collection. Ostensibly written as propaganda items, their factual merit must be balanced against more objective sources.

William J. Northen Papers, Georgia State Archives and Library, Atlanta, Georgia.

Northen, although a Democratic governor, was particularly critical about the use of violence against the blacks. But as a conservative he accepted the white dictum that "social equality" was highly undesirable to both races. This is a valuable collection for understanding why blacks would vote for a man whose party was very caustic toward the Negro. Individual currents of political reform such as Northen acted as a magnetic force to middle-class black leaders who attempted to adapt to local conditions.

Open Letter Club Correspondence, Tennessee State Library and Archives, Nashville.

A small but valuable collection of papers with several interesting pieces debating the "Force Bill" and its possible effects on the South and the Negro. After that, the collection is of little value to a study of this nature.

Leonidas L. Polk Collection, Southern Historical Collection.

The Polk papers provided a rich source of information about the Farmers' Alliance movement in the larger context of agrarian reform. The comments of Polk's contemporaries concerning political conditions and the progress of the agrarian movement proved to be of particular value in analyzing the South's slow philosophical shift toward independent political activity. Also, these same references provided an illuminating insight into the ideological struggle taking place in the southern mind over the Negro question and the consequences of a third party.

N. T. N. Robinson Letter, Tulane University Library and Archives, Tulane University, New Orleans.

Robinson was a United States Marshall in Louisiana's Fifth District. This letter contains his description of the widespread fraud and violence that was occurring during the state elections in April, 1892.

Charles A. Roxborough Letter, Louisiana State University, Archives, Baton Rouge.

A letter of resignation by a black Republican leader from Louisiana. Roxborough includes some interesting reasons for possible black defection from the Republican party. By way of innuendo and nuance, he hints that the Negro should support the Democrats. He subsequently joined the Louisiana Populist party and was nominated for the office of state treasurer at the party's first convention in 1892.

Oliver P. Temple Papers, Special Collections, University of Tennessee Library, Knoxville.

Outside of some interesting material on southern white Republican attitudes toward the Negro, the collection was of little value to a study of this nature. The Temple papers are primarily concerned with the political activities of the two major parties. The absence of correspondence concerning the third party in Tennessee is largely indicative of the state's minor role in the Populist revolt.

Tom Watson Papers, Southern Historical Collection.

Unusually disappointing for a collection with its reputation as a source of information on Populist activities. Because of Watson's prominence as a Southern liberal in race relations, it is regrettable that the collection, despite its size, contains so little useful for the period before 1900. "It is a testimony to C. Vann Woodward's thoroughness," Norman Pollack has written, "that he was able to reconstruct so ably Watson's activities in the 1890s, for the papers themselves were of little help." Despite this weakness, however, these papers constitute an indispensable starting point for any study of Southern Populist racial attitudes.

2. *Official Government Records and Documents*

Bureau of the Census. *Negro Population, 1790–1915*. Washington, Government Printing Office, 1918.

Congressional Directory, 1891–1896. Washington, Government Printing Office.

Congressional Record, 1890–1896. Washington, Government Printing Office.

Office of Recorder of Deeds, Corporation Division, Instrument No. 1606, *Incorporation Liber 4*, Folio 354, Washington, D.C.

State of Georgia. *Georgia Laws*, 1889–1894.

3. *Election Returns*

All election data (1891–1900) were unselfishly supplied by Dr. Sheldon Hackney, History Department, Princeton, New Jersey. Dr. Hackney's computerized compilation includes all eleven states of the Old Confederacy. All economic and racial statistics were taken from the 1900 census. These data were supplemented by my earlier analysis in a Master's thesis, which used 1890 census data. Due to the fraudulent nature of southern politics, particularly during this period, any conclusion drawn should be balanced against manuscript material.

4. *Newspapers*

Nashville *Banner* (Nashville, Tennessee). 1891–1896.

> An independent daily which provided objective coverage on Farmers' Alliance and Populist activities as they occurred in the Nashville vicinity. An indispensable aid to any study of the Tennessee order despite its almost total neglect of the Negro's role in the state movement.

The Caucasian (Clinton and Raleigh, North Carolina). 1892–1897.

> Under the tutorage of Marion Butler, a former Republican turned Populist, this paper, ironically, was not as sympathetic in tone to the Negro as its counterpart, *The Progressive Farmer*. It was, however, exceedingly valuable as an aid in gleaning the state's conservative white Populist opinion toward the Negro.

Atlanta *Constitution*. 1890–1896.

Daily News (Birmingham, Alabama). February 8, 1894.

> This issue contains the 1894 state platform of the Alabama Jeffersonian-Populist party. Of particular interest, is the proposal to "set apart sufficient territory to constitute a state, given exclusively to the colored race."

Louisiana Populist (Natchitoches, Louisiana). 1894–1899.

> Under the editorship of Hardy Brian, the Populist state secretary, this paper served as the official organ of the Louisiana movement. Brian was particularly vituperative, making hostile comments about Bourbons and blacks alike.

National Economist (Washington, D.C.). 1890–1893.

> The official organ of the Southern Alliance, this weekly quoted extensively from various grassroots Populist papers in a "reform press" section thereby providing a good insight into the diversity of racial attitudes within the region.

People's Party Paper (Atlanta, Georgia). 1891–1896.

> The personal organ of Tom Watson, providing an illuminating example of the white Populist liberal ideology toward the black community. Except during political campaigns, however, other states received only superficial commentary on racial and social conditions.

People's Weekly Tribune (Birmingham, Alabama). 1894–1897.

> With John W. DuBose as editor and Reuben Kolb as business manager, this was easily the most influential Populist newspaper in the state. Of all the newspapers examined, the *Tribune* was the most hostile toward Negroes—an attitude perhaps prompted by its readership, which seemed less interested in banding together politically with the blacks than did other southern states.

The Progressive Farmer (Raleigh, North Carolina). 1890–1895.

> Founded by L. L. Polk, president of the Southern Alliance, this weekly was of particular interest for its broad critical evaluation of the South's contributions to the agrarian movement. In the course of its perusal, important data were also gathered due to its wavering between a conservative and conciliatory line toward the Negro.

Public Opinion (New York, Public Opinion Quarterly Press). 1889–1895.

> This is a collection of newspaper excerpts arranged topically. The use of these volumes gave a wide geographical and philosophical overview of the Farmers'

Alliance and third party movement. Coverage for political events in the Gulf Coast
South was particularly good.

The Southern Mercury (Dallas, Texas). 1893–1897.

The official organ of Texas Populism, this newspaper was valuable for its regional
perspective of the South's political history. Exceedingly important in evaluating the
Populists' psychology toward the Negro voter in the South.

New York *Times.* May 21, 1891; March 23, 1965.

Weekly Toiler (Nashville, Tennessee). 1888–1892.

The Tennessee Farmers' Alliance organ under the editorship of J. H. McDowell,
this paper was almost the sole source of information on the history of the state's
Colored Alliances and Wheels. Despite the *Toiler's* official connotation, the Nashville
Banner provided a more intricate study of the white Alliance movement during this
period.

5. *Periodical Articles*

Cable, George W. "The Convict Lease System in the Southern States," *Century
Magazine, XXVII* (February, 1888), 582–99.

————. "The Freedman's Case in Equity," *Century Magazine,* XXIX (January, 1885),
409–18.

————. "The Silent South," *Century Magazine,* XXX (September, 1875), 674–91.

————. "A Simpler Negro Question," *Forum,* VI (December, 1888), 392–403.

————. "What Shall the Negro Do?" *Forum,* V (August, 1888), 627–39.

Diggs, Annie L. "The Farmers' Alliance and Some of Its Leaders," *Arena,* V (April,
1892), 590–604.

Flower, Benjamin O. "The General Discontent of America's Wealth Creators as Illustrated
in Current Cartoons," *Arena,* XVI (1896), 298–304.

Lloyd, Henry D. "The Populists at St. Louis," *Review of Reviews,* XIV (September,
1896).

Lodge, Henry Cabot, and Terrence V. Powderly. "The Federal Election Bill," *North
American Review,* CLI (September, 1890), 257–73.

"National People's Party Platform," *The World Almanac,* 1893 (New York, 1893), 83–85.

Reed, Thomas B. "The Federal Control of Elections," *North American Review,* CLI (June,
1890), 671–80.

Shaffer, A. W. "A Southern Republican on the Lodge Bill," *North American Reviw,* LI
(November, 1890), 601–09.

Smith, Hoke. "Disastrous Effects of the Force Bill," *Forum* XIII (August, 1892), 686–92.

Watson, Thomas E. "The Negro Question in the South," *Arena,* VI (October, 1892),
540–50.

6. *Edited Documents and Letters*

Aptheker, Herbert, ed. *A Documentary History of the Negro People in the United States.* 2
vols. Citadel Press, New York, 1964.

Bracey, John H., Jr., August Meier, and Elliot Rudwick, eds. *Black Nationalism in
America.* Bobbs-Merrill Company, Indianapolis, 1970.

Cotner, Robert C., ed. *Addresses and State Papers of James Stephen Hogg.* University of
Texas Press, Austin, 1951.

Foner, Philip S., ed. *Life and Writings of Frederick Douglass,* 4 vols. Citadel Press, New
    York, 1955.
Hendrick, Burton J. *The Training of an American: The Earlier Life and Letters of Walter
    Hines Page, 1855–1913.* Houghton Mifflin, New York, 1938.
Katz, William Loren. *Eyewitness: The Negro in American History.* Pittman, New York,
    1967.
Pollack, Norman, ed. *The Populist Mind.* Bobbs-Merrill Company, New York, 1967.
Tindall, George B., ed. *A Populist Reader.* Harper Torchbooks, New York, 1966.
Van Noppen, Ina W., ed. *The South: A Documentary History.* Van Nostrand, Princeton,
    1958.
Williamson, Joel, ed. *The Origins of Segregation.* D. C. Heath, Boston, 1968.
Winkler, Ernest William, ed. *Platforms of Political Parties in Texas.* University of Texas
    Bulletin No. 53. University of Texas, Austin, 1916.

7.   *Miscellaneous*

Cable, George W. *The Silent South.* Scribner, New York, 1890.
————. *The Negro Question.* Scribner, New York, 1890.
Dunning, Nelson A., ed. *The Farmers' Alliance and Agricultural Digest.* The Alliance
    Publishing Company, Washington, 1891.
Haley, James T., ed. and comp. *Afro-American Encyclopaedia.* Haley and Florida,
    Nashville, 1895.
Manning, Joseph. *The Fadeout of Populism.* T. A. Hebbons Company, New York, 1928.
Otken, Charles H. *The Ills of the South; or, Related Causes Hostile to the General
    Prosperity of the Southern People.* G. P. Putnam and Sons, New York, 1894.
Skaggs, William H. *The Southern Oligarchy: An Appeal in Behalf of the Silent Masses of
    Our Country Against the Despotic Rule of the Few.* Devin-Adair, New York, 1924.
Watson, Thomas E. *The Life and Speeches of Thomas E. Watson.* N. P., Nashville, 1908.

B.   SECONDARY SOURCES
1.   *Biographies*

Broderick, Francis L. *W. E. B. DuBois: Negro Leader in a Time of Crisis.* Stanford
    University Press, Stanford, 1966.
Cotner, Robert C. *James Stephen Hogg: A Biography.* University of Texas Press, Austin,
    1959.
Foner, Philip S. *Frederick Douglass: A Biography.* Citadel Press, New York, 1964.
Hare, Maud Cuney. *Norris Wright Cuney: A Tribune of the Black People,* ed. by Robert
    Cotner. Steck-Vaughan Company, Austin, 1913; 1968.
Harlan, Louis R. *Booker T. Washington: The Making of a Black Leader, 1865–1901.*
    Oxford University Press, New York, 1972.
Holmes, William F. *The White Chief: James Kimble Vardaman.* Louisiana State University
    Press, Baton Rouge, 1970.
Lynch, John Roy. *Reminiscences of an Active Life: The Autobiography of John Roy Lynch,*
    ed. by John Hope Franklin. University of Chicago Press, Chicago, 1970.
Noblin, Stuart. *Leonidas Lafayette Polk.* University of North Carolina Press, Chapel Hill,
    1949.

Robison, Dan M. *Bob Taylor and the Agrarian Revolt*. University of North Carolina Press, Chapel Hill, 1935.

Simkins, Francis Butler. *Pitchfork Ben Tillman: South Carolinian*. Louisiana State University Press, Baton Rouge, 1944.

Talmadge, John E. *Rebecca Latimer Felton: Nine Stormy Decades*. University of Georgia Press, Athens, 1960.

Torrence, Ridgely. *The Story of John Hope*. Macmillan, New York, 1948.

Woodward, C. Vann. *Tom Watson: Agrarian Rebel*. Rinehart and Company, New York, 1938; 1963.

2. *State Studies*

Arnett, Alex M. *The Populist Movement in Georgia*. Columbia University *Studies in History, Economics, and Public Law*, CIV, No. 1. Columbia University Press, New York, 1922.

Barr, Alwyn. *Reconstruction to Reform: Texas Politics, 1876–1906*. University of Texas Press, Austin, 1971.

Brewer, J. Mason. *Negro Legislators of Texas and Their Dependents*. Mathis Publishing Company, Dallas, 1935.

Clark, John B. *Populism in Alabama, 1874–1896*. Auburn Printing Company, Auburn, 1927.

Coulter, E. Merton. *Georgia: A Short History*. University of North Carolina Press, Chapel Hill, 1960.

Edmonds, Helen. *The Negro and Fusion Politics in North Carolina, 1895–1901*. University of North Carolina Press, Chapel Hill, 1961.

Going, Allen J. *Bourbon Democracy in Alabama, 1874–1900*. University of Alabama Press, University, 1951.

Hackney, Sheldon. *Populism to Progressivism in Alabama*. Princeton University Press, Princeton, 1969.

Hair, William Ivy. *Bourbonism and Agrarian Protest: Louisiana Politics, 1877–1900*. Louisiana State University Press, Baton Rouge, 1969.

Hamilton, Joseph G. de R. *North Carolina Since 1860*. University of Chicago Press, Chicago, 1919.

Hart, Roger L. *Redeemers, Bourbons, and Populists: Tennessee, 1870–1896*. Louisiana State University Press, Baton Rouge, 1975.

Kirwan, Albert D. *Revolt of the Rednecks: Mississippi Politics, 1876–1925*. Harper, New York, 1951.

Lander, Ernest M., Jr. *A History of South Carolina, 1865–1960*. University of North Carolina Press, Chapel Hill, 1960.

Lefler, Hugh Talmadge, and Albert Ray Newsome. *North Carolina: The History of a Southern State*. University of North Carolina Press, Chapel Hill, 1963.

Logan, Frenise A. *The Negro in North Carolina, 1876–1894*. University of North Carolina Press, Chapel Hill, 1964.

Mabry, William A. *The Negro in North Carolina Politics Since Reconstruction*. Duke University Press, Durham, 1940.

Martin, Roscoe C. *The People's Party in Texas, A Study in Third Party Politics*. University of Texas *Bulletin* No. 3308. University of Texas Press, Austin, 1933.

Moger, Allen W. *Virginia: Bourbonism to Byrd, 1870–1925*. University of Virginia Press,

Charlottesville, 1968.

Moore, Albert Burton. *History of Alabama and Her People*. University of Alabama Supply Store, Tuscaloosa, 1934.

Morton, Richard L. *The Negro in Virginia Politics, 1865–1902*. University of Virginia Press, Charlottesville, 1919.

Rice, Lawrence D. *The Negro in Texas, 1874–1900*. Louisiana State University Press, Baton Rouge, 1971.

Rogers, William Warren. *The One-Gallused Rebellion: Agrarianism in Alabama, 1865–1896*. Louisiana State University Press, Baton Rouge, 1970.

Scott, Mingo, Jr. *The Negro in Tennessee Politics and Government Affairs, 1865–1965*. Rich Printing Company, Nashville, 1964.

Shadgett, Olive Hall. *The Republican Party in Georgia: From Reconstruction Through 1900*. Uniersity of Georgia Press, Athens, 1964.

Sheldon, William DuBose. *Populism in the Old Dominion: Virginia Farm Politics, 1885–1900*. Princeton University Press, Princeton, 1935.

Simkins, Francis Butler. *The Tillman Movement in South Carolina*. Duke University Press, Durham, 1926.

Tindall, George B. *South Carolina Negroes, 1877–1900*. University of South Carolina Press, Columbia, 1952.

Wardlaw, Ralph W. *Negro Suffrage in Georgia, 1867–1930*. University of Georgia *Bulletin, XXXIII*. University of Georgia Press, Athens, 1932.

Wharton, Vernon Lane. *The Negro in Mississippi, 1865–1890*. Harper Torchbooks, New York, 1965.

Wynes, Charles E. *Race Relations in Virginia, 1870–1902*. University of Virginia Press, Charlottesville, 1961.

3. *Miscellaneous*

Allport, Gordon W. *The Nature of Prejudice*. Doubleday, New York, 1958.

Appleton's Annual Cyclopedia, 1886–1898. Appleton and Company, New York.

Bell, Daniel, ed. *The Radical Right*. Anchor, New York, 1964.

Brawley, Benjamin. *A Short History of the Negro American*. Macmillan, New York, 1950.

Brown, William Garrott. *The Lower South in American History*. Macmillan, New York, 1902.

Carmer, Carl. *Stars Fell on Alabama*. Farrar and Rhinehart, New York, 1934.

Cash, Wilbur J. *The Mind of the South*. Knopf, New York, 1941.

Degler, Carl N. *Out of Our Past*. Harper Colophon Books, New York, 1970.

De Santis, Vincent P. *Republicans Face the Southern Question: The New Departure Years, 1877–1897*. Johns Hopkins Press, Baltimore, 1959.

Dollard, John. *Caste and Class in a Southern Town*. Doubleday, New York, 1949.

DuBois, William E. B. *The Souls of Black Folk: Essays and Sketches*. Fawcett, Greenwich, 1961.

————. *Dusk of Dawn: Essay Toward an Autobiography of a Race Concept*. Harcourt Brace, New York, 1940.

Elkins, Stanley M. *Slavery: A Study in American Institutional and Intellectual Life*. Grosset's University Library, New York, 1961.

Factor, Robert L. *The Black Response to America: Men, Ideals, and Organization from Frederick Douglass to the NAACP*. Addison-Wesley, Reading, 1970.

Fine, Sidney. *Laissez Faire and the General-Welfare State: A Study of Conflict in American Thought, 1865–1901*. University of Michigan Press, Ann Arbor, 1950; 1966.

Frazier, E. Franklin, *The Negro in the United States*. Macmillan, New York, 1949.

Friedman, Lawrence J., ed. *The White Savage: Racial Fantasies in the Postbellum South*. Prentice Hall, Englewood Cliffs, 1970.

Gaston, Paul. *New South Creed: A Study in Southern Myth Making*. Knopf, New York, 1970.

Green, Fletcher, ed. *Essays in Southern History*. University of North Carolina Press, Chapel Hill, 1949.

Grob, Gerald. *Workers and Utopia*. Quadrangle Books, New York, 1969.

Hicks, John D. *The Populist Revolt*. University of Nebraska Press, Lincoln, 1931; 1961.

Hirshson, Stanley P. *Farewell to the Bloody Shirt: Northern Republicans and the Southern Negro, 1877–1893*. Indiana University Press, Bloomington, 1962.

Hofstadter, Richard. *The Age of Reform: From Bryan to F. D. R*. Knopf, New York, 1955.

Hopkins, Charles Howard. *The Rise of the Social Gospel in American Protestantism*. Yale University Press, New Haven, 1940.

Kelsey, Carl. *The Negro Farmer*. Jennings and Pye, Chicago, 1903.

Key, V. O., Jr. *Politics, Parties and Pressure Groups*. Crowell, New York, 1964.

————. *Southern Politics in State and Nation*. Vintage, New York, 1949.

King, C. Wendell. *Social Movements in the United States*. Random House, New York, 1969.

Lewinson, Paul. *Race, Class, and Party*. Oxford University Press, New York, 1932; 1965.

Lipset, Seymour. *Political Man: The Social Basis of Politics*. Doubleday, New York, 1963.

Logan, Rayford W. *The Negro in American Life and Thought*. Dial, New York, 1954.

Meier, August. *Negro Thought in America, 1880–1915*. University of Michigan, Ann Arbor, 1966.

————, and Elliot Rudwick. *From Plantation to Ghetto*. G. P. Putnam and Sons, New York, 1960.

Morris, Willie. *North Toward Home*. Delta, New York, 1970.

Quarles, Benjamin. *The Negro in the Making of America*. Macmillan, New York, 1965.

Raper, Arthur F. *The Tragedy of Lynching*. University of North Carolina Press, Chapel Hill, 1933.

Redkey, Edwin S. *Black Exodus: Black Nationalist and Back-to-Africa Movements, 1890–1910*. Yale University Press, New Haven, 1969.

Rochester, Anne. *The Populist Movement in the United States*. International Publishers, New York, 1943.

Rose, Arnold. *The Negro in America*. Harper and Row, New York, 1948.

Rozwenc, Edwin C., and John C. Malton, eds. *Myth and Reality in the Populist Revolt*. D. C. Heath and Company, Boston, 1967.

Saloutos, Theodore. *Populism: Reaction or Reform?* Rinehart and Winston, New York, 1968.

Scarborough, Dorothy. *In the Land of Cotton*. Macmillan, New York, 1923.

Schlesinger, Joseph A. *Ambition and Politics: Political Careers in the United States*. Rand, McNally, Chicago, 1966.

Sherrill, Robert. *Gothic Politics in the Deep South: Stars of the New Confederacy*. Grossman Publishers, New York, 1968.

Simpson, George Eaton, and J. Milton Yinger. *Racial and Cultural Minorities*. Harper and

Row, New York, 1965.

Stampp, Kenneth M. *The Peculiar Institution*. Vintage, New York, 1965.

Swann, William F. G., *et al. Essays on Research in the Social Sciences: Papers Presented in a General Seminar Conducted by the Committee on Training of the Brookings Institution, 1930–31*. Steiger and Company, New York, 1931.

Thorpe, Earl E. *The Mind of the Negro: An Intellectual History of Afro-Americans*. Negro University Press, Westport, 1970.

Vander Zanden, James W. *American Minority Relations*. Ronald Press, New York 1963.

Watters, Pat. *The South and the Nation*. Pantheon Books, New York, 1969.

Williams, T. Harry. *Romance and Realism in Southern Politics*. Louisiana State University Press, Baton Rouge, 1966.

Woodward, C. Vann. *American Counterpoint: Slavery and Racism in the South Dialogue*. Little, Brown and Company, Boston, 1971.

————. *Origins of the New South, 1877–1913*. Louisiana State University Press, Baton Rouge, 1951; 1966.

————. *The Strange Career of Jim Crow*. Oxford University Press, New York, 1957.

Wyllie, Irwin G. *The Self-Made Man in America*. Rutgers University Press, New Brunswick, 1954.

Wynes, Charles E., ed. *Forgotten Voices: Dissenting Southerners in an Age of Conformity*. Louisiana State University Press, Baton Rouge, 1966.

4. *Periodical Articles*

Abramowitz, Jack. "Agrarian Reformers and the Negro Question," *Negro History Bulletin,* XI (March, 1974), 138–39.

————. "John B. Rayner—Grass-Roots Leader," *Journal of Negro History, XXVI* (April, 1951), 160–93.

————. "The Negro in the Agrarian Revolt," *Agricultural History,* XXIV (April, 1950), 89–95.

————. "The Negro in the Populist Movement," *Journal of Negro History,* XXXVIII (July, 195:), 257–89.

Alvord, Wayne. "T. L. Nugent, Texas Populist," *Southwestern Historical Quarterly,* LVII (July, 1953), 65–81.

Atkins, Leah R. "Populism in Alabama: Reuben F. Kolb and the Appeals to Minority Groups," *Alabama Historical Quarterly,* XXXII (Fall and Winter, 1970), 167–80.

Bacote, Clarence A. "Negro Proscriptions, Protest and Proposed Solutions," in *Understanding Negro History,* ed. by Dwight Hoover. Quadrangle Books, Chicago, 1968, 200–23.

Barnhart, John D. "Rainfall and the Populist Party in Nebraska," *American Political Science Review,* XIX (August, 1925), 527–40.

Bode, Frederich A. "Religion and Class Hegemony: A Populist Critique in North Carolina," *Journal of Southern History,* XXXVII (August, 1971), 417–38.

Bryant, Girard T. "J. B. Rayner, A Negro Populist," *Negro History Bulletin,* III (May, 1940), 125–26.

Carter, Purvis M. "Robert Lloyd Smith and the Farmers' Improvement Society, a Self Help Movement in Texas," *Negro History Bulletin,* XXIX (Fall, 1966), 175–76, 190–91.

Casdorph, Paul Douglas. "Norris Wright Cuney and Texas Republican Politics, 1883–1896," *Southwestern Historical Quarterly,* LXVIII (January, 1965), 455–64.

Chafe, William H. "The Negro and Populism: A Kansas Study," *Journal of Southern History*, XXXIV (August, 1968), 402–19.

Clark, Thomas D. "The Furnishing and Supply System in Southern Agriculture Since 1865," *Journal of Southern History*, XII (February, 1946), 22–44.

Crowe, Charles. "Tom Watson, Populists and Blacks Reconsidered," *Journal of Negro History*, LV (April, 1970), 99–116.

Daniel, Lucia E. "Louisiana People's Party," *Louisiana Historical Quarterly*, XXVI (October, 1943), 1055–1149.

Degler, Carl N. "Racism in the United States: An Essay Review," *Journal of Southern History*, XXXVIII (February, 1972), 101–09.

De Santis, Vincent P. "Negro Dissatisfaction with Republican Policy," *Journal of Negro History*, XXVI (April, 1951), 148–59.

Dethloff, Henry C., and Robert R. Jones. "Race Relations in Louisiana, 1877–1898," *Louisiana History*, IX (Fall, 1968), 301–23.

Drew, Frank M. "The Present Farmers' Movement," *Political Science Quarterly*, VI (June, 1891), 282–310.

Fishel, Leslie H., Jr. "The Negro in Northern Politics, 1877–1900," *Mississippi Valley Historical Review*, XLII (December, 1955), 466–89.

Franklin, John Hope. "History of Racial Segregation in the United States," *Annals of the American Academy of Political and Social Science*, CCCIV (March, 1956), 1–7.

Going, Allen J. "Critical Months in Alabama Politics, 1895–1896," *The Alabama Review*, V (October, 1952), 269–81.

Grantham, Dewey W., Jr. "Dinner at the White House: Theodore Roosevelt, Booker T. Washington and the South," *Tennessee Historical Quarterly*, XVII (June, 1958), 112–30.

————. "Georgia Politics and the Disfranchisement of the Negro," *Georgia Historical Quarterly*, XXXII (March, 1948), 1–21.

Graves, John William. "Negro Disfranchisement in Arkansas," *Arkansas Historical Quarterly*, XXVI (Autumn, 1967), 199–255.

Grob, Gerald. "Terence V. Powderly and the Knights of Labor," *Mid-America*, XXXIX (January, 1957), 39–55.

Hammond, Marcus B. "The Southern Farmer and Cotton," *Political Science Quarterly*, XII (September, 1897), 450–75.

Hicks, John D., and John D. Barnhart. "The Farmers' Alliance," *North Carolina Historical Review*, VI (July, 1929), 254–79.

Hovland, Carl Iver, and Robert R. Sears. "Minor Studies of Aggression: VI. Correlation of Lynchings with Economic Indices," *Journal of Psychology*, IX (1940), 301–10.

Ingle, Larry H. "A Southern Democrat at Large: William Hodge Kitchin and the Populist Party," *North Carolina Historical Review*, XLV (Spring, 1968), 169–84.

Janowitz, Morris, and Dwaine Marvick. "Authoritarianism and Political Behavior," *Public Opinion Quarterly*, XLVII (Summer, 1953), 185–201.

Jones, Rhett. "Proving Blacks Inferior, 1870–1930," *Black World*, XX (February, 1971), 4–19.

Kendrick, Benjamin B. "Agrarian Discontent in the South, 1880–1900," American Historical Association, *Annual Report*, 1920, 267–72.

Kessler, Sidney H. "The Organization of Negroes in the Knights of Labor," *Journal of Negro History*, XXXVII (July, 1952), 248–76.

Krauss, James O. "The Farmers' Alliance in Florida," *South Atlantic Quarterly*, XXV

(July, 1926), 300–15.

Kutner, Bernard, Carol Wilkins, and Penny Yarrow. "Verbal Attitudes and Overt Behavior Involving Racial Prejudice," *Journal of Abnormal and Social Psychology,* XLVII (July, 1952), 649–52.

Le Piere, Richard T. "Attitudes vs. Actions," *Social Forces,* XIII (December, 1934), 230–37.

Linn, Lawrence S. "Verbal Attitudes and Overt Behavior; A Study of Racial Discrimination," *Social Forces,* XLV (March, 1965), 353–64.

Lipset, Seymour. "Working-Class Authoritarianism," *American Sociological Review,* XXIV (August, 1959), 482–502.

Mabry, William A. "Negro Suffrage and Fusion Rule in North Carolina," *North Carolina Historical Review,* XII (April, 1935), 79–102.

MacKinnon, William, and Richard Centers. "Authoritarianism and Urban Stratification," *American Journal of Sociology,* LXI (May, 1956), 610–20.

Malof, Milton, and Albert Lott. "Ethnocentism and the Acceptance of Negro Support in a Group Situation," *Journal of Abnormal and Social Psychology,* LXV (October, 1962), 254–58.

Marshall, R. "Precipitation and Presidents," *Nation,* CXXIV (March, 1927), 315–16.

Paisley, Clifton. "The Political Wheelers and the Arkansas Election of 1888," *Arkansas Historical Quarterly,* XXV (Spring, 1966), 3–21.

Powdermaker, Hortense. "The Channeling of Negro Aggression by the Cultural Process," *American Journal of Sociology,* XLVIII (May, 1943), 750–58.

Proctor, Samuel. "National Farmers' Alliance Convention of 1890 and Its 'Ocala Demands'," *Florida Historical Quarterly,* XXVIII (January, 1950), 161–81.

Reeves, Richard. "The New Populism and the Old: A Matter of Words," *Saturday Review* (April 8, 1972), 46–47.

Reynolds, Alfred W. "The Alabama Negro Colony in Mexico, 1894–1896," *The Alabama Review,* V (October, 1952), 243–68.

————. "The Alabama Negro Colony in Mexico, 1894–1896," *The Alabama Review,* VI (January, 1953), 31–58.

Robinson, Dan M. "Tennessee Politics and the Agrarian Movement, 1886–1896," *Mississippi Valley Historical Review,* XX (December, 1934), 365–80.

Rogers, William Warren. "The Negro Alliance in Alabama," *Journal of Negro History,* XLV (January, 1960), 38–44.

————. "Negro Knights of Labor in Arkansas: A Case Study of the 'Miscellaneous' Strike," *Labor History,* X (Summer, 1969), 210–17.

————. "Reuben F. Kolb: Agricultural Leader of the New South," *Agricultural History,* XXXII (April, 1958), 109–19.

Saunders, Robert M. "The Southern Populists and the Negro in 1892," in University of Virginia *Essays in History,* XII (Charlottesville, 1966–1967), 7–25.

————. "Southern Populists and the Negro, 1893–1895," *Journal of Negro History,* LIV (July, 1969), 240–61.

————. "The Transformation of Tom Watson, 1894–1895," *Georgia Historical Quarterly,* LIV (Fall, 1970), 339–56.

Scott, Roy V. "Milton George and the Farmers' Alliance Movement," *Mississippi Valley Historical Review,* XLV (June, 1958), 90–109.

Shannon, Fred A. "C. W. Macune and the Farmers' Alliance," *Current History,* XXVIII (June, 1955), 330–35.

Shapiro, Herbert. "The Populists and the Negro: A Reconsideration," in Meier, August, and Elliot Rudwick, eds. *The Making of Black America*. 2 vols. Atheneum, New York, 1969, II, 27–36.

Sharp, J. A. "Entrance of the Farmers' Alliance into Tennessee Politics," East Tennessee Historical Society's *Publications*, No. 9 (1937), 72–92.

Shoftner, Jerrell H., and William Warren Rogers. "Joseph C. Manning: Militant Agrarian, Enduring Populist," *Alabama Historical Quarterly*, XXIX (Spring and Summer, 1967), 7–37.

Shugg, Roger Wallace. "The New Orleans General Strike of 1892," *Louisiana Historical Quarterly*, XXI (April, 1938), 117–24.

Simkins, Francis Butler. "Ben Tillman's View of the Negro," *Journal of Southern History*, III (May, 1937), 161–74.

Simms, L. Moody, Jr. "A Note on Sidney Lanier's Attitude Toward the Negro and Toward Populism," *Georgia Historical Quarterly* (September, 1968), 305–07.

Smith, Ralph. "The Farmers' Alliance in Texas, 1875–1900," *Southwestern Historical Quarterly*, XLVIII (October, 1948), 346–69.

_____. " 'Macuneism' or the Farmers of Texas in Business," *Journal of Southern History*, XIII (May, 1947), 220–44.

Smith, Willard H. "William Jennings Bryan and Racism," *Journal of Negro History*, LIV (April, 1969), 127–49.

_____. "William Jennings Bryan—A Reappraisal," Indiana Academy of the Social Sciences, *Proceedings*, NS, X (1965), 56–69.

_____. "William Jennings Bryan and the Social Gospel," *Journal of American History*, LIII (June, 1966), 41–60.

Steelman, Joseph H. "Republican Party Strategists and the Issue of Fusion with Populists in North Carolina, 1893–1894," *North Carolina Historical Review*, XLVII (July, 1970), 244–69.

_____. "Vicissitudes of Republican Party Politics: The Campaign of 1892 in North Carolina," *North Carolina Historical Review*, XXXIII (Autumn, 1966), 430–44.

Suderman, Elmer F. "The Social Gospel Novelists' Criticisms of American Society," *Midcontinent American Studies Journal*, VII (Spring, 1966), 68–74.

Summersell, Charles G. "The Alabama Governor's Race of 1892," *Alabama Review*, VIII (January, 1955), 5–35.

_____. "Kolb and the Populist Revolt as Viewed by Newspapers," *Alabama Historical Quarterly*, XIX (Fall and Winter, 1957), 375–95.

Tarr, Joel A. "Goldfinger, the Gold Conspiracy and the Populists," *Midcontinent American Studies Journal*, VII (Fall, 1966), 49–52.

Taylor, Joe B. "Populism and Disfranchisement in Alabama," *Journal of Negro History*, XXXIV (October, 1949), 410–27.

Taylor, Joe Gray. "The Democratic Idea and the Deep South: An Historical Survey," *Mississippi Quarterly*, XVIII (Fall, 1965), 76–83.

Turner, Arlin. "George Washington Cable's Beginning as a Reformer," *Journal of Southern History*, XVII (May, 1951), 135–61.

_____. "George Washington Cable, Novelist and Reformer," *South Atlantic Quarterly*, XLVIII (October, 1949), 539–45.

Vander Zanden, James W. "The Ideology of White Supremacy," *Journal of the History of Ideas*, XX (June-September, 1959), 385–402.

Weatherford, W. D. "Race Relationship in the South," *Annals of the American Academy of Political and Social Science,* XLVIII (September, 1913), 164–72.

Welch, Richard E. "The Federal Elections Bill of 1890. Postscripts and Preludes," *Journal of American History,* LII (December, 1965), 511–26.

Wellborn, Fred. "The Influence of the Silver-Republican Senators, 1889–1891," *Mississippi Valley Historical Review,* XIV (March, 1928), 402–80.

White, Melvin V. "Populism in Louisiana During the Nineties," *Mississippi Valley Historical Review,* V (June, 1918), 3–19.

Wilhoit, Francis M. "An Interpretation of Populism's Impact on the Georgia Negro," *Journal of Negro History,* LII (April, 1967), 116–27.

Wirth, Louis. "Race and Public Policy," *Scientific Monthly,* LXVIII (April, 1944), 302–12.

Woodward, C. Vann. "Tom Watson and the Negro in Agrarian Politics," *Journal of Southern History,* IV (February, 1938), 14–33.

Wynes, Charles E. "Charles T. O'Ferrall and the Virginia Gubernatorial Election of 1893," *Virginia Magazine of History and Biography,* LXIV (October, 1956), 437–53.

————. "Lewis Harvie Blair, Virginia Reformer: The Uplift of the Negro and Southern Prosperity," *Virginia Magazine of History and Biography,* LXXII (January, 1964), 3–18.

5.   Theses and Dissertations

Abramowitz, Jack. "Accommodations and Militancy in Negro Life, 1876–1916." Unpublished Doctoral dissertation, Columbia University, 1950.

Blackburn, Helen M. "The Populist Party in the South." Unpublished Master's thesis, Howard University, 1941.

Boras, Mary A. "A Case Study of the Speeches of the Birmingham, Alabama Populist Party Convention, September 15–16, 1892." Unpublished Master's thesis, University of Alabama, 1952.

Budd, Harrel. "The Negro in Politics in Texas, 1867–1898." Unpublished Master's thesis, University of Texas, 1925.

Byrd, Ruth E. "The History of the Force Bill of 1890 and Its Effect Upon State Constitutions." Unpublished Master's thesis, University of North Carolina, 1932.

Cartwright, Joseph Howard. "The Negro in Tennessee Politics, 1880–1891." Unpublished Master's thesis, Vanderbilt University, 1968.

Church, Joseph. "The Farmers' Alliance and the Populist Movement in South Carolina, 1887–1896." Unpublished Master's thesis, University of South Carolina, 1953.

Gaither, Gerald. "The Negro in the Ideology of Southern Populism, 1889–1896." Unpublished Master's thesis, University of Tennessee, 1967.

Harris, David Alan. "The Political Career of Milford W. Howard, Populist Congressman from Alabama." Unpublished Master's thesis, Auburn University, 1957.

Hearn, Thomas K. "The Populist Movement in Marshall County Alabama." Unpublished Master's thesis, University of Alabama, 1935.

Jones, Theron Paul. "The Gubernatorial Election of 1892 in North Carolina." Unpublished Master's thesis, University of North Carolina, 1949.

Lewis, Robert David. "The Negro in Agrarian Uprisings, 1865–1900." Unpublished Master's thesis, State University of Iowa, 1938.

McCain, William D. "The Populist Party in Mississippi." Unpublished Master's thesis,

University of Mississippi, 1931.

McKay, Herbert S. "Convict Leasing in North Carolina." Unpublished Master's thesis, University of North Carolina, 1947.

Perry, Douglass Geraldyne. "Black Populism: The Negro in the People's Party in Texas." Unpublished Master's thesis, Prairie View University, 1945.

Quillian, Bascom Osborne, Jr. "The Populist Challenge in Georgia in the Year 1894." Unpublished Master's thesis, University of Georgia, 1948.

Reddick, Jamie Lawson. "The Negro in the Populist Movement in Georgia." Unpublished Master's thesis, Atlanta University, 1937.

Roberts, William P. "The Public Career of William Harrel Felton." Unpublished Doctoral dissertation, University of North Carolina, 1952.

Rogers, William Warren. "Agrarianism in Alabama, 1865–1896." Unpublished Doctoral dissertation, University of North Carolina, 1959.

Smith, Florence. "The Populist Movement and Its Influence in North Carolina." Unpublished Doctoral dissertation, University of Chicago, 1928.

Smith, Robert Wayne. "A Rhetorical Analysis of the Populist Movement in North Carolina, 1892–1896." Unpublished Doctoral dissertation, University of Wisconsin, 1957.

(A microfilm copy of this dissertation is available in the North Carolina Collection, University of North Carolina.)

Sparkman, John. "The Kolb-Oates Campaign of 1894." Unpublished Master's thesis, University of Alabama, 1924.

Summersell, Charles G. "A Life of Reuben Kolb." Unpublished Master's thesis, University of Alabama, 1930.

Westphal, Corinne. "The Farmers' Alliance in Tennessee." Unpublished Master's thesis, Vanderbilt University, 1929.

Zimmerman, Helen J. "Penal Systems and Penal Reforms in the South Since the Civil War." Unpublished Doctoral dissertation, University of North Carolina, 1947.

INDEX